Encyclopedia of Practical Photography

Volume 10

Mo-Pan

Edited by and published for
EASTMAN KODAK COMPANY

AMPHOTO
American Photographic Book Publishing Company
Garden City, New York

Note on Photography

The cover photos and the photos of letters that appear elsewhere in this encyclopedia were taken by Chris Maggio.

Library of Congress Cataloging in Publication Data

Amphoto, New York.
  Encyclopedia of practical photography.

  Includes bibliographical references and index.
  1. Photography—Dictionaries. I. Eastman Kodak Company. II. Title.
TR9.T34   770′.3   77–22562

ISBN 0–8174–3050–4 Trade Edition—Whole Set
ISBN 0–8174–3200–0 Library Edition—Whole Set
ISBN 0–8174–3060–1 Trade Edition—Volume 10
ISBN 0–8174–3210–8 Library Edition—Volume 10

Manufactured in the United States of America

Editorial Board

The *Encyclopedia of Practical Photography* was compiled and edited jointly by Eastman Kodak Company and American Photographic Book Publishing Co., Inc. (Amphoto). The comprehensive archives, vast resources, and technical staffs of both companies, as well as the published works of Kodak, were used as the basis for most of the information contained in this encyclopedia.

Symbol Identification

 Audiovisual

 Color Processing and Printing

 Picture-Making Techniques

 Biography

 Equipment and Facilities

 Scientific Photography

 Black-and-White Materials

 Exposure

 Special Effects and Techniques

 Black-and-White Processing and Printing

 History

Special Interests

 Business and Legal Aspects

 Lighting

 Storage and Care

 Chemicals

 Motion Picture

 Theory of Photography

 Color Materials

 Optics

 Vision

Guide for the Reader

Use this encyclopedia as you would any good encyclopedia or dictionary. Look for the subject desired as it first occurs to you—most often you will locate it immediately. The shorter articles begin with a dictionary-style definition, and the longer articles begin with a short paragraph that summarizes the article that follows. Either of these should tell you if the information you need is in the article. The longer articles are then broken down by series of headings and sub-headings to aid further in locating specific information.

Cross References

If you do not find the specific information you are seeking in the article first consulted, use the cross references (within the article and at the end of it) to lead you to more information. The cross references can lead you from a general article to the more detailed articles into which the subject is divided. Cross references are printed in capital letters so that you can easily recognize them.
Example: *See also:* ZONE SYSTEM.

Index

If the initial article you turn to does not supply you with the information you seek, and the cross references do not lead you to it, use the index in the last volume. The index contains thousands of entries to help you identify and locate any subject you seek.

Symbols

To further aid you in locating information, the articles throughout have been organized into major photographic categories. Each category is represented by a symbol displayed on the opposite page. By using only the symbols, you can scan each volume and locate all the information under any of the general categories. Thus, if you wish to read all about lighting, simply locate the lighting symbols and read the articles under them.

Reading Lists

Most of the longer articles are followed by reading lists citing useful sources for further information. Should you require additional sources, check the cross-referenced articles for additional reading lists.

Metric Measurement

Both the U.S. Customary System of measurement and the International System (SI) are used throughout this encyclopedia. In most cases, the metric measurement is given first with the U.S. customary equivalent following in parenthesis. When equivalent measurements are given, they will be rounded off to the nearest whole unit or a tenth of a unit, unless precise measurement is important. When a measurement is considered a "standard," equivalents will not be given. For example: 35 mm film, 200 mm lens, 4″ × 5″ negative, and 8″ × 10″ prints will not be given with their customary or metric equivalents.

How Articles are Alphabetized

Article titles are alphabetized by letter sequence, with word breaks and hyphens not considered. Example:

> Archer, Frederick Scott
> Architectural Photography
> Archival Processing
> Arc Lamps

Abbreviations are alphabetized according to the letters of the abbreviations, not by the words the letters stand for. Example:

> Artificial Light
> ASA Speed

Contents

Model and Miniature Photography

The first problem in photographing a scale model is to decide whether the picture is to look like one of a model, or if the model is to look like the actual object. The first approach might be used to display the talents and handiwork of a model builder, to show the amount of labor and effort that went into making the model. The second approach is often used in motion pictures to avoid the expense of full-scale sets and for special effects, such as a land of giants or of miniature creatures, as well as for spectacular distortion and destruction. In still photography, "real" model shots are used in illustrative and display work to show architectural concepts in a seemingly finished state, and for many other purposes.

Models as Models

Techniques for showing a model as a model are exactly the same as photographing any small object. The only serious problem is that a small model must be photographed at close range, and depth of field will be very shallow. For that reason, it is often preferable to use a 35 mm camera in order to take advantage of the depth-of-field characteristics of the short focal length of its lenses.

This must not be carried too far; using a 35 mm camera with a wide-angle lens will necessitate a very close viewpoint that somewhat negates the depth-of-field advantage and, more importantly, exaggerates perspective and distorts the shape of the model.

Lighting for this type of picture depends upon the model itself; if it is an airplane or an automobile model, it is probably best to light it just like a catalog illustration. In this case, a key light at 45 degrees is used; and plenty of fill light is added to it, from a nearly frontal position, to ensure rendition of detail into the deepest shadows.

When the model is highly detailed, as, say, a ship model with a great deal of rigging, or a locomotive model with all of its external piping, valve gear, and so on, a softer, flatter lighting will help to bring out detail rather than form. The lighting in such cases should be mostly frontal, from diffused light sources; in extreme cases it may be necessary to use a tent, as for jewelry and other bright metal objects. (*See:* TENT LIGHTING.)

Making a Model Look Real

When a model must look like the real thing, there is a different photographic problem. The illu-

Type of lighting depends upon the nature of the model to be photographed. (Left) Models like these motorcycles are best lighted as for a catalog illustration; a key light and plenty of fill light bring out shadowed detail and add depth and contour. (Right) Highly detailed models, such as heavily rigged ships, should be lighted to bring out fine detail. Light should be mostly frontal and fairly diffused. Photos by Neil Montanus.

sion of reality depends to a very large extent upon the perspective of the photograph, and this, in turn, depends upon the viewpoint from which the picture is made.

Lens Viewing Distance. As a simple rule of thumb, the lens-viewing distance must be scaled down in almost exact proportion to the scale of the model. Thus, if a model is made to a scale of 1 inch = 1 foot, that is 1:12, it should be photographed from $\frac{1}{12}$ the normal distance, that is, the distance from which the full-scale original would be photographed. An automobile about 15 feet long is usually photographed from a distance of about 30 feet; then if the model is scaled down to $\frac{1}{12}$ its normal size, it must be photographed at $\frac{30}{12} = 2\frac{1}{2}$ feet. Strangely enough, if the same lens is used at the closer distance, the image will more than fill the available film area. This is because the lens must be extended to focus at the close range of 2½ feet, and that causes its field of view to become narrower, as if it were a longer-focus lens.

There are two solutions to this problem: (1) leave the lens set at infinity and use a supplementary lens of 2½-foot focal length; and (2) use a wide-angle lens on the camera, which will not upset the perspective, since perspective depends upon lens-to-subject distance, not upon focal length.

A model scale of 1:12 is fairly large, so it is not necessary to get especially close for natural perspective. But most models are not made at such large scales. For example, model railroads are always (or nearly always) built much smaller; the three most popular scales are "O," "HO," and "N" gauge, and these have the following proportions:

SCALES AND PROPORTIONS

Gauge	Scale	Size Ratio
O	¼ inch = 1 foot	1:48
HO	3.5 mm = 1 foot	1:87
N	2 mm = 1 foot	1:160

At these size ratios, the problem is more severe. To photograph an "HO" scale automobile from a scale distance of 30 feet would involve making the picture at a distance of $\frac{30}{87} = 0.34$ foot or about 4 inches, which is inconveniently close. Furthermore, even with a fairly short-focus lens, the depth of field will be insufficient at this distance, and the model will have to be photographed broadside to get even a usable picture. Most often, a greater distance is used and the picture is enlarged, but this tends to

The illusion of reality depends largely on perspective. To achieve this, the lens viewing distance must be scaled down in almost exact proportion to the scale of the original. Photo by Railroad Model Craftsman.

Model and Miniature Photography

Scale and perspective are essential elements in creating the illusion of reality. (Above left) To simulate the viewpoint of a proportionally small person, the model should be placed on an elevation so it can be viewed at eye level from the camera. Photo at left shows the view as the camera sees it. (Above) A detail, photographed from a realistic angle, appears quite lifelike.

flatten perspective, and to some extent diminish the illusion of reality.

Perspective. There is still another problem—one instinctively photographs small objects looking down upon them, but this again gives incorrect perspective. A model should be photographed from the viewpoint of an imaginary person scaled down in the same proportion. If the imaginary real photographer is 6 feet tall, then to photograph in "HO" scale, he or she would have to shrink to $\frac{1}{87}$ of that, which is less than an inch. It is hard to find a camera small enough so that its lens can be positioned less than an inch above the ground; one solution is to set the model on an embankment or some elevation, so it can be viewed at eye level without having to place the camera so low.

Some railroad model enthusiasts have carried the idea to its ultimate—not only do they scale down the viewer, but they scale down the camera as well. One or two model railroad photographers have built tiny cameras, using 16 mm film, and having lenses of about ½-inch (12.5 mm) focal length, borrowed

Model and Miniature Photography

from an 8 mm movie camera. Allowing the necessary extension for the close viewpoint, such a lens will cover a 16 mm frame or a bit more with fairly even definition, and stopped down to $f/22$ it affords a good deal of depth of field.

Clarity of Detail. Such a small negative will not have too much fine detail, but in this case, it is a positive advantage. One of the things that gives away a model as not being real is the clarity of the detail; such small things as rivets show up with painful distinctness. At the distance you usually view a locomotive, the rivets and other small details are only barely noticeable, and the slight loss of detail in these tiny negatives actually makes the picture look more real.

Even so, some compromise is usually needed, and a model will be photographed from a point a bit farther away than that which provides exactly correct perspective. Since the eye is fairly tolerant of small perspective errors, such pictures look quite satisfactory. Obviously, depth of field is still a problem with regard to the surroundings. A common solution is either to make an artificial background that can be placed close behind the model, or else have natural backgrounds far enough away to be completely out of focus.

Motion Pictures of Models

Aside from an occasional film of a model made simply to demonstrate the art of modeling, models in motion pictures are usually used to simulate the real thing.

When a model is built especially for this purpose, you can take certain liberties with it to enhance realism. For one thing, most of the models used in Hollywood movies are large—much larger than the usual railroad or ship model. Using a scale of 1 inch = 1 foot, a 600-foot ocean liner will be as much as 50 feet long, and models this large are frequently used in Hollywood features. The studio tank in which these models are floated is the size of a small lake. Train models are generally smaller, but still bigger than most hobby railroad scales.

The problem of perspective is exactly the same as in still photographs, but the large scale of the model and the wide variety of focal lengths available in lenses for professional motion-picture cameras tend to simplify the problem considerably.

However, a new problem enters when the model is being photographed in motion—the *speed* of the model must be reduced in the same proportion as the scale of the model. This would not be difficult if only the motion of the model needed to be considered, but there are matters of inertia that complicate the problem.

For instance, an "O" gauge train, which is $\frac{1}{48}$ full size, can be operated quite easily at a speed of about 110 feet per minute, which is exactly $\frac{1}{48}$ of 60 miles per hour. But if run at this speed and photographed at the normal 24 frames per second, it will

Light from the background puts a model into silhouette. A piece of opal glass is used for the sky; the water is textured glass. Floodlight bounced from blue paper behind the opal glass provides the overall blue in the sky and water. A spotlight behind the opal glass forms the moon. Photo by Frank Pallo.

Model and Miniature Photography

not look right—the motion will be jerky, starts and stops will be abrupt, and the whole thing will look faked.

With ship models, the problem is even more severe; a 600-foot ocean liner has a very slow, ponderous roll; by comparison, its model in a studio tank will bob around like a cork. In addition, the waves, while possibly correct in size, will be moving far too fast.

The usual solution is to photograph the model in slow motion. In professional motion pictures, rates of from 128 to 256 frames per second are often used in model shots; this makes the rolling of a ship slower by factors of as much as 10 times, and the picture is much more natural looking.

The same thing is done with train models, but the train is run at several times its normal speed to counteract the slowing down of its travel by the camera. The result is that the train takes much longer to get up to speed and to slow to a stop, and its rocking motions are slower and more natural looking. Most "O" gauge models can easily be run at "scale speeds" as high as the equivalent of 240 miles per hour, and can easily be slowed to the apparent 50 or 60 miles per hour by any camera that can be run at 96 to 128 frames per second. The sound track, which contains the noises of a real train, not of a model, is added later.

One does not see a great deal of fine detail at the usual viewing distance of an ocean liner or a train; and in many models made especially for film work, much small detail can be deliberately omitted from the model. Such models viewed at close hand do not appear quite natural, but in the final film, they look much more realistic than ones containing full detail.

• *See also:* ARCHITECTURAL PHOTOGRAPHY; PERSPECTIVE; TABLETOP PHOTOGRAPHY; TENT LIGHTING.

Model Release

A model release is a legal form that grants a photographer the right to publish, exhibit, sell, or otherwise use specified photographs in which the person signing the release (the subject) appears. The rights assigned may be unlimited, or may be restricted to certain uses specified in the release. The person signing the release must be of legal age to execute a contract; the signature of a parent or legal guardian is required in the case of a subject who is a minor. The release must be dated at the time of signing and, to be a legal contract, must acknowledge receipt of payment or other consideration of value paid by the photographer to the subject.

Commercial or Advertising Purposes

As a general rule, any photograph made for commercial or advertising purposes in which a person appears requires written permission of that person before it may be used, sold, or published. As a matter of routine, all professional models who are paid to pose for pictures are expected to provide a legal release for the use of such pictures.

Formerly, such releases were fairly broad, allowing the use of the picture for any purpose whatever. Today, there is a tendency to limit the scope of a release. Thus, a model may refuse to allow a picture to be used in any type of advertising that would tend to lower his or her standing or subject him or her to ridicule—for example, poses or situations that are undignified. It is therefore necessary to have a complete understanding with the model and to inform him or her of the purpose of the photograph before taking it.

Publication of Photos

In theory, photographs made of news events while they are happening do not require releases when used in newspapers. But this usage is quite limited; if a news photograph is later used in an advertisement, then releases will be required of all recognizable persons therein.

By the same token, a casual snapshot of a person, taken while touring, needs no release; however, if it is anticipated that it may later be used, say, in a book of travel photographs, prudence would dictate obtaining a release. In recent years, courts have developed a doctrine of "invasion of privacy," and it is not safe to assume that a release is unnecessary merely because the publication does not involve advertising.

The rule is: When in doubt, get a release from each and every recognizable person in a picture. For a release to be legally binding, it must involve a "consideration"; that is, the person signing a release must receive some kind of remuneration for it. In most cases, the release will state "for value received" or similar phrasing. This may be only for prints of the pictures taken. In the case of professional models, the fee is usually agreed upon in advance.

Content and Form of a Model Release

The content of a model release is more or less standard, but the form may vary. It is perfectly legal to use a printed form, filling in only the name of the model, and if desired, the fee paid, as well as the date, the time, and information identifying the pictures to be made. If there are to be exceptions or limitations on the end use of the pictures, these should be carefully stipulated and signed by both the model and the photographer. Such stipulations may be in the form of an addendum to the release itself, or if you are printing your own forms, space should be provided in the body of the form for such exceptions.

A suggested form for releases accompanies this article. If you prefer to write your own, it would be wise to have it checked by a lawyer to be sure it is binding and legal.

• *See also:* BUSINESS METHODS IN PHOTOGRAPHY; LEGAL ASPECTS OF PHOTOGRAPHY; MODELS AND MODELING; SELLING PICTURES.

Models and Modeling

Working with models is a skill that makes unique demands upon the photographer. Assuming that the photographer is experienced, such tasks as obtaining models, understanding something of human nature, being able to select the right model for the photography to be done, and dealing with the legal and financial aspects of working with models should be accomplished with ease.

While the word "model" may suggest glamorous women and handsome men, the fact is that the appropriate subjects for modeling are many and varied. In addition to the young, slim, and beautiful, the ranks of models include children, senior men and women, weight lifters, characters, and animals. Models, in addition, are specialized into many different categories depending on the nature of the photographic assignment—fashion models, product models, or models needed for a certain type of scene, service, or subject.

Obtaining Models

For the professional or freelancing amateur, the use of a model can be a successful adjunct to a

---

EASTMAN KODAK COMPANY MODELING • PERFORMING NARRATION • WRITTEN EXTRACT RELEASE	SUBJECT _____ PRINT PROJ. # _____ HRS. WORKED

For value received and without further consideration, I hereby consent that all photographs taken of me and/or recordings made of my voice and/or written extraction, in whole or in part, of such recordings or musical performance

at _____ on _____ 19 ____

by _____ for Eastman Kodak Company, may be used by Eastman Kodak Company, or/and others with its consent, for the purposes of illustration, advertising or publication in any manner.

SUBJECT _____
SIGNATURE
SUBJECT'S SOC.SEC.No.

Street _____ City _____ State _____ Zip _____

IF SUBJECT IS A MINOR UNDER LAWS OF STATE WHERE MODELING IS PERFORMED

GUARDIAN _____ GUARDIAN _____
SIGNATURE   PRINT

Street _____ City _____ State _____ Zip _____

Date _____

A typical model release. This particular form is quite general in terms of the use to be made of the model/performer's work. Other forms may be more specifically restrictive.

photographic career. The demand for this kind of photography is certainly evident; models are used to advertise products, services, and recreational facilities. By the same token, models need photographic assignments. Standard working equipment for every model is his or her "book." This is almost always a portfolio of photographs showing the model in poses and situations that demonstrate to prospective clients that the model photographs superbly. And all but the most famous models will also need a supply of composite photographs, which show a variety of poses, to leave behind for the potential client's files. So the photographer who aspires to model photography can, with the necessary time and effort, find a model to meet his or her requirements.

It is worth repeating that models are not all young and glamorous; the pipe-smoking oldster next door might have a photogenic quality that will launch a photographer's career. Do not, by the same token, neglect to make photographs of children and animals.

Before taking any photographs of models, the photographer must first find a subject. Basically there are three ways to go about this: (1) work with a modeling school and/or modeling agency, (2) use a friend or acquaintance, or (3) use an entertainer—actress, dancer, singer—either amateur or professional.

Modeling Agency. A modeling agency supplies models for a fee that varies with location, the type of modeling involved, and the degree of the model's skill.

In small communities, fees range from $5 an hour up to $15, with an occasional agency charging a flat $25 an hour. Next in size are secondary markets. These are cities such as Chicago, Cleveland, Atlanta, and other industrial centers where models earn as much as $60 an hour for posing. Finally there are the major markets of New York and Los Angeles, where a skilled model *starts* at $60 an hour and can expect to get as much as $120 an hour. A few "names" in the major markets earn as much as $1500 to $2000 per day.

In order to utilize the services of a modeling agency, a photographer must have either a specific assignment in mind, an established reputation as a professional, or other proof that he or she is "legitimate." For example, if an advertisement for a restaurant is being photographed, and an attractive woman sitting at a table is needed, an agency will be able to supply one for an hourly fee. The same is true for a fashion photograph or any other assignment for specific clients.

An established professional photographer does not need an assignment in order to hire a model. He or she can explain to the agency that some test work is going to be done or perhaps some pictures are to be taken for sample work. A model will be provided either for a fee, or in exchange for prints for the model's portfolio. The latter is commonly done when the work is for the photographer's samples rather than for resale; the photographer gets fresh, new images to show potential clients, and the model gets new prints for his or her portfolio.

Amateur photographers thinking of going professional, at least on a part-time basis, can also utilize modeling agencies. However, they are going to have to prove themselves to the agencies' satisfaction. This usually involves showing a representative sample of work that will testify to the photographer's skill.

Although the standards for agencies vary around the country, in theory the use of a professional model will insure that the photographer is working with someone who knows how to pose and is relaxed in front of the camera; a professional model can often compensate for a photographer's lack of experience. However, the cost can be fairly high, especially if the photographer is just building a set of sample photographs and must personally absorb the costs. The photographer might be able to pay the model in photographs instead of cash, but the model will expect quality enlargements.

Modeling School. Modeling schools are more numerous than modeling agencies because they are paid a fee by would-be models; the agencies earn their fees only from working models—those with at least a foothold in the commercial modeling world.

Modeling schools are happy to work with legitimate photographers, including advanced amateurs, without being overly concerned about charging for the time. The schools know that, in most cases, the students are not professional enough to handle the jobs for which agency models are expected to pose each day. However, they also know that having the opportunity to appear before a camera is exciting for the students as well as giving them needed experience; it is "glamorous" and a big selling point when seeking new students. Thus, the schools are even more cooperative than the agencies, although the models may lack professional talent.

Friend or Acquaintance. If the photographer is willing to have a friend or acquaintance pose, this can be a highly satisfactory relationship, because such a person will not be overly concerned with hours spent posing, payment, and other matters. Often such an individual will cooperate because he or she is flattered to be asked or simply because of friendship. The photographer should provide the model with photographs of the session. Because this

A specific assignment is not necessary in order to hire a model; the photographer may need a model for portfolio photographs or for experimental work. Sometimes the model will take photographs as payment in lieu of cash for use in his or her own portfolio. Photo by Norman Mosallem for Editorial Photocolor Archives.

Models need not be professionals; friends or acquaintances may be flattered to be asked to model. The photographer should realize, though, that nonprofessionals may require extra direction and coaxing. The photographer met this young woman, a college student, while covering pre-season football tryouts for his newspaper. Photo by Jim Peppler. ▶

Models and Modeling

means of obtaining a model is so convenient and usually satisfactory, it is perhaps used more frequently than any other method.

Entertainers. Another source of models can be found among entertainers. Singers, dancers, and actors are relaxed on stage, they know how to move effectively, and they are delighted to pose in many cases. The top stars of Broadway and Hollywood are not going to pose for such photographs, but there are thousands of amateur and lesser known professionals who will be pleased to pose. These people are found in smaller clubs and lounges, little theater groups, working as apprentices for major production companies, and even in high school and college dramatic productions.

If working with an amateur or professional entertainer, the most effective approach is the same as is used when dealing with a modeling agency for the first time. A photographer should have high-quality samples of past work, even if a model has never been used, to show his or her skill and seriousness about becoming professional. Entertainers know what it means to knock on doors trying to land that first assignment, and will usually be happy to help in exchange for some prints.

The Photographer-Model Relationship

The best photographers of models seem to bring to their work many interpersonal skills; they have the ability to calm nervous individuals, reassure shy people, get the best poses from veteran professionals, and work with individuals who have none of these problems. In many ways, working with models requires the photographer to become, in effect, a director-photographer. In fact, a number of successful fashion photographers have become motion-picture directors, and a number of models have had a second career as actors.

Skills in human relations can be strained to the utmost, for example, when making photographs of a friend. Many people are extremely attractive and vivacious in person; however, in front of a camera and lights they become tense. Their movements are wooden, their faces strained, and they suddenly discover they haven't the slightest idea where to put their hands. This is when the photographer's ability to put the model at ease comes into play.

An equally bad situation can arise with the individual who is completely relaxed and natural in front of the camera, allowing the photographer to picture exactly what he or she sees. A friend is often "seen" on several levels when talking. There is the physical appearance, which will be photographed, but there is also the intangible "personality." The way the model talks and reacts to the photographer can be an important part of what makes that particular individual appealing. Since the camera only records the physical features of the model, someone who seems unusually attractive when talking may photograph less pleasantly, even though he or she is relaxed and cooperative. This problem does *not* usually arise with a professional.

It is important to maintain a professional demeanor and relationship. Have business cards printed if possible, with your name, studio name if any (even if the "studio" is in your home), address, and telephone number. Pass these cards out liberally to prospective co-workers and clients.

The photographer always asks the potential model to telephone to set up an appointment if he or she is approaching the individual for the first time and not working through an agency.

Equipment for Photographing Models

The photographer living in geographical areas where it is usually warm and sunny should consider handling assignments outdoors—taking advantage of wilderness, urban backgrounds, buildings with character, and so on. It is always a good idea to be on the lookout for unusual locations prior to obtaining any assignments.

Whether or not the photographer relies on location settings for work, sooner or later he or she will need a studio and some equipment for it.

Backdrop. A backdrop is needed, which can be made from seamless paper that is available through large photography dealers. Seamless paper is typically placed on a special holder that is usually free-standing (some holders are spring-loaded poles, wedged between the ceiling and the floor). Cost of this equipment varies between $30 and $50. An inexpensive substitute can be rigged by screwing strong hooks or screw eyes into the ceiling. A sturdy nylon cord is then run through the roll of seamless paper and knotted to the hooks or eyes.

Lighting. There are many types and varieties of lights available for photographers to use, ranging from the most inexpensive reflector flood lamps to

(Left) The photographer should always be on the lookout for good locations; interesting backgrounds and settings often enhance fashion photographs and may give model and photographer new ideas for their work. (Right) Studio backdrops of seamless paper are essential to the photographer's work. The paper is readily available and comes in many colors and patterns. Photos by Norman Mosallem for Editorial Photocolor Archives.

very sophisticated and expensive electronic flash units. Quartz-halogen bulbs are an improvement over photofloods. They have a longer life and do not blacken with age the way floodlights do, and they maintain exact color temperature, which can be a blessing with color film. However, both the bulbs and the stands are relatively expensive and not essential. The same is true for such lighting control extras as barn doors, umbrella reflectors, and other tools.

To soften light when using simple photofloods (if the budget does not allow for umbrella reflectors), buy an inexpensive, large wooden frame on which

artists stretch canvas. Take an old white sheet and stretch it taut across the frame. Then staple the sheet to the frame and place it far enough in front of the flood so that it does not overheat or burn, yet close enough so the light passes through the material. The frame can be clamped to a chair or suspended from the same type of cup hooks used for holding seamless paper. This diffuses and softens the light.

Electronic flash is the ultimate in lighting equipment. A minimum of three units plus modeling lights is essential. The modeling lights enable the photographer to preview the effect the flash will have in terms of light and shadow.

If a photographer's budget is low and location photography is being handled with flash, portable electronic flash units will serve the purpose well. These can be mounted on stands adapted for either ac or dc, preferably with a high-powered battery pack and a holder for an accessory modeling light. At this writing, fairly complete systems of this type, including reflectors and a flash meter, will run in the neighborhood of $400. More powerful, less mobile studio types can run double or triple this figure.

Working space will vary with the type of photography involved. A long room in which furniture can be pushed to one corner makes an ideal small studio for models: Full-length fashion poses can easily be handled and simple props can be utilized; however, elaborate settings involving furniture or large products will not be possible in such confined space.

Getting Started

Posing the Model. The biggest problem most photographers have when working with models is finding appropriate ways for them to pose. A professional model knows numerous techniques for posing. A beginning model is not likely to have such skills.

One way to help a new model learn to pose, and at the same time suggest ideas, is for the photographer to collect clippings of pictures showing models in situations similar to those that the photographer is trying to achieve. These clippings will provide a starting point. As the model experiments with poses, new situations will suggest themselves. Clippings will also suggest ideas for clothing, sets, props, and accessories.

Many models have one or more unusually attractive features. Instead of posing full figure, only their lips, hands, or legs are shown. Such models are used to promote cosmetics, shoes and boots, jewelry, and similar items.

There are several ways to photograph a model who specializes in posing only one or more unusually attractive features. Lips, for example, can be photographed extremely close-up with relatively shallow depth of field. This can be done with a macro lens, extension tubes, bellows, or even close-up lenses fitted over a normal lens.

Accessories can be of tremendous help when working with models. Jewelry, scarves, hats, and shoes can be generally utilized in any way the imagination can create. Again, clippings can give ideas of how to use these accessories.

Consideration of the Model. The photographer should always consider the model's well being. It is easy for the photographer to become so absorbed when looking through the camera that he or she

Accessories—hats, scarves, and so forth—can be invaluable when working with models. As the model experiments with the accessories, new situations and poses will suggest themselves. Photo by Norman Mosallem for Editorial Photocolor Archives.

Models and Modeling

The photographer's client will generally provide clothing only if a fashion assignment is being done. Otherwise, the model supplies the clothing. These details should be worked out between model and photographer before the shooting session. Photo by Norman Mosallem for Editorial Archives.

forgets that the model may be perspiring under hot lights in July, or perhaps freezing in a bathing suit in the middle of January. The model should be given regular rest breaks, even if only for a few minutes at a time, during each hour of work. If the photographer plans to work for more than one hour with an amateur, he or she should be certain to allow the model some time to relax between lengthy sessions. A professional is more accustomed to the effort involved and can look attractive and alert when inwardly approaching exhaustion.

If working in a cold location, the model should be given an insulated container of hot tea, coffee, or other warm beverage. In hot weather, cold water should be accessible. The photographer should also plan on treating the model to a meal when the session is long and lasts through the normal lunch or dinner hour. This is an expense chargeable to a client when working on assignment and is deductible as a legitimate business expense (at this writing) if the model is working strictly for the photographer.

Models will usually supply their own clothing, but this is something that should be worked out between the model and the photographer. The only time the client is likely to provide clothing is for a fashion layout.

Models and Modeling

Nude Models

Nude photography is a specialized area of model photography. Markets have traditionally been calendars and special-interest magazines; although there is a growing art photography market, nudes are appearing more widely in advertising, and there is even interest in nude portraits. However, nudes are among the most difficult subjects to handle tastefully and effectively because of the need to utilize form, light, and color in ways that are frequently more sophisticated than for clothed models.

Whatever the intended use of nude photographs, the photographer must obtain a signed model release that includes any conditions or reservations on the use of the photographs, or that spells out the model's willingness for general publication of the nude photographs.

Financial and Legal Aspects

Modeling Fee. Handling of modeling fees varies depending on the source from which the model was obtained. If the photographer is working with an agency, the fee for the model is usually paid on a 30/60-day basis. This means that the photographer is normally expected to pay the fee 30 days after the work is done. This gives the photographer time to collect from the client; however, if there is a delay in collecting this fee, most agencies extend the pay period another 30 days (60 days total from the date of the session). At that point the photographer must pay out of his or her own pocket if payment from the client has not been received. Otherwise the agency assesses a charge for late payment.

In dealing with a modeling school, the photographer will find that there is a wide divergence between schools in the handling of fees. Some do not assess a fee at all, believing instead that the opportunity for their students to work is compensation enough. At any rate, the school will detail the handling of their particular modeling fees. If the photographer is working directly with an individual and there is no intermediary such as a school or an agency, rates are typically spread over a spectrum ranging from low to medium to high. Low rates are usually paid to children, medium rates to individuals who are adults but not professional, and high rates to those individuals who are not only professional but who bring a high degree of expertise or unusual effort to the job.

Model Release Form. Photography of models always requires a signed model release. It is almost impossible to sell a photograph without a release from the model. This also serves as protection for the photographer. The release form is available from photographic equipment stores. One type of model release is a simple 3″ × 5″ card that, when signed, gives permission to use pictures made on a specified day. This form is adequate for most purposes.

While there is a variety of release forms that may be appropriate, the photographer should use a release that is comprehensive and uncomplicated. It is important to remember that photographs of models have one of the longest life spans of any picture a photographer might take, and these photographs can often be resold. The signed release from the model involved should be saved if there is a possibility of reselling these photographs at a later date.

Care of Photographs. A photographer should always file photographs carefully, indexing with cards according to type, clothing, location, props, and so on. Thorough records are invaluable in the event of future legal questions. Also, it is possible to establish a mini-stock agency for the purpose of supplying pictures to magazines, calendar companies, and others from photographs taken in the past. If records are kept, it is easy to locate negatives or slides in the future.

Selling Work

What types of markets can be exploited in a photographer's particular area? This will vary according to the size, location, and industry base. Here are some suggestions.

Photograph models for fashion ads. If the stores do not run photos with their ads in a particular area, they may still want in-store fashion shows and similar events to be recorded using models for their publicity department.

Advertising agencies are potential clients. Even small agencies will need model photography from time to time.

Talk with restaurant owners. They might want a photo of the restaurant interior featuring a pretty waitress or handsome waiter.

High school, college, amateur, and professional theater groups can use model photography skills, as can entertainers, especially those appearing in the lower-paying clubs. They can be contacted directly,

Department stores and other clothing stores may not use photographs in their advertising. However, they may want in-store fashion shows and similar events recorded for publicity purposes. Photo by Norman Mosallem for Editorial Photocolor Archives.

through club managers, and through area talent agencies.

Model portfolios can be taken by making arrangements with modeling schools, agencies, and even by advertising in area high school and college newspapers that accept outside advertising. Students who have modeling aspirations may respond to such an ad.

Finally, there are the magazines that buy portraits of pretty girls. These range from confessions magazines (for cover use), to men's magazines, to family publications that like demurely clothed, pretty girls in scenic settings.

The photography of models can be a part of almost every picture a photographer takes, the only limitations being personal ability. With hard work and careful planning of photographs, a photographer can add an extremely rewarding, new experience to amateur or professional photographic work.
• *See also:* DANCE PHOTOGRAPHY; FASHION PHOTOGRAPHY; GLAMOUR PHOTOGRAPHY; MODEL RELEASE; THEATRICAL PHOTOGRAPHY.

Further Reading: Farber, Robert. *Images of Woman.* Garden City, NY: Amphoto, 1976; ———. *Professional Fashion Photography.* Garden City, NY: Amphoto, 1978.

Moiré Pattern

Moiré is the interference effect created when two or more screen patterns are superimposed out of register. If the screens are identical, the moiré is visible as a uniform crosshatching, spotting, mottling, or similar pattern. If the screens differ, a modulated

A moiré pattern can be created intentionally for expressive effect, most easily during the printing process. For this moiré effect, the original portrait was duplicated on color transparency film. Then two high-contrast black-and-white negatives of a radial-line moiré pattern, aligned to center on the eyes, were double-exposed onto the duplicate through a yellow filter. Photo by Jerry O'Neill.

moiré will be visible, one that grows darker as the screens are progressively farther out of register. This is because the lines or dots of one screen block more and more of the spaces in another.

Moiré can be created intentionally for expressive effect by using suitable screens (1) on the camera, (2) in the enlarger, or (3) in contact with the printing paper. It is most easily observed and controlled during printing.

Moiré is an unwanted effect in halftone reproduction. It often arises when a halftone image is rephotographed through a halftone screen to make a duplicate reproduction negative or plate. For this reason, unscreened copy is preferred for reproduction. When halftone color separations are made, the screen must be at a different angle for each plate so that moiré will not occur when the images are superimposed in printing.

• *See also:* GRAPHIC ARTS PHOTOGRAPHY; HALFTONE; SPECIAL EFFECTS.

Monckhoven, Desiré Charles Emanuel van

(1834–1882)
Belgian chemist and photographer

Monckhoven was a leading photographic scientist who made contributions in the fields of optics, emulsions, chemistry, and printing processes. In the mid-1860's, he devised an improved solar (sun-illuminated) enlarger that used a meniscus lens between the condenser and the negative to correct spherical and chromatic aberrations and to provide more even illumination. He incorporated such an enlarger in a studio he constructed for a Viennese photographer, making possible life-size portraits, which became a sensation of the day. He later perfected a system of artificial illumination for the enlarger.

Monckhoven's discovery of the use of ammonia to prepare silver bromide-gelatin emulsions led him to manufacture and supply emulsion to leading dry-plate factories. He also manufactured pigment papers, used for the forerunners of the carbon, carbro, and similar processes. Other researches led to contributions to spectral analysis by photography and to astronomical photography.

Monobaths

A monobath is a single solution containing both developer and fixer, intended to process a negative emulsion in a single step. The idea is far from new; the possibility of combining development and fixation was first investigated by Richmond in 1889. The monobath is a superficially attractive idea; it would appear that the process would always come to the same conclusion, and that neither time nor temperature control would be required.

Unfortunately, this is not true in practice. The major stumbling block is that development and fixation are not affected by temperature in the same way. At low temperatures, a monobath will complete fixation before development is finished, and the negative will have low contrast. At high temperatures, the negative will develop too long before fixation, and it will have high contrast. Thus, temperature control is just as important in a monobath as in conventional processing.

There are additional difficulties; fixer reacts with most developing agents, causing a good deal of chemical fog, as well as sulfur stain and other defects. Furthermore, even when a satisfactory combination of developer and fixer concentration is found, it may work well only with a single film emulsion; no such thing as a universal monobath has yet been developed.

Still another serious problem exists with monobaths; because the developer must necessarily be highly alkaline, it cannot be combined with an acid hardening fixing bath, and monobaths tend to soften emulsions severely. Often the result is reticulation, frilling, and other damage to the gelatin.

Experimentation with monobaths can be a source of pleasure and amusement to those so inclined. One approach is to try developing agents other than Metol and hydroquinone; some experimenters report promising results with Phenidone® and Dimezone developing agents. Another approach is the use of fixing agents other than sodium thiosulfate; however, this is less promising. Sodium thiocyanate, for instance, has an even more severe softening effect upon gelatin than does sodium thiosulfate.

The following is a typical monobath formula:

Developer-Fixer

Sodium sulfite	50 g
Hydroquinone	15 g
Phenidone	10 g
Potassium alum	18 g
Sodium hydroxide	18 g
Sodium thiosulfate, anhydrous	130 g
Water (distilled) to make	1 litre

Use the developer-fixer full strength or dilute 1:1 with water. Process at least 7 minutes at 15–27 C (60–80 F); wash thoroughly, typically 5 to 20 minutes. Handle the film with care since the emulsion will be soft. Use a wetting agent before drying. Typically, monobaths cause decreased film speed and increased graininess with most films. Mix the solution shortly before use since it will lose its effectiveness if kept more than a few days.

• *See also:* DEVELOPERS AND DEVELOPING.

 Montage

A montage is a composite image made by assembling pieces of two-dimensional images. The elements may be both photographic and non-photographic (drawings, engravings, printed reproductions, and so on); often the term *photomontage* is used to designate a composite in which all elements are photographic. Unlike *collage,* which may attempt to make expressive use of the cutting apart or disassembly of an image, montage brings all elements into a single, unified composition. Often, great care is taken to conceal the fact that different images have been used; elements are blended to look like a single photograph. In other cases the use of different images is apparent.

The term "montage" is also used to mean a kind of dynamic motion-picture editing; it is the French word meaning the combined process of motion-picture assembly and editing.

Uses of Montage

Montage has been used for expressive, commercial, and scientific purposes. Laszlo Moholy-Nagy made montage assignments a major teaching device in his design classes at the Bauhaus in Germany in the 1920's and later at the New Bauhaus in Chicago. John Heartfield achieved strong anti-Nazi political statements with photomontages in the 1930's. Barbara Morgan and others have explored its use in the United States. Montage is often used to create an image that cannot be made by multiple exposure or combination printing. Montages are widely used for advertising and display purposes. A primary scientific use is in assembling large numbers of aerial photographs into mosaics for mapping.

Basic Methods of Montage

Paste-Up Montage. Where the sections of a montage must match exactly, the separate photographs must all be made to the same scale. In aerial work, contact prints from the large (9″ × 9″) negatives are commonly used, so there is no scale problem. In advertising and other work in which it is not at all necessary that the various separate images match for scale, prints are usually made by enlargement. It is well to plan the montage in advance in such cases, and to make a full-scale sketch of the finished montage for scaling and assembly.

Prints should be made on single-weight or light-weight paper, so that the overlaps of the separate prints will be less conspicuous. It is not possible to butt the adjacent prints; they will pull apart as the paper shrinks in drying.

A method often used for making aerial mosaics is to cut the paper only part way through by scoring it on the face with a very sharp razor blade. Then the paper is lightly dampened along the score line, and the part to be discarded is pulled up and away from the print. This causes the paper base to tear away from the edge, producing a very thin area right at the edges. When this is pasted down, the join is nearly invisible.

Assembly is done on a sheet of Homasote material or flakeboard. The adhesive generally used in aerial work is a solution of gum arabic (commercially available as "mucilage"). This is brushed liberally on the back of the print and also on the mount. Prints can easily be moved about while they are wet, until exact register is attained; then the prints are rubbed down with a squeegee made of a piece of Lucite material, polished to a round edge. Any adhesive that gets on the front face of the prints can easily be removed with a damp sponge before it dries.

After drying, any misregisters, damages at the prints' edges, and other flaws are corrected by painting out with tempera water colors, applied with an

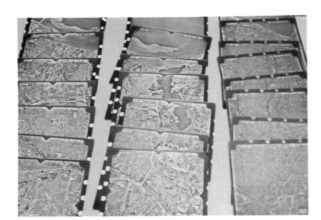

(Below) An aerial mosaic is constructed by first lining up overlapping prints so they match exactly. (Right) They are then pasted down on Homasote material or flakeboard; while they are wet, they can be moved around until exact register is attained.

To make this montage, a black-and-white continuous-tone negative was contact printed onto a high-contrast paper to produce the high-contrast positive of the boat. Then the positive was sandwiched with a slide containing two flowers. Photo by Barbara Jean. ▶

artist's sable brush, or for large areas, an air brush. The final montage is then copied to a single large negative, and final prints are made from this.

Other backing materials and adhesives may be equally suitable, depending upon whether the montage is to be exhibited directly, or rephotographed so that prints with completely uniform surfaces can be made. (*See:* PANORAMIC PHOTOGRAPHY.)

Another use of the paste-up montage is to make a non-realistic derivation, called a mosaic picture, from one or two prints. The print is sliced into thin strips and reassembled with alternate sections out of phase with each other. When two prints are used, strips from the two pictures are alternated.

Montage from Different Negatives. When the final print size is not too large, a montage can be made from a number of different negatives on a single sheet of paper. The design is marked out to size on a blank sheet of paper. The negatives are put in the enlarger one at a time, and each is sized to the area assigned to it. A small overlap (¼ to ½ inch) is allowed between the pictures. The marked master sheet is removed and photographic paper is carefully located in the easel. While the exposure is being made, the edges of the picture are dodged so that they will fade. In this way one image blends into the next. Test strips determine the correct exposure for each negative, and the photographic paper is marked so that it goes into the easel the same way each time. Most workers make two or three prints in case an error is made on one.

While this method may seem like quite a bit of work, the time saved by not having to mount individual prints and not having a great deal of print retouching to do later, saves time in the long run. Many people prefer the blended tones where separate prints come together to the abrupt joins of a paste-up montage.

• *See also:* COLLAGE; SPECIAL EFFECTS.

  Moonlight Photography

There are two separate problems in moonlight photography. The first is the question of photographing a landscape or city scene by moonlight; the other is photographing the moon itself. The two are quite different, photographically. The moon itself is a grayish object, illuminated by full sunlight; since it reflects about 7 percent of the light falling upon it, it is roughly half as bright as a normal earth landscape, and is thus easily photographed with short exposures. On the other hand, since an earth scene illuminated by moonlight receives sunlight only by reflection from the moon, it is much less brightly illuminated, and exposures must be long.

Moonlit Landscapes

Moonlight shots almost always require time exposures, and this in turn requires the use of a tripod.

As a starting point, try an exposure of 50 seconds at $f/5.6$ with Kodak Tri-X pan film normally rated at ASA 400. You can shorten the required exposure time by opening the aperture of the camera or by rating the film at a higher index, such as 1250, and push-processing the film. An exposure for Tri-X film rated at 1250 would be 16 seconds at $f/5.6$. Since the effect produced is somewhat unpredictable, bracketing exposures by one and two stops over and under the starting point is advisable. Underexposure tends to give a more subjective impression of a moonlit scene.

When exposures exceed one second, there is some loss of photographic response, due to reciprocity effect. This means that with these exposure times, a proportionate increase in exposure time will not produce a proportionate increase in density. For this reason, it is best to keep the exposure time uniform and change only the lens aperture wherever this is possible.

Reciprocity compensation always involves increasing the exposure over the calculated one. If, for instance, you have an exposure meter that can read in moonlight, you will still have to compensate for reciprocity effect; you cannot simply take the readings off the meter calculator when exposures exceed one second. Approximate corrections are as follows:

If the exposure time is:	*Increase exposure given by the meter by:*
1–2 seconds	½ stop
3–6 seconds	1 stop
7–16 seconds	1½ stops
17–35 seconds	2 stops
36–70 seconds	2½ stops

In addition, you need some compensation for the character of the scene and its reflectance. Thus, when estimating exposures (without a meter) you will find the above starting point will have to be increased by one stop for a landscape without water in it or a medium close-up. On the other hand, a scene with snow on the ground will require one stop less than the estimate. City scenes, containing street lights, building lights, and other light sources, will probably require two stops less than the estimate. In any case, these exposures are just starting points; you will always have to bracket above and below, at least until you have had considerable experience.

If you include the moon itself in the scene, you will have to keep exposures short; remember the earth and the moon are both in motion, and if you make a long time exposure with the moon in the scene, it will turn out egg-shaped instead of round; in extreme cases, it will be drawn out into a fat sausage. Furthermore, because the moon itself is much brighter than the landscape, it will be badly overexposed and will contain no detail at all.

• *See also:* AVAILABLE-LIGHT PHOTOGRAPHY; EXISTING-LIGHT PHOTOGRAPHY; MOON, PHOTOGRAPHY OF.

Moon, Photography of

To photograph the moon, remember that the surface of the moon is mainly grayish volcanic material; it is illuminated by full, bright sunlight, and since its reflectance is about 7 percent, exposures will be only very slightly longer than an earth scene in bright sun. (The earth has about 18 percent reflectance.)

As a starting point, try the rule of thumb for normal bright sunlit scenes (shutter speed of 1/ASA, film speed at $f/16$). That would be 1/400 sec. at $f/16$ for a high-speed black-and-white film, or 1/25 sec. at $f/16$ for a slow color slide film. If you are

making the exposure through a telephoto lens or telescope, use a higher shutter speed. Then try several more exposures on the overexposure side at one-stop intervals. With Tri-X film or a high-speed color film, try exposures of 1/500, 1/250, 1/125, and 1/60 sec. at $f/16$. The exposures can vary a good deal because they are affected by the state of the earth's atmosphere, your altitude, and other factors. A hazy night will call for one stop more exposure than normal, while shooting at altitudes above 7000 feet may require one stop less than normal.

The moon's image is smaller than it appears to be, and on a 35 mm negative with a 50 mm lens, it is likely to be nothing more than a dot. To get a sizable moon image, use a fairly long-focus lens on your camera. If you have a small telescope, such as a Questar, Celestron, or others, finely detailed moon images can easily be made with it. If you do not have one, a mirror telephoto lens of about 500 mm to 1000 mm focal length will do almost as well.

A "harvest moon" effect can be obtained by making a double exposure with two different lenses. First, the landscape alone is photographed with a standard 50 mm lens, using a long exposure. Then, a short exposure is made of the moon itself. Photo by Hal Berg.

Moonlit landscapes may be simulated by photographing the scene in daylight through filters. This landscape with the moon was made by first photographing the house by daylight, underexposing it through a polarizing screen. The image of the moon was later added by making a second exposure on the same frame of film with a telephoto lens and no filter. Normal exposure was used for the moon. Photo by William Michaud.

Moon, Photography of

Some interesting effects can be had by making double exposures with two different lenses. With the standard 50 mm lens, make an exposure of the landscape without the moon in the frame, using one of the long exposures given for moonlit landscapes. Now, using the double-exposure feature of your camera—if it has this capability—rewind the shutter without advancing the film, change to a long-focus lens, aim at the moon, and place its image in a part of the frame where it will appear in the sky area of the finished negative. Now make the exposure for the moon; this will be very short and will not register any landscape at all. When the negative is developed, you will have a night landscape with a big "harvest moon" in it. A reflex camera is a must for this sort of photography.

• *See also:* ASTROPHOTOGRAPHY; ECLIPSE PHOTOGRAPHY.

Morse, Samuel Finley Breese

(1791–1872)
American inventor and portrait painter

An accomplished portraitist and first president of the National Academy of Design, Morse is best known for inventing a practical electric telegraph. On a trip to Paris in 1839, he met Louis Daguerre and was greatly impressed with the quality of daguerreotype images and the possibilities it offered in portraiture.

He had a daguerreotype camera built and brought it back to America. In September of 1839, he made some daguerreotype portraits that were purely experimental because exposures were 10–20 minutes. In 1840, improvements in the process led him to open a daguerreotype studio in New York, in partnership with John W. Draper. Because Morse, along with Draper, gave lessons to other photographers in this new method of making portraits, he is considered to have had considerable influence on the growth of photography in the United States. However, Morse dropped out of the operation shortly thereafter to devote himself to improving and promoting his system of electrotelegraphic communication.

Mosaic Systems

Most single-image methods of additive color photography have employed a mosaic, or filter screen, of multiple red, green, and blue elements. When viewed at a suitable distance, the individual elements are not visible; instead they blend together to create composite color effects. The size of the mosaic elements is chosen so that the elements are invisible at normal viewing distances; however, they become quite visible when the image is enlarged or projected.

Almost all systems operate on the same principles. An image is photographed on a black-and-white emulsion through the mosaic, which breaks it up into individual red, green, and blue density records. The image is processed or printed to a transparency. When viewed through the same mosaic or a matching one, the densities of the transparency control the amount of the transmitted light, and the mosaic filters it to reproduce an image of the original subject colors and relative brightnesses.

Random and Regular Mosaics

There are two types of mosaics: random and regular. In a random mosaic the elements are not all the same size or shape (although the variation is slight); the elements are randomly but not necessarily uniformly distributed. Such a mosaic may create mottling or color spotting because it is impossible to avoid the statistical clumping of some elements of the same color. The first commercial random mosaic system was the Lumiere Autochrome plate process; the original mosaic elements were dyed grains of potato starch bonded to a panchromatic plate.

A regular, or line-screen, mosaic consists of uniformly distributed elements of identical size and shape. The best known regular mosaic processes were Dufaycolor and Finlay color.

The face of a color television tube is a regular mosaic of red, green, and blue phosphor dots. When excited by electron beams, the dots glow red, green, and blue, creating additive full-color images.

Polavision Movie Film

The only current photographic film that uses mosaics is the Polavision movie film. It has a screen of parallel-line color-filter elements.

Earlier mosaic color films have been replaced (with the one exception noted) with subtractive color films for two reasons. The first is that mosaic transparencies are very dark. Not only does the silver image absorb a good deal of light, but the filter elements are additive filters, each subtracting two thirds of the light spectrum. When the mosaic transparencies were used as originals for halftone reproduction, this could be corrected in making the halftones, but the transparencies were very difficult to see when projected. The other disadvantage was that the mosaic pattern elements were of such size that they showed even with a moderate degree of enlargement.

The Polavision film overcomes these disadvantages in two ways. Although the film images are dark, they are only projected through an electronic system that uses a television-type tube as the viewing screen. The electronics brighten the image. Modern technology is used to make the line screens very narrow, while the locked-in projector system limits the size of the projected image.

• *See also:* ADDITIVE COLOR SYNTHESIS; COLOR THEORY; DUFAYCOLOR; LINE-SCREEN SYSTEMS; LUMIERE COLOR PROCESSES.

Motion-Picture Production

While it is true that the success of any project depends upon adequate planning, motion-picture production, because of the many elements involved, calls for very careful definition and scheduling of every step in the project. A poorly planned motion picture almost always costs more than a well-planned film, and a slipshod production also stands the chance of being ineffective. (*See:* AUDIOVISUAL PLANNING.)

The Film Treatment

The film treatment is a statement of the content of a proposed motion picture. It may be brief for a simple film, but the treatment should be detailed enough in every case to give the reader a solid idea of what the filmmaker plans to do. The film treatment should also include a statement of the film's "Communication Objective"—why it is being made, and what it will accomplish (ideally, a measurable

change in viewer behavior, attitude, knowledge, and so forth). The treatment should also include production information detailing the camera original and release print film format and type—35 mm, 16 mm, or super 8; color or black-and-white.

The treatment proper should be written in a narrative form without technical terms so that anyone can get a good idea of what the film will be like. If there is narration or dialogue planned, briefly sketch out what is to be said. Indicate to the reader that he or she is reading a first effort with phrases such as, "Now the narrator comments along these lines." The work done on a thorough treatment will be repaid many times if all concerned have a very clear idea of what it is you propose to do; and a script based on an approved treatment will, generally, be in less danger of numerous rewrites.

Visualizing the Treatment

After the treatment has been approved, many filmmakers move next to the storyboard to help in further defining their production details. Storyboard forms are available in art supply stores, particularly in metropolitan areas where there is an active motion-picture or audiovisual industry. Specially prepared 4″ × 6″ or 5″ × 7″ cards are a second option open to the filmmaker. These cards can easily be made locally and duplicated in quantity by any readily available method. If large numbers are needed, it is often practical to have them produced at a local print shop.

The large rectangle on the cards provides a frame for a rough sketch of the anticipated shot. Fine artistry is rarely needed; stick figures and general outlines of objects can serve. Before sketching each shot, visit the location where it is to be made, if at all possible; without on-the-spot viewing, you may easily visualize a shot that later proves impossible because of space limitations, immovable objects, or other restrictions. Photographs shot on scouting locations can also be attached to the frame on the card.

The number (or title) of the production is placed in the space designated "Job." If a series of films is being planned, the number "1" should be entered on each card.

"Shot" indicates the position the shot is to occupy in the final film. At this point, it is advisable to enter the number in pencil, numbering the card permanently only when it is certain that there will be no further change in the sequence of shots.

Under "Production Notes," write any suggestions for making the shot, such as camera setup, type of shot (long, medium, or close-up), and the approximate footage needed.

A summary of the purpose of the shot or some of the intended narration can be entered under "Commentary."

Each completed card represents one shot in the planned movie. Therefore, the quantity of these cards seldom corresponds to the number of "idea" cards; one idea may require several shots to make its point. (*See:* Audiovisual Planning.)

As soon as cards describing all the planned shots have been completed and placed on the board, the cost of producing the film can be estimated and presented with the storyboard for approval. After approval, numbers indicating the correct sequence are marked permanently in the upper right-hand corner of the cards.

Many short, uncomplicated movies can be filmed directly, using the approved storyboard cards for guidance. For such films, a formal script is often unnecessary. A script, however, is a requisite for most productions that incorporate narration or dialogue, especially if the film length is substantial.

The Film Script

The storyboard cards often provide the basis for writing the script, which includes both a description of each shot and the narration or dialogue that will accompany the shots.

In preparing the script for a sound film that will have voice-over narration, one becomes aware of such problems as a portion of narration that is too long for the matching shot. Very often, it is not practical to hold the shot on the screen long enough for the planned narration to be spoken. Undoubtedly, the narration needs to be rewritten to present verbal information in briefer terms, or additional shots (maybe different angles on the same subject) can be planned to lengthen the visual portion of the film.

Completion of the script makes it possible to prepare a proposed budget. The budget should be realistic, providing for contingencies such as illness of a key individual, unusually prolonged bad weather, rephotographing bad shots, rerecording, or other occurrences that can delay production and increase costs.

When the final script and budget receive the necessary approvals, the director prepares a shot breakdown—also called a script breakdown. (In many in-plant situations, one person can function as both camera operator and director.) In the script, shots are listed in their order of appearance on the screen; the shot breakdown, on the other hand, places scenes in the most practical sequence for shooting.

While it is tempting, and sometimes possible, to do shooting in the same order in which the scenes will appear in the completed motion picture, this procedure is usually wasteful of time and money, particularly for complex productions. The best practice is to group your shots by location, time of day, or whatever approach allows you to finish one set of scenes before moving on. Here is a typical shot list, with scenes grouped for maximum efficiency of the film crew:

1. 50–59 warehouse background plate.
2. 23, 24, 29, 30 department store.
3. 31–33 accounting office.
4. Building 205:
   64–72 Miracode equipment film
   38, 39 keypunch
   40, 42–44 computer.
5. Same accounting office as 3:
   34–37 IC4 operation
   45 same
   13, 22 screen.
6. Live sound:
   2 & 75 irate man
   5 & 75 diaper girl
   6 shrimp
   7 & 77 wheelchair
   8 & 78 girl
   9 & 97 grease smudge
   80 man at end in smoking jacket
   10, 14, 16, wild hat
   15 girl answering wild hat
   47–49 Recordak Microstrip reader operator
   50–58 warehouse man.
7. Exteriors:
   1 switchyard
   3, 4 store window.

8. Miscellaneous:
   (Can shoot any convenient time)
   25–28 hourglass, and so on.
   41 wastebasket
   61 display.
9. Narrator.

When shooting out of script order, keep in mind what precedes and follows the shot you are making. For example, if you are shooting a truck in one location and intend to film the succeeding shot in another location days later, make sure the truck and driver are similar enough to convince the viewer. A red truck in one location should not change to a green truck in the next shot, unless that is your intention.

Advance Preparations for Photography

Preparations for filming may be either extremely complex or relatively simple, depending on the scope of the movie. Scheduling, studio and location shooting, travel, casting, lighting, set design and construction, talent releases, music selection, sound recording, editing, and laboratory work can involve hundreds of detailed functions in producing an ambitious film.

Even for a modest film, advance preparations will result in the saving of time and money. Locations should be scouted and prepared. Electrical outlets and wiring should be checked against possible power requirements; additional electrical service may be required. Simple backdrops can be produced and erected to eliminate cluttered or undesirable backgrounds, as well as to avoid underexposed areas more distant from the camera than the subject field. Props can be ordered and placed in their prescribed positions. Working space for the camera and lights can be cleared if necessary.

Any "actors" who are to appear in the scene should be briefed in advance so that they will be ready to play their parts. Their clothing should be specified to make certain that their appearance will be suitable for the shot, and the same clothing should be available if it is necessary to rephotograph the scene at a later date.

A written release should be obtained in advance from each person who will be recognizable in a scene. Legal model release forms are available for this purpose and should be a requirement. If the model is a minor, a parent's or guardian's signature must also be secured. *See:* MODEL RELEASE.

At this stage of the production, it becomes the duty of those who have been assigned various responsibilities for the success of the motion picture to make sure that all of the details are planned and executed properly—and on schedule.

Equipment and Procedures for Shooting

The Camera. The selection of the right camera or cameras to meet the particular job requirements is most important. The choice may be yours, or you may be required to use equipment provided by others. If the choice is yours, there are a few basic points to be considered.

Hand-Held Camera. This type of camera is usually lightweight and designed for rapid operation. It can be either silent or sound. It utilizes a short or limited film load and can be either spring-wound or electrically operated. This type of camera is very adaptable where conditions demand ease of handling and rugged construction. Such situations would involve sports, news, television reporting, and shooting for in-plant films.
IMPORTANT: Some test footage from each camera that will be used during a production should be projected to make sure that the exposure, focus, image steadiness, and the frame-line-to-perforation relationship are satisfactory.

Silent Professional Production (Studio) Camera. This camera type is capable of producing the highest image quality. It usually has registration pin movement to provide maximum steadiness, interchangeable electric motor drives (wild, governor-controlled, synchronous), magazines, and through-the-lens reflex viewing. It can also be equipped with various fixed-focal-length lenses or zoom lenses.

Sound Camera. The sound camera generally includes all of the features provided on the silent professional production (studio) camera, plus the necessary equipment to produce sound motion pictures. Some models are designed to produce a minimum of noise while running (without a blimp). Other models may require a blimp or a "barney" to minimize the running noise.

NOTE: Many of the currently manufactured cameras are capable of being utilized in all categories because of their versatility.

Special-Purpose Camera. This type of camera is difficult to categorize and generally would only interest the cinematographer when he or she has to make a choice of equipment for a special assignment. Such cameras are usually designed and used with a special purpose in mind—for example, animation, time-lapse, or high-speed photography.

Purchase, Rental, or Lease. Since budget and cost are most important factors, these three possibilities should be considered very carefully. If your budget limitations prevent the purchase of necessary equipment, or if the need is only temporary, then rental arrangements can be made on a daily, weekly, or long-term basis from professional suppliers of photographic equipment. A short test of all rented or borrowed equipment should be made to make sure that the camera, lenses, and so forth, function satisfactorily.

Lens Selection. Choosing the proper lens for a specific job is also an important aspect of motion-picture production.

Wide-Angle Lens. The majority of scenes to be photographed can probably be done satisfactorily with a normal-focal-length lens. However, certain scenes will require the use of a wide-angle lens (of less than normal focal length, or approximately 9 to 15 mm).

Wide-angle shots include more of the scene than your eyes would concentrate on if you were standing next to the camera. The viewer feels farther away from the subject than he or she actually is and experiences an exaggerated feeling of depth. A wide-angle lens is especially useful when you want to include more in the scene than is possible with a normal lens, and the camera cannot be moved away from the subject because of some physical restriction such as a wall. Some producers use this lens in movie sequences for an "establishing" shot.

When extreme wide-angle lenses are used, objects that are particularly close to the camera will appear changed in perspective and often be distorted. This is because the camera is closer to the object being photographed than is proper for normal perspective. However, wide-angle shots have greater depth of field (range of sharp focus) than other types of shots, so if the camera angle is carefully chosen, a scene can be filmed with an element very prominent in the foreground and still have distant background objects in acceptably sharp focus. (*See:* WIDE-ANGLE PHOTOGRAPHY.)

Normal Lens. The lenses normally supplied with 16 mm motion-picture cameras are of 1-inch (25 mm) focal length and cover a horizontal angle of 23 degrees and a vertical angle of 16.9 degrees. Foreground, middle, and background elements photographed with a normal lens are reproduced with perspective similar to that of a scene perceived by the human eye.

It is important to bear in mind that the field coverage of motion-picture camera lenses is intentionally about one half that of equivalent still-camera lenses. The reason for this is that, when viewing a still picture, the eye can leisurely scan the entire picture from one side to the other; whereas in motion pictures, action is taking place and the image is constantly changing so that the viewer's eyes do not have the time to scan as large an area as they do when looking at still pictures. The use of a normal lens in motion pictures may add to the realism of the picture and make it possible for the producer to direct the audience's attention to the important action. (*See:* LENSES.)

Telephoto Lens. A telephoto lens has a greater-than-normal focal length (approximately 75 to 200 mm). It is generally used to narrow or concentrate the field of view without moving the camera closer to the subject. This type of shot is very useful when you want to increase the image size of the subject but cannot reduce the camera-to-subject distance. Telephoto shots produce the effect of compressing the planes in a scene so that the foreground, middle, and background elements appear very close together.

With a telephoto lens, occasional close-up shots can be made from the same camera position that is used for filming the medium shot with a lens of normal focal length, thus avoiding the need for camera repositioning. This is especially helpful when shooting time is limited.

A telephoto lens has less depth of field than does a normal or wide-angle lens. Consequently, the distance from subject to film should be very carefully measured, especially for close scenes. This limited depth of field can be used advantageously to throw the background out of focus and in this way help to put more visual emphasis on the object of primary interest.

IMPORTANT: Slight camera movement is usually not objectionably evident in films made with lenses of normal or short focal length. However, a telephoto lens will magnify unsteadiness to about the same degree as it magnifies the size of the image; therefore, when filming with a telephoto lens, it is important to use a solid tripod. (*See:* TELEPHOTOGRAPHY.)

Zoom Lens. A lens of variable focal length, commonly called a zoom lens, is capable of doing the work of several lenses of different fixed focal lengths. The focal length of the zoom lens can be varied continuously from wide-angle to telephoto, which allows the cinematographer to choose framing of a scene by zooming in close or "backing away" during filming. A typical zoom lens can have variable focal lengths from 9.5 to 95 mm, or from 12 to 120 mm—a ratio of 1 to 10 or greater.

The ability to control the area of the field being photographed by means of a zoom lens is of tremendous value. To the uninitiated, however, the novelty of the zoom capability may be irresistibly fascinating, and overuse of this feature can lead to distracting results. Plan shots carefully, and keep these most important facts in mind while shooting:

1. A zoom lens can accomplish basically the same results that fixed-focal-length lenses are capable of.
2. The optical rules that apply to lenses of fixed focal lengths also apply to zoom lenses, especially when set at the wide-angle and telephoto positions.
3. Do not pan and zoom at the same time except to maintain centering of the subject during a zoom.
4. Always focus the zoom lens at the maximum aperture and at the longest focal length, regardless of the setting to be used for filming a scene.
5. Determine whether the zoom lens focus scale is calibrated to the front lens element or to the film plane of the camera. This is a relatively simple point; however, much footage can be spoiled if the shooting distance is incorrectly determined.

6. Always set the exposure by using the T-stop calibration, when provided on the lens; this adjusts the exposure for the light loss caused by the light having to pass through the more numerous elements of the zoom lens.
7. Any camera equipped with a zoom lens should be mounted on a firm support for maximum steadiness, especially when a long-focal-length setting is to be used.
8. Special motors are available that can be attached to some nonautomatic zoom lenses to produce smooth zoom action that is difficult or impossible to accomplish when the lens is operated manually.
9. The depth of field at the longer focal lengths is quite shallow, especially at the large apertures. At times, this characteristic can be used to an advantage; it can also create problems. (*See:* ZOOM LENS.)

General Rules for Lenses. The following rules can be applied to all of the lens types mentioned:

1. Always use a lens hood when shooting.
2. Make sure that the front and rear lens elements are clean.
3. With threaded mounts, remove all dust and grit from the threads and the metal facing of the mount.
4. When mounting any lens, seat it fully and lock it securely into place.
5. Even though lenses may be interchangeable between cameras, each lens should be checked either optically or photographically on its mount before filming is begun.
6. Determine for each camera whether the focus of the lens has been established at the front taking lens element or at the camera focal plane.
7. Time permitting, check the lens for focus shift at different apertures.
8. All lenses should be protected (with lens caps) during transportation from one location to another.

Camera Support. While acceptable movies can be obtained when uncontrolled action is being shot with the camera hand-held, a steady camera support is a necessity for high-quality results when controlled action is being filmed. The focal length of the lens being used and the kind of action being photographed will in all probability dictate the type of support necessary. The following types of camera supports are available, and all have been used successfully.

Sturdy Tripods. Available in various heights, tripods can be equipped with balljoint, geared, fluid, friction, or gyroscopic heads. Additional stability and mobility can be obtained by using a tripod triangle or a three-wheel dolly attached to the feet of the tripod.

Camera Clamps. These support the camera from any available frame, railing, or fixture.

Dolly. A dolly may carry both camera and camera operator and facilitates camera movement during the shooting of a scene. It can range from a simple, sturdy materials-handling truck or possibly an office chair, to a complicated, rubber-tired custom-made vehicle with a boom attached. (The inexpensive truck dolly should be fitted with brakes, wheel chocks, or jacks to hold it in place during filming.)

Body Brace. This device holds the camera securely on the body of the user, leaving the hands free to operate the camera. The brace is especially useful for hand-held camera shooting and provides maximum mobility.

A sturdy tripod is essential for proper camera support.

(Right) A simple tripod fitted to a wheeled triangle makes a very portable dolly. The dolly is necessary for smooth camera movement. (Far right) A body brace for hand-held cameras provides a steady support and allows the cameraman to relocate quickly between shots.

Viewfinders. Many currently manufactured professional cameras have some form of reflex (through-the-lens) viewing that eliminates the parallax problem (see below) and permits accurate focusing and framing of each scene. Some finders also provide a magnified image on a fine ground-glass screen. Auxiliary attachments may include:

1. Periscopic finder—allows the cinematographer to see through the viewfinder in close or cramped quarters (swivels horizontally and vertically).
2. Rubber eye cushion—fits over the camera viewfinder eyecup.
3. Ground glass with TV framing guide and cross hair.
4. Ground glass with projector aperture framing guide and cross hair.

Some currently manufactured cameras are equipped with direct-view optically matched and, in some cases, focusing viewfinders for each lens. This type of finder is positioned either above or on the side of the camera lens and provides satisfactory framing at intermediate to far shooting distances. However, the user must be especially careful when framing a scene at close distances because of parallax. In simple terms, parallax is the difference in alignment between what you see through the viewfinder at close distances and what the camera lens "sees." This difference is caused by the position of the viewfinder lens relative to the camera lens. Generally, the camera viewfinder will have a built-in aid to overcome this problem.

Lens Turret. A lens turret is usually in the form of a round plate that is mounted on the front of a camera. It will accommodate two or more lenses and can be rotated quickly and easily to position the desired lens for shooting. The turret must position each lens accurately and then hold the lens securely so that best-quality results will be obtained. Some turrets have threaded lens mounts while others use a bayonet and locking-type mount. Both types of mounts must maintain an accurate lens flange focal distance and optically center the lens. A well-designed and accurately made turret will provide the cinematographer with some of the flexibility that is provided by a zoom lens.

Some lenses of unusually long focal length may require additional support, such as a bracket or a cradle, to provide and to maintain accurate seating and alignment on the camera turret.

Frame Rate. Silent films are usually made at the rate of 18 frames per second. Optical and most magnetic-sound pictures, however, are exposed at 24 frames per second (the standard frame rate) to obtain the greater linear film velocity necessary for high-quality sound. If there is any possibility that at some future date the footage might have a sound track added (for possible television use) or that portions of it might be edited into a sound film, then the 24-frames-per-second rate is essential.

Accessories. The following accessories may be useful in the various aspects of motion-picture production.

Slate. The slate can be simply a piece of cardboard marked with a grease pencil or crayon, a classroom slate marked with chalk, or a more elaborate

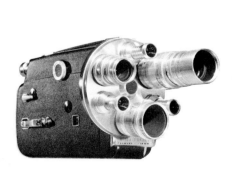

(Far left) A lens turret, mounted on the front of the camera, will accommodate two or more lenses, thus facilitating lens changes for different shots. (Left) A slate and clapstick appears on the first few frames of each shot to provide identification.

version of the classroom slate with a clapstick for use with synchronized sound filming. It provides identification on the first few frames of each shot. Usually included are the scene number, take number, and any other information necessary at the editing stage.

Exposure Meter. Available as either a reflected-light or an incident-light instrument, the exposure meter is necessary to establish consistent exposure control from one scene to the next.

Ditty Bag. This is usually a heavy canvas bag with straps to hang from a tripod for holding tapes, meters, filters, and so forth.

Tape Measure. The tape measure should be cloth or steel, 25 or 50 feet in length, and able to be wound into a case. It is essential for measuring camera-to-subject distances for critical close-up shots and for measuring preset camera distances.

Changing Bag. A changing bag is a lighttight bag with access holes for inserting hands and arms. It permits the handling of unexposed core-wound film in existing light when loading or unloading magazines, cameras, and cans of film. It is used when a darkroom is not available.

Masking Tape (Black). Masking tape is very handy for sealing film cans, holding electrical wires, and other uses.

Camera Syringe. An exceptionally safe way to remove dust from lenses and viewfinders and from the inside of cameras is with a camera syringe.

Lens Cleaner. This is excellent for cleaning coated or uncoated lenses.

Lens-Cleaning Paper. This is a soft, lintless paper specially prepared for cleaning lenses, filters, and other highly polished glass surfaces. It is satisfactory for use on coated or uncoated lenses.

General Information about 16 mm Motion-Picture Films

Film Exposure Indexes. Film exposure-index values published for use with exposure meters are intended to serve only as guides. The index figures given in the film listings are recommended for use with meters and cameras marked for ASA speeds (ASA denotes American Standards Association, which is now entitled American National Standards Institute—ANSI). Exact exposure levels should be determined by means of tests with the equipment that will be used for the production (because of differences in cameras, lighting equipment, meters, and techniques). The effective speed of films is also influenced somewhat by the particular solution, formulas, and method of processing employed. If possible, the tests should include an exposure series made with the particular film emulsion selected for the production shooting.

Perforations. Film with perforations along both edges is called "double perforated" and is generally used for silent footage, although it may have a narrow magnetic sound stripe applied to it after processing. "Single-perforated" film has perforations along one edge only and is generally used for filming single-system sound and whenever a full-width magnetic sound track is to be added. It should not be used in cameras or projectors designed only for double-perforated film—with double sprockets and double pulldown claws on both sides. Film with double perforations can, however, be used in cameras having a pulldown claw on only one side. Footage exposed on double-perforated film can and should be duplicated or printed on single-perforated stock by commercial laboratories if it is desired to add optical or magnetic (full-width) sound track to the film.

Magnetic Striping. Many 16 mm camera films are available with magnetic sound striping for use in single-system sound cameras fitted with magnetic recording heads. The films, perforated along one edge and furnished in Winding "B" (see the section on winding later in this article), are striped on the base side only, and are supplied on 100-, 200-, and 400-foot spools. The full-width 0.100-inch coating will be applied to 16 mm single-perforated film with an existing photographic track *only* when specified by the customer.

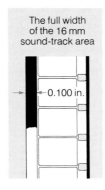

The full width of the 16 mm sound-track area

←0.100 in.

Many 16 mm films are available with magnetic sound striping for single-system sound cameras fitted with magnetic recording heads. The films are perforated along one edge and are striped on the base side only. The full-width 0.100-inch coating is applied to a film with an existing photographic track when specified by the customer.

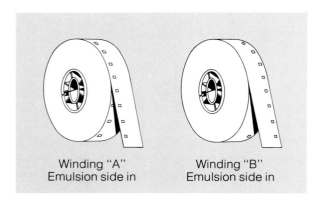

Winding "A"
Emulsion side in

Winding "B"
Emulsion side in

When a roll of film, perforated along one edge, is held so that the end of the film leaves the roll at the top and to the right, it has Winding A if the perforations are toward the observer. If the perforations are away from the observer, the film has Winding B.

Cores and Spools. Motion-picture-camera films are furnished on several types of cores and spools and in various lengths. The designs of the core and the center hole configuration in the spools are for specific types of equipment.

Winding. Two different windings of camera stock, designated as Winding A and Winding B, are used with 16 mm films that are perforated along one edge. Either type may be required for use on existing equipment, and the particular winding that is needed should be specified when single-perforated 16 mm raw stock is being ordered. The accompanying diagram illustrates the two types of windings.

The Language of Moviemaking

The motion-picture industry has evolved a basic set of terms that communicate ideas, concepts, or technical information quickly and clearly. A thorough understanding of these terms and their use will speed up planning and production work. The following is a basic glossary of these terms that will be helpful in the production of the movie.

Audience Role. Before beginning a motion-picture production, a decision must be made relative to the role the audience will play. Will they watch the action from the sidelines as observers? Or will they feel as though they are participating in the action? Which camera angles are best for a particular production?

Objective Filming. Objective filming shows the scene from a spectator's viewpoint—on an impersonal basis. The viewer is not brought into the scene; he or she views it from the outside. That is why camera angles for objective filming provide an excellent way to show what is happening.

Subjective Filming. Subjective filming brings the viewer into the action. The camera lens assumes the position of the eyes of the person performing the action. This camera angle is of special value in training films where small-scale hand operations are concerned, since the student sees the action as he or she will when performing the operation. The effect is usually achieved by shooting over the student's shoulder to the hands and immediate surroundings.

Types of Shots. A motion picture should be shot from various distances to maintain interest, to provide variety, to provide transition, and to direct the attention of the viewer to the precise details you want them to see. Generally speaking, the shooting distances fall into four categories.

Long Shot (LS). To tell a simple story with motion pictures, the viewer must be introduced to the scene with a general shot that gives an overall view of the setting and its surroundings, a shot that shows the basic relationship between the parts making up the whole. For this reason, long shots are often referred to as "establishing shots"—they help orient the viewer to the subject's environment.

It is not uncommon to make this first shot with a wide-angle lens. Devices such as maps, layout sketches, and cartoons can also be used to introduce a sequence where the true long shot is impractical to make, or to give some variety to the introduction. The length of this scene should be sufficient to allow the viewer to scan the whole setting and to form his or her own reference image of it.

Medium Shot (MS). After the location has been established with the long shot, the camera is usually moved in, or a lens of longer focal length is used to bring the main element of the scene into full-frame size. This type of shot narrows the center of interest for the viewer.

Close-Up (CU). With close-ups, the camera is near enough to permit one element of the scene to dominate the full frame. A close-up shot includes

Top row: (Left) A long shot, often made with a wide-angle lens, is frequently used as the "establishing shot" for a scene. (Right) The medium shot narrows the center of interest for the viewer. Bottom row: (Left) The close-up shot shows only the action of primary interest. (Right) The extreme close-up will accentuate small but essential detail.

only the action of primary interest. Routine and related subsidiary motions are eliminated as much as possible.

Extreme Close-Up (ECU). Some extreme close-up shots may require supplementary lens attachments to the standard camera lens. The choice of a supplementary lens depends upon the size of the subject. The extreme close-up is most helpful in accentuating minute, but important, detail.

Basically, this is the technique of telling a motion-picture story in its most fundamental form. However, this sequence of shooting does not have to be rigidly followed from scene to scene. It should be understood that the terms "long shot," "medium shot," and so forth, are relative to the size of the subject being photographed. A close-up of a door

might well be a long shot of a sign attached to the door. A close-up of a laboratory table could be a long shot of a test tube on the table.

Camera Angles. When one sequence is finished and another is started, especially if the same background is used, it is wise to change the camera angle or distance, or both. This accomplishes the desirable objectives of reviving the audience interest by giving them a fresh viewpoint, and by making them subconsciously aware that one sequence is completed and a new one has begun.

The term "camera angle" merely refers to the camera's view of the subject or its relation to the principal planes of the scene. Normally, the basic camera viewpoint should be from eye level. Variations are considered from this starting point.

Motion-Picture Production

How high or low should you position your camera to shoot a scene? The answer to that question stems from another question. If a viewer were watching the actual scene, what would be the best vantage point? Would eye level be best, or would it be better to look up or down at the action?

Eye-Level Shot. The camera is horizontal with reference to the ground. When long and medium *objective* shots are being filmed, the camera should usually be at a height of 5 to 5½ feet—the height of the average unseen observer. *Subjective* eye-level shots should be made from the height of the person performing the action, whether he or she is standing, sitting, or on a ladder.

High-Angle Shot. The camera is tilted *downward* at the subject. High-angle shots help orient the viewer because they show the relationships among all elements of the setting and can produce a psychological effect by minimizing the subject and its setting. High-angle "establishing" shots are useful if the action occurs in great depth, such as a jet airliner discharging passengers or a fire engulfing a waterfront. High angles will help keep all the important elements in sharp focus.

Low-Angle Shot. The camera is positioned below the point of primary interest and points *upward.* Low-angle shots tend to give strength and dominance, dramatizing the subject. Low shots will probably be used when such things as massive machinery, church interiors, or football action—where dramatic impact is desired—are being filmed. This angle shot is also useful for separating the subject from the background, for eliminating unwanted foreground and background, and for heightening the illusion of size, speed, and perspective.

Selection of Camera Angle. The majority of subjects in front of the camera will be three-dimensional and should be photographed at an angle (to the left or right and higher or lower than the subject) that lets you see more than one side of the subject.

Camera angles must be chosen and altered judiciously and with some restraint. Changes in angle from scene to scene should be subtle, since large, striking changes in angle or very unusual angles can be disturbing to the viewer. To create impact, camera angles should be changed dramatically. For example, in a safety film illustrating an unsafe practice, the culmination showing the accident occurring might be made with a gross change in angle to add

(Top) Eye level shots place the subject in direct relationship with the unseen observer. (Center) High-angle shots show the relationships of all elements and help orient the viewer. (Bottom) Low-angle shots dramatize the subject and help concentrate the attention on one particular element.

to the startling effect when the tool suddenly breaks, the worker falls to the floor, or a fire starts. For normal filming, changes in camera angle should be made in a subtle manner so that the viewer's attention will not be diverted from the story or action to a puzzled consideration of the new viewpoint.

For examples of the many points made here, simply turn on a television set, and watch how the camera shows action from a variety of angles. Notice how the viewing angle is changed from an overall view into an informative close-up. The commercials on television are, in a way, single-concept films designed to get a key message across to the viewer in a dramatic, memorable way—all in a matter of a few seconds.

Descriptive Shots. The following shooting techniques provide descriptive shots.

Panning. The technique of panning consists in pivoting the camera while it is operating, in such a manner that it will scan a scene that is too extensive horizontally to be included in the frame if the camera is motionless. Panning should be done with the camera on a good solid tripod and at a very smooth, slow rate of movement. Make sure that the tripod is level so that the horizon line will be level throughout the pan. Start the camera before beginning to pan, and continue running it after the pan has been completed.

An often expressed rule of thumb for panning is that the camera operator should move the camera at about half the speed that he or she imagines the finished pan should appear on the screen. If there is no action in the scene, the frame rate can be advanced to slow the panning rate as it appears on the screen. A stroboscopic effect can be obtained by panning too rapidly. The faster the panning rate, the greater the image smear or stroboscopic effect that will occur.

One of the instances where a pan can be used effectively is in following action. If by panning, a moving object is held in its same position relative to the frame edges, the viewer's eyes will rest on the subject and accept the moving background. An example of this action would be an individual moving through a crowd of people or parts moving along on a conveyor belt. Also see the section in this article on follow shots.

Tilting. Tilting is vertical panning. This camera movement is used to follow action or to cover the

(Top) When the scene is static, panning should be done slowly. In photo at center, panning is too fast, causing the scene to blur. (Bottom) For action subjects, blurring is no problem; the subject and the camera move at the same time.

height of an object that is too great to be included entirely in the camera viewfinder, such as the steeple of a church or the bottom of a deep gorge. If extreme wide-angle lenses are used during this movement, tall buildings will appear to tip over backward as the tilting action progresses. Care should be exercised when using this technique.

Zooming. Zooming refers to the continuous changing of image size from small to large (zoom in) or from large to small (zoom out). This increase or decrease in image size is accomplished by continuously changing the focal length of the zoom lens— not by moving the camera. Zooming should be done smoothly and slowly, and used sparingly. One of the most important advantages of a zoom lens is that it lets the photographer frame the subject at different magnifications before filming a scene without moving the camera.

Follow Shot. A continuous shot that follows moving action is called a "follow shot." The camera is moved flexibly (panning, tilting, or dollying) to keep the subject always in the same relative position in the viewfinder. Follow shots are useful when filming unbroken action such as people walking along a sidewalk, and so forth.

Inserts. An insert is any segment of film, such as a full-screen close-up of a printed article, a machine nameplate, a Mathew Brady Civil War photo, and so forth, that is filmed separately and then spliced into the finished film at the most appropriate spot. Inserts are useful for expanding on the primary subject matter or for helping to clarify the continuity of action.

Cutaway Shots. Cutaways are used to depict a secondary action. They may show something that occurs simultaneously with the main action, whether it is a few inches or many miles away. They should always be related to the primary subject. A cutaway may also be used when it is necessary to condense an extended flow of action. For instance, if a sequence began with a close-up of a clock face and then cut to the main action, a cutaway back to

The follow shot is a continuous shot that follows moving action, always keeping the subject in the same relative position to the camera.

Motion-Picture Production

the clock would show the elapsed time of the main action.

Continuous Run. When the action takes place within a small area and during a short period of time, it may be desirable to film the action continuously. However, if the action is lengthy and repetitive, continuous-run shots would be boring—and unnecessary. It would be best to use cutaways, inserts, titles, or to change the audience's role. That is one of the advantages of motion pictures—they can condense time by eliminating the unnecessary. If the action is short, it might be better to film it with more than one camera, or recreate the action and film it again from a different vantage point. The resulting footage can then be edited into a logical sequence. While continuous-run filming simplifies photography and reduces shooting time, greater variety and interest are achieved by using the camera to create frequently changing series of images. Generally speaking, the longer the sequence and the more complex the subject, the greater the need for a change of pace. However, an involved operation may be observed more clearly by a continous-run shot, so that the viewer may see it in actual time.

Sequence Shooting. When events are shot in chronological sequence (even though some time passes between "takes"), this is called shooting *in sequence.* It is also called *editing in the camera.* For variety, these shots might be taken from several different camera positions and angles.

Professionally produced films are generally *not* shot in chronological sequence. All of the action that is to take place at a particular location, or on a particular set, or with a particular group of talent, is done at the same time. This means that the actors have to change costumes and use the appropriate part of the script, but this saves time and money. The scenes are shot *out of sequence.* Then, after all of the scenes have been filmed, they are assembled into the proper sequence. One vital word of advice about this technique: A scene-by-scene record must

Cutaways depict a secondary action related to the main action. In this sequence, by using a cutaway shot to the pan of chicken, the cinematographer has condensed the action which began with opening the picnic basket and ended with eating the basket's contents.

Motion-Picture Production

be kept of what has been shot including as much detail as possible. This will make editing simpler.

Continuity. Before starting the initial production, it would be advisable to consider two things that will lead to better continuity in the finished film.

Matching the Action. When changing from a long to a medium to a close-up shot, it is important to make each new scene appear to be a continuation of the preceding one. The action at the end of each shot must be duplicated at the beginning of the next shot so that there is an overlap. This permits the final cutting to be done at the most effective frames. Thus, if a long shot ends with a hand and arm reaching for a vial of crystals, the following medium shot should show the hand grasping the vial, and the close-up will be the vial held in the fingertips as the crystals are poured onto a balance. In order to make smooth transitions from one shot to the next, overlap the action and change the camera angle slightly. Move the camera up or down, to the side, or both. If this is done, the viewer will lose precise orientation of the hand within the scene, so the change in screen image will appear smooth and natural. This is called *matching the action.*

Screen Direction. Screen direction is the direction of motion on the screen—the direction of movement on the screen in relation to the camera. If a subject walks into the scene from the left and out toward the right, the next shot should show the subject entering from the left and walking to the right, or screen direction will be lost. Confusion will also result if a continuous straight-line motion is shown going from left to right one time, and right to left the next (as it would appear if a long shot were made of someone feeding a board into a table saw from one side, and the photographer then moved to the other side of the saw for a close-up). If screen direction is to be reversed intentionally, show in the film how it is reversed (such as the person going to the other side of the saw), with one or more shots inserted between reversals to give the viewer time to become oriented.

Film Editing. Editing a motion picture is the process of eliminating and rearranging shots and sequences to do a better job of putting across those ideas that the picture is intended to convey. There is, or can be, much creative work in editing so that the finished picture is more than merely the total of the film clips going into the picture. Editing is a skill that is generally acquired through observation, personal experience, and practice.

Initial Steps. The first steps of editing actually precede the physical process of cutting the film. For instance:

1. Conferences, a written script, and a shooting schedule will simplify all stages of editing.
2. Whenever practical, on any one set or location, schedule shots in sequence to save editing time later. Allow additional footage at the beginning and end of each shot for unexpected script changes, overlapping action, optical effects, and so forth.
3. Photograph a slate at the beginning of each shot for identification purposes. The slate should contain such information as date, scene number, take number, and so on. Make sure that the corresponding data is included on the shot record.
4. Keep an accurate shot record. It should include the information listed on the slate, the camera-film roll number, a list of the good and bad takes, and so on. This information can be invaluable when selecting usable footage. A script person may be needed to keep these records.

The responsibility of editing can also be allocated to someone else. There are a number of independent editors, editing companies, and laboratories who will take over the film after it has been processed and make a coordinated motion picture of it. Some of the laboratories may even accept the responsibility of making a film from a miscellaneous collection of scenes; however, no amount of editing can make a good film from poor material.

Sending the film to someone else for editing has advantages. The professional editor will probably be an experienced person, working with adequate equipment and doing a competent job both aesthetically and mechanically. Having the editing done outside also frees the photographer for other work and relieves him or her of the necessity for operating on his or her own creation.

There are also disadvantages. Contact between the client and the editor for discussion of changes must often be made by mail or telephone. If the editing can be done by the photographer or an associate, there is less opportunity for misunderstanding and fewer details need to be written down.

Cost may be higher if the work is done outside, although the chances are that there will be little difference if time is charged against the film edited by in-plant personnel. (*See:* A AND B ROLL EDITING; EDITING MOVIES; SYNCHRONIZATION.)

Sound

Narration. A method of supplementing visual images most commonly used with short motion pictures that are to be shown only a few times is live commentary, similar to that used in an illustrated lecture. The treatment may be simply an extemporaneous running commentary by the producer; or it can be a formal reading from a carefully timed manuscript, exactly like a narrative sound track, except for the manner of delivery.

Writing narration for motion pictures differs considerably from straight expositional writing in that it should not be written to carry the entire weight of the story. Rather it should be supplementary to the film. The picture should generally tell the story. The narration should clarify points made by the pictures, call the viewer's attention to the vital points in the action, and explain or bridge gaps in the story or scene changes. It *should not* simply repeat the obvious or merely identify scenes with such phrases as: "This is a picture of . . ." or "In this scene . . ." or "This shot shows . . ."

Whether for recorded or live delivery, narration may be written in its final form only after the film is in its final stages of editing. The story can be firmly delineated in the original script, but the final exact fitting and timing of the narration to the film, or film to the narration, can be done only after the workprint is in nearly finished form. Probably the most important single point to be observed in writing narration is that of timing. The narrative covering a scene or sequence should not take longer to read than the screen time of the footage. The visual and audible thoughts must be presented simultaneously. The viewer should not be viewing one scene while the narrator is still describing the preceding one; and, conversely, the narration usually should not refer to a scene before it appears on the screen. Also, avoid using a steady stream of narration—"loading the sound track"—from the opening fade-in to the end title. The audience may stop listening. The language used in the narration should be concise and lucid. Complete sentences can often be dropped in favor of apt descriptive phrases or single words.

The narrator should be chosen carefully on the basis of intelligibility, authority, suitability, and neutral quality. Good narrators are to be found in almost any locality, especially among radio or television announcers. A test of several voices may be necessary to find one with the desired qualities.

Music and Sound Effects. When music or sound effects are being planned for a motion picture, careful consideration should be given to the role each will play. Care in the choice of background music can greatly enhance the vocal portions of a film. Music, when properly used, can create a mood more quickly than any other means of communication. Generally, it takes only a few bars to establish a mood for the scene. A study of how music is used in television, commercials, and feature films will point up the role it plays in establishing mood.

Music can be used in a film in several ways: alone, as a general background, alternately with narration, or as background for narration. When used with narration, the music is often recorded at a high level on sections of the film—such as for titles, as bridges during scene transitions, and for action that is simple and self-evident. When music is used as a background for the narration or dialogue, it is often more or less continuous and is recorded at a much lower level than the voice. Remember, it is intended as background to the narration.

Recorded music for which clearance or use rights can be obtained is available from music libraries. Catalogs from the libraries list titles, themes, moods, and exact playing times. For legal reasons, no music tape or record should be rerecorded for film unless it has proper clearance.

Sound effects, which can add greatly to the realism of films, are commercially available in a wide variety, but can be made artificially or recorded live with a tape recorder or a magnetic-sound recording projector. The potential of such effects as a useful part of the sound track should be planned for when scripts for sound motion pictures are being prepared.

Background sounds can be recorded on location and used nonsynchronously with a film to good effect. For example, a shot of a busy schoolroom, business office, or machine shop can be backed up by sound recorded on a portable tape recorder and later rerecorded onto the sound track without any attempt to synchronize sound and picture. The sound of a crowd, a city street, a busy airport, or wind and insect noises outdoors can be obtained similarly on location.

Magnetic Sound. Magnetic-sound films may involve simply photographing a desired action, then having a magnetic sound track coated on the film and postrecording the necessary narration and/or music. For the educator, this type of picture and sound treatment might be ideal when recording a critical experiment in the laboratory for presentation to a class. For the business or industrial photographer, a magnetic sound track on the film can broaden the use of films.

A magnetic coating or stripe is applied to the edge of the film and can be placed on either originals or duplicates of black-and-white or color films, single or double perforated. When magnetic sound is to be used, particularly if there are a large number of splices in the film, it is best to have a duplicate made of the entire film after it is edited (assuming the film

to be of good duplication quality), and then add the sound stripe to this print. Once this coating has been applied, live or previously recorded speech, music, and sound effects can be recorded on the magnetic stripe with a sound projector that is designed for magnetic recording and reproduction. The sound can then be played back immediately, erased, or rerecorded.

Single-System Sound. This is the method used for the recording of both picture and sound track (either optical or magnetic) simultaneously in a camera at 24 frames per second. If the recorded sound is to be magnetic, then the film must have a 100-mil magnetic sound stripe applied to the base side before it can be used to record sound in the camera. When the film is processed, it can be projected with the sound synchronized.

A magnetic or an optical single-system sound camera is equipped with a built-in sound-recording device. The microphone and recording amplifier are connected by a cable to the recording head in the camera body. This system is portable, compact, and relatively easy and economical to operate. However, it has some limitations when it becomes necessary to

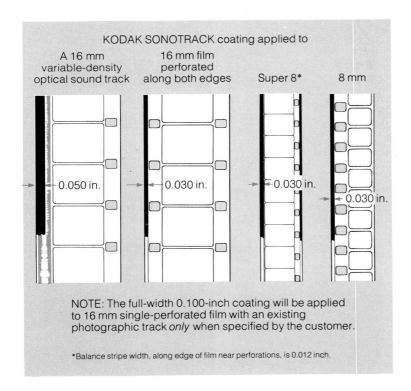

KODAK SONOTRACK coating applied to

A 16 mm variable-density optical sound track — 0.050 in.

16 mm film perforated along both edges — 0.030 in.

Super 8* — 0.030 in.

8 mm — 0.030 in.

NOTE: The full-width 0.100-inch coating will be applied to 16 mm single-perforated film with an existing photographic track *only* when specified by the customer.

*Balance stripe width, along edge of film near perforations, is 0.012 inch.

A magnetic coating or stripe that is applied to the edge of processed film is used in single-system sound-on-film production. The stripe can be placed on the original, or on duplicate prints of color or black-and-white films, single or double perforated. With the super 8 film, the balance stripe width, along the edge of the film near the perforations, is 0.012 inch.

edit the film. With a 16 mm magnetic-sound film, the sound is recorded 28 frames ahead of the picture; it is recorded 26 frames ahead of the picture for optical sound recording. This 28-frame advance causes the picture and sound to play back in synchronization when projected. However, during the editing process, it may be necessary to edit only the sound track and disregard the picture because of the separation between picture and sound. Otherwise, complete words or phrases can be inadvertently omitted. Television news interviews are often edited in this manner.

Double-System Sound. This is the most widely used professional technique for recording sound. The camera should be properly blimped or otherwise soundproofed, and the frame rate should be a constant 24 frames per second. The sound is recorded on a separate tape or magnetic-film recorder at the time of filming. If the recording is made on magnetic tape, it is later transferred to sprocketed magnetic film for final synchronization of the picture and sound during editing.

There are various methods of obtaining synchronism between sound and picture. It is necessary that a sync pulse be recorded on the magnetic-tape sound track, in such a manner that it will not interfere with the audio portion. The sync pulse is the control used when transferring sound on tape to sprocketed magnetic film. This is accomplished by a variety of means, such as:

1. A cable connecting the recorder to a sync generator attached to the camera.
2. Synchronous ac motors on both camera and recorder, with the signal taken from the power source by the use of a transformer on the recorder.
3. Battery-operated, quartz-crystal-controlled camera and recorder motors. These motors operate with such extreme accuracy that the recorder is capable of placing a sync signal on a tape without a connecting cord to the camera. This method provides extreme portability and flexibility during filming.

Periodic maintenance of the recording equipment, such as cleaning and demagnetizing of the recording heads, will minimize the possibility of recording unwanted sounds and distortion of sound. It is also a good practice to erase all tape before recording.

Double-system sound recording permits complete freedom in the final editing of sound and picture. (*See:* MAGNETIC SOUND FOR MOTION PICTURES.)

Optical Sound. This is the most commonly used type of sound track for 16 mm release prints. It is printed directly on the film with the photographic image. In other words, pictures and sound track can be duplicated photographically, whereas with magnetic sound, each film must have the sound track recorded on it. It is for this reason that optical sound is the choice when many duplicate prints are to be made.

Optical sound tracks can also be produced with a single-system motion-picture camera equipped to record an optical sound track. This system may be convenient when recording interviews or documenting evidence that will be presented in court.

The application of optical sound is, in general, a professional motion-picture laboratory technique. When it is applied to in-plant films, the mechanics of the sound track—rerecording, editing, and reproduction—are handled by commercial motion-picture service organizations. The film producer who wants an optical sound track may rough-edit the workprint and then send it, together with the original film, script, and final magnetic recording, to an outside laboratory where he or she orders conforming. The producer may also order additional background music and sound effects. The original film and optical sound track are then printed for release.

• *See also:* A AND B ROLL EDITING; AUDIOVISUAL PLANNING; LENSES; MAGNETIC SOUND FOR MOTION PICTURES; MODEL RELEASE; SYNCHRONIZATION; TELEPHOTOGRAPHY; WIDE-ANGLE PHOTOGRAPHY; ZOOM LENS.

Further Reading: Adams, William B. *Handbook of Motion Picture Production.* New York, NY: John Wiley & Sons, Inc., 1977; Cushman, George M. *Movie-Making in 18 Lessons.* Garden City, NY: Amphoto, 1971; Eastman Kodak Co. *Magnetic Sound Recording for Motion Pictures,* pub. No. S-75. Rochester, NY: Eastman Kodak Co., 1977. Glimcher, Sumner and Warren Johnson. *Movie-Making: A Guide to Film Production.* Irvington-on-Hudson, NY: Columbia University Press, 1975; Horvath, Joan. *Filmmaking for Beginners.* New York, NY: Cornerstone Library, Inc., Div. of Simon & Schuster, Inc., 1977.

Motion Study

Still photography and motion-picture photography are both used in the study of motion. Motion-picture photography is now accepted as one of the fundamental tools for motion and methods analyses, but in some instances it is unsuitable. When several different movements of a subject are occurring at the same time, it may be difficult to analyze the event, even with motion pictures. In such instances, still photography, with trace lights on the subject, may prove to be the best way to analyze the motion. This article covers motion-study techniques with both still and motion-picture photography.

Motion Pictures for Methods Measurement

The technique most often used by industrial engineers in motion and methods studies is called micromotion. In this technique, motion pictures are taken of an industrial operation with a camera operating at a known constant speed. (Or, if the speed is unknown or not constant, a precise timer is included in the scene.) Micromotion studies are most useful in providing information for:

1. Improving work methods;
2. Establishing work-measurement standards in assembly operations;
3. Analyzing man-machine operations (punch press, drill press, brake, and so on);
4. Analyzing operations that consist of highly skilled, rapid hand motions.

Equipment. Although 16 mm equipment has been the generally accepted film size for studies of this nature, many industrial engineers are now using super 8 motion pictures for methods studies. Super 8 equipment can challenge 16 mm equipment in this field because new and more versatile cameras and projectors are available, and black-and-white films are now made in the super 8 size.

Because it has been the accepted professional standard for nontheatrical motion pictures, a much wider selection of film stock is available for 16 mm than for super 8 cameras. The tables in this article primarily cover 16 mm film and equipment; however, this information is also adaptable to super 8 equipment.

If a spring-wound 16 mm motion-picture camera is used, it should have a governor-controlled motor with a film pull of at least 40 feet per winding. The film capacity should be at least a 100-foot spool. Three lenses are suggested: a 25 mm (normal), a 15 mm (wide-angle), and a 50–60 mm (long-focus or telephoto). A synchronous or other electric motor drive is recommended but not necessary.

A heavy-duty, elevator-type tripod and a good exposure meter are essential. If much work in color is anticipated, or if plant lighting levels are low, three or four photoflood lamps with reflectors and stands will probably be required.

Still Photography for Motion Study

Fastening lights to various parts of the subject and recording the trace of these lights with a still camera can provide a "graph" of the relationship and path of the subject's movements. For example, place a light on the right front fender of several vehicles and take an overhead view to show a comparison of the turning radius of each.

When it is necessary to know how much time has elapsed during the movement being studied, use lamps that flash at a known frequency, and count the separate blips in the picture.

Equipment. Use a good, sturdy tripod. Make sure that the camera does not move during the exposure. This is especially important if, for comparison purposes, more than one exposure is made on the same sheet or frame of film.

Use lamps that will provide a point source of light. The filament in a small, clear lamp provides a good point source. Almost any lamp of this type will work, but a 12-volt lamp will probably be most convenient because power is readily available from batteries used in most vehicles, and the lamps are stocked by automobile service stations. If a person's hands or small objects are being photographed at close range, consider using a small lamp (1.5- to 6-volt) that can be powered by flashlight batteries. Small penlights also provide a good point source of light and can be used very satisfactorily.

When color film is used, wrap cellophane of various colors over the lamps so that the different traces of light can be recorded.

The movements being studied may need to be related to some reference or baseline. A grid drawn on a background will work well for many applications. Or, for portability, a grid can be made by stringing wire or cord on a frame.

Setup for Continuous Traces. The surrounding light level must be as low as possible. If the photographs must be taken outdoors, take them at night in a dark area.

Fasten the lamps on the subject at locations that will trace the maximum movements of the various parts to be studied. The lamps should be positioned to move in a plane parallel with the film. In some cases, it will be helpful to use a number of different camera positions rather than just one, in order to record different planes of action.

Be sure to place at least one lamp, as a reference or base point, in a position that will provide either as little movement or as straight a line as possible. For additional references, have grid lines or some other type of good reference either in the background or superimposed on the photograph.

If comparison tests are required, make careful measurements of the setup and keep good records. Reliable comparisons are difficult to achieve because of problems of parallax between the camera, the subject, and the reference grid. For accurate comparisons, the angles and distances from reference grid to subject and subject to camera must be kept constant. The light traces may often move in planes other than the one parallel to the film. Stereo or multiple cameras can be employed if the studies are extremely critical. Another technique is to use a grid at a 90-degree angle to the film plane, and equidistant from the camera and the subject. Place a dichroic, beam-splitting mirror in front of the camera lens in order to record both the subject and the reference grid. This technique is often used in anthropometric studies, but since it is so highly specialized it will not be covered in detail in this article.

Taking the Picture. Be sure to position the camera so that its field of view covers the area in which the total action is to take place. The camera shutter should be left open during the action.

If the action to be photographed is a recurring cycle, the shutter should be closed after one cycle. This will provide one complete cycle and the lights will not continue to trace over the same path. Use as small an aperture as possible in order to eliminate ghosting and to provide maximum depth of field.

The highlights and a minimum amount of detail of the subject should be shown in the photograph.

The subject image should be underexposed—just dense enough to barely register on the film. The subject exposure can be made at any time during the trace exposure, or it may be taken separately. Use electronic flash or blue flashbulbs for this exposure.

Tests must be made to determine the proper exposure for the final picture. If possible, make these test exposures under the same conditions that will occur during the actual shooting session. Or, if a number of people and a lot of equipment are required, the shooting conditions can be simulated instead. Be sure that the same number and type of lamps are used and placed at the same distance as in the final picture. Remember to make a flash exposure (to simulate the minimum-detail exposure) at a lamp-to-subject distance equal to that in the final picture.

Pulsating or Intermittent Light Traces. The same basic procedures used for photographing continuous light traces apply to this type of trace. A control device is needed to flash the lamps at variable frequencies. An electronics plant or an electrical shop should be able to fabricate such a device with a range from about 8 to 30 flashes per second. Discuss with the shop personnel the quantity of lamps needed and the voltage desired. If the lamps are to be used to study hand movements, be sure to keep the voltage in a safe 1.5- to 12-volt range.

Other sources of pulsating light are neon or argon lamps. Depending on their construction, these

Light traces on parts of a road grader indicate relationships of various moving parts as the machine traverses a particularly rough piece of terrain.

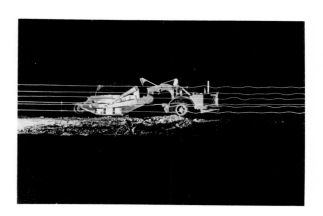

lamps flash at the frequency, or at double the frequency, of the supply source. Because the frequency of the usual ac supply is 60 Hz, the rate will be either 60 or 120 flashes per second. Lamps of this type may be useful for controlled tests in a very dark room; but because of their low level of illumination, their value is limited. Also, their emission is in an area of the spectrum where photographic film is not very sensitive, and if an attempt is made to filter them to obtain color differences, the sensitivity is reduced even more. Also, relatively high voltage is required to fire lamps of this type, and under some conditions they can create a potential shock hazard.

Even with all of the disadvantages noted, neon or argon lamps can be quite useful in a controlled laboratory experiment, such as determining the rate of fall of an object, the time elapsed in an elliptical pendulum swing, or the changing pattern of successive pendulum spirals. These lamps have the advantage of being inexpensive, readily available, and they do not require a separate flashing-control apparatus.

A third method of providing intermittent light traces involves the use of a stroboscopic electronic flash unit and reflective tape, such as Scotchlite. The tape has a reflectance of about 200 times that of a white card. Place strips of tape on the areas of the subject to be studied, and set the stroboscopic flash to a frequency that will show the movement desired. Since the entire subject is being illuminated by the repeating flash, any other highly reflective surfaces or highlights should be dulled.

Luminous Path of an Electrical Discharge. The procedures and techniques for photographing this type of discharge are very similar to photographing the path of any light movement. The exception in this case is that the light is supplied by the discharge and additional illumination is seldom needed.

The approximate moment that the discharge will occur can be predicted, so the shutter should be open for a fairly brief period. Use as small an aperture as possible to provide maximum depth of field and to minimize problems from surrounding light. Exposure must be determined by trial-and-error.

The phenomenon shown in the accompanying illustration is the electrical discharge in a piece of lead silicate glass that has been irradiated with directional gamma rays. The electrical discharge supplied the only light used.

In some applications, it may be desirable to make a minimum-detail exposure of the subject, as is done in other types of light-trace photography.

When electrical discharges are photographed at very close range, use a fast film and a very small aperture for maximum depth of field.

One major objective of the study of the electrical discharge shown in the illustration was to determine the length of time the discharge lasted. To the unaided eye, it appeared to last about $\frac{1}{10}$ second. A high-speed motion-picture camera filming at 3200 frames per second revealed that the duration of the discharge was actually less than 10 microseconds.

Films. A reversal-process film is almost always best, since there is seldom any need for duplicates. The accompanying table suggests appropriate films for several lighting conditions. Since optimum color

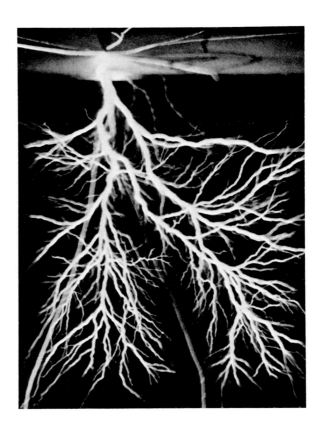

The light supplied by the luminous path of an electrical discharge is itself sufficient for illumination.

SUGGESTED MOTION-PICTURE FILMS FOR METHODS STUDY

Type of Photography	Type of Lighting	Suggested 16 mm *Kodak* Film
Black-and-white photography	Any (up to about 30 footcandles)	*2475 recording (*Estar-AH* base) *2485 high-speed recording (*Estar-AH* base)
	Any (30 footcandles or more)	†*4-X* reversal, 7277 †*Tri-X* reversal, 7278 †*Plus-X* reversal, 7276
	No visible illumination	High-speed infrared 2481
Color photography	Daylight or fluorescents (white, cool white)	*Ektachrome* EF, 7241 ‡*Ektachrome* MS, 7256
	Tungsten or fluorescents (warm white, deluxe warm white, deluxe cool white)	†*Ektachrome* EF, 7242
	3400 K tungsten (photofloods)	*Kodachrome* 40 movie (type A)

*125 feet of *Estar* base film is actually spooled on a 100-foot spool. This provides 25 percent more running time per roll.
†These films are also available in super 8 cartridges.
‡This film is also available on *Estar* base, 2256.

---

balance is usually not required for methods studies, color filters are not specified in the table. If optimum color balance is required, see the articles COLOR PHOTOGRAPHY and FILTERS.

When the lighting level is very low—30 footcandles or less—try using one of the super-fast films. You might try Kodak 2475 recording film (Estar-AH base), which has a speed of ASA 1000, but an index of 1600 is recommended for most applications; or Kodak 2485 high-speed recording film (Estar-AH base), which has an exposure index of 8000 for flat-lighted subjects.

Kodak industrial engineers are even making methods-study motion pictures in darkrooms. They are using Kodak high-speed infrared film 2481 and infrared lamps.

Camera Speed. Some industrial engineers prefer a speed of 1000 frames per minute, so that each frame has a time value of 1 time unit (1 T.U. = .001 minute). This makes the data derived from micro-motion studies compatible with studies made by other methods, such as stopwatch studies or methods-time-measurement (MTM).

Motion-picture camera specialty houses will modify a motion-picture camera to run at 1000 frames per minute. However, unless very precise synchronous electric motor drives are used to power the camera, this modification is seldom worthwhile because each camera must be calibrated under conditions identical to those of actual use.

Most industrial engineers use 16 frames per second (fps—a standard speed setting on many adjustable motion-picture cameras), which works out to 960 frames per minute (fpm). If desired, time values derived from methods-study motion pictures made at 16 fps can be converted to time units by multiplying by 1.04. Motion-picture cameras marked "silent speed" probably operate at 18 fps to conform with the USASI standard PH22.9 of 1976. An 18 fps rate can be converted to time units by multiplying the number of frames used by 0.926. The following equation can be used to convert time units to other frame rates.

$$\text{Time Units} = \frac{1000}{\text{Actual speed (fpm)}} \times \frac{\text{Number of frames used}}{}$$

FRAMES PER FOOT OF FILM

Camera-Setting Conversion to Frames per Minute*	Frames per Foot of Film
8 fps = 480 fpm	16 mm = 40
16 fps = 960 fpm	8 mm = 80
18 fps = 1080 fpm	Super 8 = 72
24 fps = 1440 fpm	35 mm = 16
32 fps = 1920 fpm	
48 fps = 2880 fpm	
64 fps = 3840 fpm	

*fps = frames per second; fpm = frames per minute.

Use the accompanying table to convert camera speed setting to frames per minute, and to determine the number of frames per foot of film.

If motions are rapid or extremely rapid, it will be helpful to double or even quadruple camera speed. If motion pictures made at 64 fps are projected and viewed at 16 fps, time will appear to have been expanded by a factor of 4. This allows easier analysis of rapid or very small motions. The following time magnification equation can be used to determine time expansion for any combination of camera speed and projection speed.

$$\text{Time Magnification} = \frac{\text{Camera speed}}{\text{Projector speed}}$$

Camera Calibration. The only way to make precise methods-measurement motion pictures is to know the camera speed and how much that speed might vary while one roll of film is being shot. Also, the speed should be tested on several rolls in order to determine whether speed variations exist between rolls.

The simplest method of calibrating a camera is to use close-up techniques to photograph an accurate stopwatch. (Many industrial engineering departments have a stopwatch that has been calibrated by the National Bureau of Standards.) Use as long a film run as possible—at least 1 minute's worth—and the whole roll of film if electric drive is used. Ignore several frames at the beginning and the end because these will be exposed at a slower frame rate while the camera is starting and stopping.

Some special cameras that have been designed for instrumentation have provisions for putting a timing signal on the film. A signal generator triggers a small timing light inside the camera. Each time the light blinks, a small spot is exposed at the edge of the film. If the timing light blinks at a known frequency, then the average camera speed between any two spots can easily be calculated according to the following equation.

$$\text{Camera Speed} = \frac{\text{Frames between signals}}{\text{Time interval between signals (seconds)}}$$

One of the easiest and simplest techniques puts an image of a clock in the picture. Place a large clock in the camera's field of view but out of the operator's view. A clock with a fast sweep hand (say one revolution every 15 seconds), or a large-dial darkroom timer, such as the Gralab, works very well.

Lastly, a double-exposure technique can be used to superimpose the face of a stopwatch over the picture. Photograph the watch face against a black velvet background and underexpose by one stop. The watch image can be placed in one corner of the frame or in the center, as desired. Expose the entire roll of film. In the dark, rewind the film onto the camera spool in such a way that the head end of the film is out. The event can now be photographed normally. *Be sure to use the same camera, camera speed, and type of camera drive for both exposures.* This effect is particularly useful for dramatic presentations.

Lighting. Simple lighting is best. If the lighting level is high enough for proper exposure with high-speed films, then try available lighting first. Watch out for dark areas that may require some supplementary light to avoid loss of details.

One of the most important aims in engineering studies is accurate results. Changes in lighting or other conditions can affect the subject's normal per-

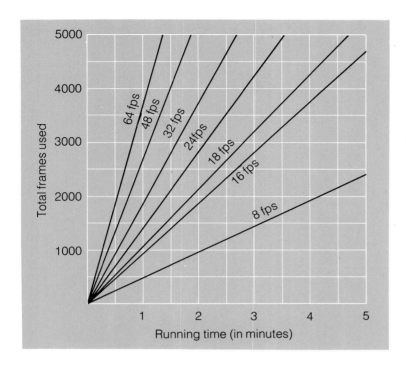

To make precise methods-measurement motion pictures, the camera speed and how much that speed might vary while one roll of film is being shot must be known. By plotting the running time against the total frames used, the number of frames per second can be calculated, and speed variations can be seen.

formance. For this reason, only essential changes in lighting should be made. The variety of fast films available today and the lighting level of most industrial operations are such that additional lighting should seldom be required. (See the table on the following page.)

When additional light is necessary, try to place the extra lamps in positions where their light will fall like the normal illumination. Background lighting is not usually required, but try to provide some separation between the subject and the background. Remember, the objective is to study normal motion and not necessarily to make "pretty pictures."

Sampling. Sampling techniques can be successfully employed with methods-measurement motion pictures. The motion-picture camera can be used in some operations as an observer to make sampling observations according to a predetermined random schedule. In other operations, it is better to record continuous observations with the camera and to sample the resulting film. If a clock is included in the picture, sampling can be done on a time schedule; otherwise, a frame counter and a random-number table are usually employed. Sampling from the film has an advantage over other techniques, in that the

size of the sample can be increased without restudying the operation.

Analysis. Good analysis techniques and equipment are most important in obtaining useful results. The best way to view methods-measurement movies is with a stop-motion projector. This projector should have both forward and backward projection, variable speed, single-frame viewing, and a frame counter. A heavy-duty blower and heat-absorbing glass condensers are essential, and a single-frame advance is also quite useful.

The industrial engineer working with a photographer may find these suggestions on analysis techniques helpful:

1. View the film several times for overall impressions. If the event is cyclic, select the best cycle for study.
2. Break down the portions of the film selected for detailed study by preparing a chart of the motions and the times required. Use a man-machine chart, a chart showing the motions of each hand, or some other graphic analysis technique.

INCIDENT-LIGHT EXPOSURE TABLE

Kodak 16 mm Film	Exposure Source	Exposure Index	Footcandles Required at:						
			f/1.4	f/2	f/2.8	f/4	f/5.6	f/8	f/11
*Kodachrome 40 movie (type A) *Plus-X reversal, 7276	Tungsten	40	40	80	160	320	640	1250	2500
Ektachrome MS, 7256	Daylight	64	25	50	100	200	400	800	1600
Ektachrome ER, 7258 *Ektachrome EF, 7242	Tungsten	125	12.5	25	50	100	200	400	800
Ektachrome ER, 7257 *Tri-X reversal, 7278 Ektachrome SM, 7244 Ektachrome 160 (type A) Ektachrome 160 (type G)	Daylight Tungsten Tungsten Tungsten Tungsten	160	10	20	40	80	160	320	640
*4-X reversal, 7277	Tungsten	320	5	10	20	40	80	160	320
†2475 recording (Estar-AH base) For normal contrast subjects, develop in Kodak developer DK-50 for 5 min. at 20 C (68 F).	Tungsten	1000	1.6	3.2	6.4	12.5	25	50	100
For low-contrast or flat-lighted subjects, develop in Kodak developer DK-50 for 8 min. at 20 C (68 F).		3200	0.5	1	2	4	8	16	32
†2485 high-speed recording (Estar-AH base) For normal contrast subjects, develop in Kodak developer 857 for 1 ½ min. at 35 C (95 F).	Tungsten	630	1.3	2.5	5	10	20	40	80
For low-contrast or flat-lighted subjects, develop in Kodak developer D-19 for 2 ½ min. at 35 C (95 F).		3200	0.5	1	2	4	8	16	32

*These films are also available in super 8 cartridges.
†Kodak 2475 and 2485 recording films are negative films. They can be viewed as negatives or printed as positives.
NOTE: Shutter speed: 16 fps (normal 175° opening), approximately equivalent to 1/30 sec.

3. Go through the detail several times to make sure that all motions and times have been recorded. A single-frame advance is especially useful here.

4. Check the other cycles in the film for operator consistency—especially for difficult motions, fumbles, idle time, operator shortcuts, or inherent problems in the operation itself.

Important Considerations. The following procedures should be carried out when making methods-measurement motion pictures.

AVERAGE LIGHTING LEVELS IN MODERN INDUSTRY

Footcandles	Types of Seeing Tasks	Typical Examples
30	Extra rough (easy or casual seeing)	Loading (inside freight cars or truck bodies), labeling, cartoning, plating, warehousing (large, bulky stock).
50	Rough (rough material, difficult seeing)	Auto-frame assembly, reading gauges or meter panels, most rough foundry tasks, rough inspection, rough bench or machine work, sheet-metal punches, presses, shears.
100	Medium	Most general inspection, medium bench work, machine tasks, drilling, riveting, screw fastening, auto-chassis assembly, body-parts manufacturing, electrical-equipment testing, foundry grinding and chipping, glass grinding, polishing, beveling.
200–500	Fine	Auto final assembly and inspection, embossing, cloth cutting, sewing and pressing, glass etching, decorating and inspection, very difficult inspection tasks.
1000 or more	Extra fine (intricate detail)	Cloth inspection, the most difficult or critical inspection, extra-fine bench and machine work, precision manual arc welding, hospital surgery, autopsy, and so forth.

1. Check the viewfinder carefully for good coverage of the event. Usually, a high camera angle is best if the subject is standing or walking; an eye-level angle is preferable if the subject is sitting.
2. Select a camera viewpoint that will allow the most important motions to be perpendicular to the camera axis.
3. At the start of each roll of film, shoot a few frames of a card showing the date, plant number, machine number, and so forth.
4. Always use a tripod.
5. Consider using a high camera speed, especially for close-ups of intricate and rapid finger motions.
6. Make arrangements with production people to have material in process, operators, and so forth.
7. If supplementary lighting is used, check the electrical supply and make sure that sufficient power is available.
8. Explain your intentions to the shop steward and/or foreman and get permission to invite him or her to be present at the shooting.
9. Sell the operators on the idea. If possible, show a movie from a previous study. Offer to let the operators see the movies of themselves.
10. Tell the operators to dress normally, and get a release from those being photographed.
11. Make as few changes as possible in normal working conditions. Do not move people or things around, or change the lighting more than is absolutely necessary. Motion pictures of operations performed under normal conditions provide more reliable data than those made under changed conditions.

• *See also:* TIME-LAPSE PHOTOGRAPHY.

Further Reading: Eastman Kodak Co. *Basic Production Techniques for Motion Pictures,* pub. No. P-18. Rochester, NY: Eastman Kodak Co., 1976; _____. *High Speed Photography,* pub. No. G-44. Rochester, NY: Eastman Kodak Co., 1977;

Mounting

Since the inception of photography, finished images have been mounted in a variety of ways for physical protection and for aesthetic purposes. Albums for mounting and protecting photographs came into use as soon as paper prints became common—about 1850.

Today, slides and transparencies are usually mounted in cardboard, plastic, or metal frames, which may include cover glass on each side of the film. Prints are usually mounted on stiff board; they may also be laminated between sheets of plastic for maximum protection.

The primary function of a mount is to provide a safe handling area. This is especially important with slides and transparencies because there is virtually no border area on the film. In addition, the mount serves to hold the film flat and to absorb the impact of changing movements during projection. Mounting prints on stiff cardboard or plastic material protects them against cracks, folds, bends, and edge dents. Lamination in plastic also provides protection against atmospheric attack.

The aesthetic function of a mount is to provide a uniform field, or surround, within which the image can be seen. Generally speaking, a deep matte black enhances color images, while a clean white or a light ivory color shows black-and-white images to best advantage. Mounts with strong or unusual colors tend to call attention to themselves and to compete with the image for attention. The mount must be large enough so that it blocks out surrounding details in the immediate field of view, permitting attention to focus on the image without distraction. Mount borders that are too narrow become useless stripes around the edges of the picture.

The materials used for mounting must be sturdy enough to absorb normal physical handling. They must also be free of chemicals or other substances that could attack the image; this is an especially important consideration in selecting an adhesive for mounting prints.

Specific mounting materials and procedures are covered in the articles LAMINATING; PRINTS, MOUNTING; and SLIDES AND TRANSPARENCIES, MOUNTING.

  Movie Films, Storage and Care of

This article contains information about proper storage, care, and handling of motion-picture films. Unexposed, unprocessed, and processed films are covered. Most of the information presented deals with safety-base films, but a section on nitrate films is also included.

Everyone concerned with the handling and storage of motion-picture film should be interested in prolonging its useful life. After the primary consideration of first-quality processing, long service for films depends on proper care.

Handling of Processed Movie Film

Care should be exercised when handling and projecting motion-picture films because they can be easily damaged in a variety of ways. Listed below are some of the more common causes of damage to processed movie film.

1. Dirt in the projector gate and other parts that guide the film through the projector.
2. Improper threading or operation of the projector.
3. Lack of inspection and failure to repair the film before projection.
4. Improper rewinding of the film. Much damage can be done by rewinding onto bent reels, rewinding too rapidly, overloading the reels, or cinching the film.
5. Use of projection equipment that has worn parts that are in contact with the film, such as pulldown claws, gate, or sprocket teeth.
6. Poor splicing.
7. Accidents due to carelessness in handling, such as dropping a reel of film, damage to film cans, or breakage during projection.
8. Improper handling of film, resulting in fingerprints, crimping, and so on. (Film should be handled by edges only.)
9. Lack of film lubrication.
10. Improper storage.

Long film life can be expected if the suggestions listed below are followed:

1. The projector gate and other parts that guide the film through the projector should be kept clean.
2. Film should be threaded correctly and the projector operated properly.
3. Film should be inspected and repaired periodically before use.
4. Film should be cleaned and lubricated properly.
5. Splices should be made with care and accuracy.
6. Sufficient leader should be attached at the start of a reel, with a trailer at the end. The leader will protect the first few feet of film from scratches and tears that can occur during threading and start-up. Also, a leader is easy to replace when damaged. Similarly, the trailer allows projection of the last frame and also protects the last scene from damage that might occur during rewinding and cleaning.
7. Reels should not be filled to maximum capacity. The outside convolution of film should be at least 13 mm (½ inch) in from the edges of the flanges. Film from an overloaded reel can be easily damaged and may not take up properly when projected.
8. Bent reels should be discarded.
9. Care should be exercised in rewinding films. The tension should be high enough to produce a tight roll, but not so high that it will cinch the film.
10. Films should be stored at the recommended temperature and relative humidity. Storage in an excessively dry atmosphere can cause film to become brittle and, therefore, easily broken.
11. Libraries should include instruction leaflets with each shipment of film to advise customers of the best method of handling.
12. Libraries should also warn customers that they will be charged for the replacement of film that is damaged while it is in their possession. Some libraries require a deposit for rental films; others insure the films against damage and add the cost to the rental fee.
13. Film should be packed in rigid containers that will withstand rough handling and provide ample protection for the film reels. Reinforced-fiber, plastic, and light metal cases are commercially available and are excellent for this purpose.

Cleaning and Lubrication

The recommended procedure in the professional motion-picture industry is to lubricate all films after processing to permit smooth operation in projectors.

The Cleaner. Film can be cleaned and lubricated by drawing it between soft, lintless cloths moistened with a preparation such as Kodak movie film cleaner (with lubricant).* This should be done whenever a film becomes dirty. If a film is unsteady and noisy during the first projection, it may not have been adequately lubricated at the processing laboratory. In this case, the film should be lubricated not only to reduce noise but also to minimize film damage during use.

The Cloth. Cleaning cloths of the following types are usually satisfactory: a good grade of Canton flannel, a short- or medium-pile rayon or nylon plush, or a soft cotton batiste. These should be white, undyed, and free of fabric fillers and additives for stiffening. If in doubt, the cloths should be laundered before use.

The Method. To clean the film, place it on a rewind and thread the leader strip onto a take-up reel. Rewind the film, drawing it between two cloths that have been moistened with the cleaner/lubricant. Constant light pressure with one hand will provide continual contact between the film surfaces and the cloths. This operation must be performed slowly enough to permit the cleaner to evaporate *completely* before the film reaches the take-up reel.

---

*Kodak movie film cleaner (with lubricant) does not contain carbon tetrachloride. Even so, the cleaner should be used with adequate ventilation. If used for more than a few minutes at a time, forced-air ventilation should be provided. No matter what type of cleaner is being used, the instructions on the container should be followed.

Frequent remoistening of the cloths is recommended because the solvent evaporates rapidly. To avoid scratching the film with accumulated dirt particles, it is advisable to refold the cloths frequently, so that only clean areas will be in contact with the film. If streaks are noticed on the film after lubrication, they can usually be removed by buffing with a soft cloth.

Cleaning and lubrication should be accomplished with *continuous,* smooth rewinding of the whole reel. If stopping is necessary to refold the cloth and apply more cleaner, reverse the film about 30 cm (1 foot), and resume the cleaning operation.

Any color that appears on a cloth used for cleaning Kodak color film can be disregarded. It is a film-surface accumulation, not a part of the dye in the image.

Cleaners such as Kodak film cleaner and Kodak movie-film cleaner (with lubricant) are satisfactory for cleaning and lubricating both film to which Kodak Sonotrack coating has been applied and pre-striped sound film.

Another lubricant that gives good results consists of 0.1 gram of wax, such as PE Tetrastearate (Pentaerythrityl Tetrastearate), Practical Grade,* in 100 ml of a solvent such as Chlorothene (1,1,1-Trichloroethane).

If the film has a magnetic sound stripe, a test should be made on a discarded piece of film before cleaning it with a solvent. This is to ascertain whether the solvent in the cleaner dissolves the binder in the magnetic stripe. In case the stripe softens or smears, another type of cleaner will have to be used.

CAUTION: Water detergent cleaners are not recommended for color films because under certain conditions, they can cause fading of the dyes.

Storage of Motion-Picture Film

The sensitometric characteristics of virtually all photographic films are subject to change because of ambient conditions such as high temperature, high relative humidity, and harmful gases. Color films are more seriously affected than black-and-white films, because these conditions usually alter the three emulsion layers to different degrees, causing a change in speed, color balance, or contrast, or possibly all three. Improper storage conditions can cause a much larger change in the color quality and the speed of the film than does any permissible variation in manufacturing. Sensitized films (raw stock) should be protected from: (1) moisture, (2) heat, (3) harmful gases, (4) x-rays and radioactive materials, and (5) physical damage.

Storage of Raw Stock in Original Package. All motion-picture raw stock should be kept in the original package to prevent any exchange in moisture between the rolls and their surroundings up to the time that they are to be exposed. Motion-picture films are sold in heat-sealed foil pouches and taped metal or plastic cans to provide this protection.

Relative Humidity. A small amount of moisture leakage through the closure of a taped can is unavoidable. The problem becomes more serious when a small amount of film is involved because of the greater amount of air space in the can. For this reason, motion-picture color films should be given additional water-vapor protection if they are to be kept longer than a month in a region having high relative humidity. Such regions include not only those commonly thought of as tropical but also any localities where relative humidities of 70 percent or higher prevail (as in a number of areas in the continental United States), or in damp basements or refrigerators. This additional water-vapor protection can be obtained by tightly sealing as many unopened rolls as possible in a second plastic container or can.

NOTE: It is the *relative* humidity, *not* the *absolute* humidity, that determines the moisture content of the films. Relative humidity is best measured with a sling psychrometer. In a small storage chamber, a humidity indicator, such as those sold for home use, is satisfactory.

Temperature. In general, the lower the temperature at which a film is held, the slower will be the rate of change of its sensitometric properties during aging. For periods of storage up to 6 months, both color and black-and-white motion-picture raw stock should be stored at a temperature of 13 C (55 F) or lower. This temperature should not be exceeded dur-

---

*Available as Chemical No. P7421, from Eastman Organic Chemicals, Rochester, New York 14603; or as Hercules B-16 Synthetic Wax, from Hercules, Inc., 917 King Street, Wilmington, Delaware 19899.

ing the entire storage period if optimum film properties are to be retained.

Store raw stock at −18 to −23 C (0 to −10 F) in a freezing unit if it must be kept longer than 6 months or if the film is intended for a critical use that requires uniform results. Sensitometric deterioration will not be prevented by such storage, but it will be minimized.

IMPORTANT: After a package of raw stock has been removed from cold storage, it should be allowed to warm up until its temperature is above the dew point of the ambient (outside) air before the can is unsealed; otherwise, moisture condensation, and spotting of the film can occur.

WARM-UP TIME FOR COLOR FILM

| Type of Color Film Package | Warm-up Time (Hours) | |
	For 14 C (25 F) Rise	For 55 C (100 F) Rise
8 mm	1	1½
Super 8	1	1½
16 mm	1	1½
35 mm	3	5

Any moisture condensation that may occur *inside* a taped can of film when it is refrigerated is harmless. The only possibility of damage from moisture condensation occurs when the can is removed from the cold storage and opened without allowing sufficient warm-up time.

Protection Against Harmful Gases and Rays. Gases such as formaldehyde, hydrogen, sulfide, sulfur dioxide, ammonia, illuminating gas, exhaust fumes; vapors from solvents, mothballs, cleaners, turpentine, mildew, or fungus preventives; and mercury can damage photographic emulsions. The cans in which motion-picture film is packaged provide protection against some gases, but others can slowly penetrate the adhesive tape seal. Keep film away from any such contamination.

Raw stock should not be stored or shipped near x-rays or other radioactive materials. Some scanning devices used by postal authorities and overseas airlines may be harmful to raw stock. Special storage precautions should also be taken in hospitals, industrial plants, and laboratories where radioactive materials are in use. It is also advisable to label packages of unprocessed films to be mailed across international borders:

Contents: Unprocessed photographic film.
Please do not x-ray.

Commercial-film-processing mailers are generally recognized by customs and postal inspectors and are not x-rayed.

Physical Damage. Storage rooms for motion-picture raw stock should be designed so that accidental flooding from storms, water pipes, or sewers cannot damage the product. All film should be raised at least 15 cm (6 inches) off the floor for storage.

Rooms that are artificially cooled should be constructed and insulated so that moisture does not condense on the walls. If the building itself is not fireproof, sprinklers should be installed. As indicated, relative humidity control below 70 percent is unimportant as long as the film cans remain sealed. The temperature should be maintained as uniformly as possible throughout the storage room by means of adequate air circulation, so that any sensitometric changes that occur do so uniformly among the stored rolls.

Film should not be stored near heating pipes or in sunlight coming through a window, regardless of whether the room is cool or not.

Storage of Unprocessed Film Before and After Exposure. After a film package has been opened, the film is no longer protected from the outside atmosphere. High relative humidities and high temperatures often cause undesirable changes in the latent image. Exposed film, particularly color film, changes more rapidly than unexposed film. Therefore, film should be processed as soon as possible after exposure.

Film in original packages or film loaded in cameras, cartridges, magazines, on reels, and in carrying cases should be protected from direct sunlight and should never be left in closed spaces that may trap heat from the sun or from other sources, even in temperate climates. The temperatures in closed automobiles, parked airplanes, or the holds of ships, for example, can easily reach 60 C (140 F) or more. A few hours under such conditions, either before or after exposure, can severely impair the quality of the film.

The films must be kept away from the harmful gases previously mentioned. Since the vapors from mothballs and mildew or fungus preventives can adversely affect film, keep all films away from clothes closets and drawers containing these preparations.

Satisfactory drying of motion-picture films by means of desiccation is not possible because of the slow transfer of moisture through a large roll. It is easier, therefore, to avoid excessive moisture take-up when handling motion-picture film in high relative humidities than it is to do an adequate job of removing the excess moisture once it has been absorbed. If there are delays of a day or more in shooting, a magazine containing partially used film should be removed from the camera and placed in a moisture-tight, dry chamber. This will prevent any absorption of moisture by the film during the holding period. Immediately after exposure, the film should be returned to its can and retaped to prevent any increase in moisture content over that picked up during actual exposure. If processing facilities are not immediately available, exposed films should be stored at −18 C (0 F).

Storage of Processed Film. Storage of processed motion-picture film differs from the storage of raw stock because the film is no longer photosensitive, and much longer storage periods are generally involved.

The dyes used in color films are as stable as is consistent with the optical and chemical requirements of the color processes. The primary factors affecting their life are light, moisture, and heat. For maximum permanence, processed color films should be stored in areas where it is dark, dry, and cool.

Processing is one of the most important factors contributing to the ultimate permanence of photographic records. A thorough washing is particularly important because thiosulfate salts (hypo) left in the processed material can fade the silver image of black-and-white films by converting it partially to silver sulfide, especially under conditions of high humidity and temperature. Thiosulfate salts allowed to remain in color film can also fade the dye images.

In color films, it is likely that one dye will be affected more than another, causing an undesirable change in color balance and deterioration of the image. Therefore, color films require more care in handling and storage than do black-and-white films.

Black-and-White Film. For short-term storage of processed black-and-white motion-picture film, the storage temperature should be kept below 24 C (75 F), and the relative humidity should be kept below 60 percent. If processed black-and-white film is to be kept for archival purposes, it should be stored at a temperature below 21 C (70 F), and at a relative humidity between 15 and 50 percent. Very low storage temperatures are desirable (− 18 C [0 F] or lower) when infrequent use of the film is expected and maximum useful life is the primary concern.

Color Film. For short-term storage of processed color motion-picture film, the storage temperature should be kept at around 21 C (70 F), and the relative humidity should be kept between 40 and 50 percent.

For archival keeping of processed color film, the following suggestions are offered:

1. Make black-and-white separation masters for protection against total loss of valuable original color-negative or optical-effects footage through dye fading. Store all three separations under the same conditions, with a temperature of 21 C (70 F) or lower and a relative humidity of approximately 50 percent.
2. Store color film for which separations have *not* been made in hermetically sealed containers. Acetate-base films should be moisture-conditioned to a relative humidity of between 15 and 30 percent, and polyester-base films to a relative humidity of between 25 and 30 percent prior to placement in the sealed containers.
3. Store the film in a vault at 1.5 C (35 F) with a relative humidity of between 15 and 30 percent.
4. Store the film in taped cans at − 18 C (0 F) or lower. The film should first be moisture-conditioned and then placed in the cans, which should then be sealed with several laps of a moisture-resistant

tape. Although moisture leakage will occur in time, it can be kept to a minimum by reconditioning and repackaging the film after a period of several years. Better moisture resistance is also obtained by heat-sealing the taped cans in foil envelopes. The storage of film in untaped cans offers no humidity control, and there is the risk that high humidities may eventually have adverse effects, even at low temperatures.

Storage Cabinets. All modern motion-picture films are produced on safety base and can be stored on wooden shelves or in wooden cabinets. However, most libraries store film on metal shelves or in metal cabinets made especially for this purpose. Such metal cabinets are usually supplied with adjustable shelving for standard-size reels. The can of film should be stored on edge for easy access.

Storage Conditions. Storage cabinets should be separated enough to permit free circulation of air on all sides. Storage areas should be located on the intermediate floors of buildings—never in damp basements, on the top floors of uninsulated buildings, or near radiators, hot-air ducts, and other sources of heat and humidity.

Film storage and handling areas should be kept as free as possible from dust and dirt. Ideally, such rooms should be supplied with conditioned and filtered air. Precautions should be taken to prevent the entrance of dust and dirt through ventilators, heating ducts, and windows.

Film with a Magnetic Sound Track. The same precautions that apply to the storage of any other safety motion-picture film should be used for film with a magnetic-sound coating on which sound has been recorded. Heat and humidity cause deterioration of the film and, to a certain extent, of the magnetic track. A magnetic sound track, as far as is now known, is as permanent as the film base to which the coating has been applied. Storing the film in a metal container, such as a film cabinet or an aluminum or steel film reel, will not adversely affect the recorded sound.

NOTE: The film must not be stored near a permanent magnet or electrical wiring that carries a heavy current.

Storage cabinets should be arranged to permit free circulation of fresh air to avoid damage from both heat and moisture. The storage area should be kept immaculately clean; preferably, it should be air-conditioned. Films with magnetic sound track must not be stored near magnetic sources or heavy electrical wiring.

Nitrate-Base Films

Since no nitrate-base films were manufactured after about 1951, the information that follows is of primary interest to the film archivist, the librarian, or the person finding a roll of nitrate-base film with other materials. The handling of nitrate-base films, although not likely to be a commonplace occurrence, requires special care and precautions.

Cellulose-nitrate film base is relatively unstable, and in any considerable quantity it constitutes a fire

Nitrate films turn up in unlikely places. This toy motion picture projector and films were found in an attic; the films, ranging in length from 25 feet to 100 feet, are all nitrate base, and at least 40 or 50 years old. Even in small quantities like this, nitrate film can pose a real danger; piled up with other inflammables in an attic, the ignition of a small quantity of film can set off a much larger blaze.

hazard. It is chemically similar to guncotton, but contains somewhat less nitrogen in the molecule. Cellulose-nitrate base is not explosive, but it is highly flammable.

Nitrate film base decomposes slowly under ordinary conditions, and the rate of decomposition is accelerated by increasing temperature and relative humidity. The products of decomposition—nitric oxide, nitrogen dioxide, and others—hasten the process unless allowed to escape from cans, boxes, and other packages. The usual effects of such decomposition are a yellowing of the film base and the gelatin of the emulsion, softening of the gelatin, and oxidation of the silver image. As decomposition proceeds, the base cockles, becomes extremely brittle, and then sticky. Finally, disintegration is complete.

The actual life of nitrate-base films has varied widely; examples 50 or even 60 years old are still in a fair state of preservation, while others have deteriorated seriously in a much shorter time. Such wide differences in the rate of decomposition cannot be fully explained; however, rapid decomposition is most likely to have been caused by high temperature coupled with high relative humidity and by lack of ventilation. There seems to be little relationship between the rate of decomposition of nitrate base and the amount of residual processing chemicals—hypo and silver—present in the material.

Probability of Rapid Decomposition. Observations of old films on nitrate base show that aside from the adverse effects of excessive heat and humidity, the quantity of cellulose nitrate present in a container and the ability of the products of decomposition to escape have a definite bearing on the rate of decomposition. For example, a roll of motion-picture film—which represents a considerable bulk of cellulose nitrate—stored in a sealed can deteriorates fairly rapidly.

Segregating Nitrate-Base Negatives. Some of the products of deteriorating nitrate film are powerful oxidizing agents; consequently, these products attack other materials, such as any acetate-base film and prints that might be in contact with, or in the immediate vicinity of, decomposing nitrate film. This attack takes the form of yellowing and fading of the silver image and softening of the gelatin.

Also, nitrate film base poses a serious fire hazard. Nitrate negatives should therefore be segregated and stored under the best conditions available until they can be duplicated and the originals destroyed.

Identifying Nitrate Base. Unless some deterioration has set in, it may not be readily apparent whether film is on nitrate or acetate base. Generally speaking, any film that was made before 1950 may be suspect, although many films were made with an acetate base long before that time. Generally, 16 mm and 8 mm movie films were not made on nitrate base.

One indication of the presence of cellulose nitrate is a characteristic nitric oxide odor. This odor is usually present when a quantity of nitrate film has been packaged in a closed container.

A test to distinguish nitrate base from any of the acetate bases is to take a 6 mm (¼ inch) square piece of dry film and place it in a test tube containing trichloroethylene. Shake the tube to make sure that the film sample is completely wetted. If the sample sinks, it is cellulose nitrate; if it floats, it is acetate or polyester. Although trichloroethylene is not flammable, it is volatile and the vapor should not be inhaled. Trichloroethylene is obtainable from most suppliers of laboratory chemicals.

Evaluating Extent of Deterioration. It should not be assumed from this discussion that all films on nitrate base are on the verge of total loss. If properly cared for, they can be expected to last a considerable number of years. It is important, however, to recognize the first signs of decomposition. First, the film base becomes yellowish and then amber. At this stage the base is brittle and it breaks easily on being bent double. Also, the gelatin has become soft enough to melt readily if the negative is wetted. To make a simple test, cut a small strip from the film, fold it to check for brittleness, and then soak the strip for a minute or so in water. Scrape the gelatin from the surface. The degree of discoloration can then be observed by placing the strip on a sheet of white paper. This procedure is necessary in order to discover the degree of discoloration of the film base, because most old films appear to be slightly yellow due to sulfiding of traces of silver in the emulsion and to some yellowing of the gelatin itself.

Clearly, films in the process of decomposition must be handled with care and kept dry. Also, they should be duplicated as soon as is convenient. In the later stages of decomposition, which take the form of buckling and stickiness of the gelatin, duplication becomes much more difficult.

Spontaneous Combustion. In the days when motion pictures were made on nitrate-base film, many fires occurred due to spontaneous ignition of this material. So far as is known, fire has not been caused by cellulose nitrate that is in good condition; however, in the advanced stages of decomposition, self-ignition can take place at temperatures greater than 38 C (100 F) if such temperatures are sustained for a considerable time.

The conditions under which still-picture negatives on nitrate base would ignite spontaneously are rare, but the possibility does exist, however remote it might be. Generally, self-ignition of the material has been caused by sustained high temperature coupled with low relative humidity, and where the heat generated by the process of decomposition was unable to escape. Moreover, a considerable amount of material would have to be in a closed container to make spontaneous ignition possible. Tests show that a 1000-foot roll of decomposing motion-picture film ignited after being subjected to a temperature of 41 C (106 F) for 17 days. The film was enclosed in a can wrapped in mineral wool to retain the heat generated by the process of decomposition.

Temporary Storage. Examine all films known to be on nitrate base. If any are badly buckled or sticky, they are in an advanced stage of decomposition. It may be possible to duplicate some of these; if duplication is not feasible, they often yield a fair quality print. If the film base is heavily stained and moisture from the breath makes the gelatin slightly sticky, the film must be duplicated within one or two years.

On no account should a nitrate-base film be wetted, because the gelatin may be soft and readily dissolved if the film has decomposed. If surface dirt must be removed, use a commercial film cleaner such as Kodak film cleaner. Many old negatives have some dichroic or silver-sulfide stain; this iridescent stain is usually on the surface of the gelatin. It may be removed or reduced by rubbing the film with Du Pont white polishing compound, which is obtainable from most automotive supply stores. Be very careful not to damage the image. Also be careful not to bend the film sharply, because the base is usually very brittle and easily broken.

The following instructions are intended for the

storage of films until such time as they can be duplicated on a more stable film base. Note that the instructions are for small quantities of material only. Large quantities should be stored in vaults that meet the specifications of the National Fire Protection Association.

Nitrate-base material should not be stored in closed containers without ventilation, because the products of decomposition cannot escape and they increase the rate of decomposition. The negatives should be packed loosely in ventilated metal boxes or cabinets and stored in a room apart from other negatives or photographic materials.

The temperature in the storage area should not exceed 21 C (70 F), and a lower temperature is desirable if it can be achieved without increasing relative humidity above 45 percent. From the standpoint of retarding decomposition, relative humidity below 40 percent is desirable, but there is a risk of negatives becoming very brittle if conditions are too dry. With the nitrate-base material, relative humidity is critical because a compromise must be reached between making the base too brittle and making the gelatin so tacky that it might adhere to the negative enclosure.

Disposal. When films on nitrate base have been duplicated, they should be destroyed. Only small numbers of films in *good condition* can be discarded into normal trash-disposal channels. Do not incinerate nitrate films with office wastepaper.

Unstable or deteriorated nitrate films present hazards similar to explosives and must be handled with the same respect. Such films should be kept *underwater* in a suitable steel drum until disposal can be arranged. Any substantial quantity of films should be regarded as unstable, whatever the apparent condition.

The safest method for disposing of nitrate films is by carefully controlled burning by qualified personnel in the open air. In most cases, environmental or fire-prevention regulations will require that such disposal be supervised by the proper authorities. A large area removed from any building or combustible material, such as gases, brush, or litter, should be selected, and only a small quantity of film burned at one time. Nitrate films should never be burned in a furnace or other enclosed space, because the gases generated by burning produce high pressure and are highly toxic as well. However, if buildup can be prevented by controlled-rate feeding, it may be possible to dispose of nitrate film in a good incinerator equipped with pollution-control devices.

• *See also:* SPLICING FILM; STORAGE OF SENSITIZED MATERIALS AND PROCESSING SOLUTIONS.

  Multimedia Presentations

Multimedia shows are usually one-of-a-kind, custom-produced presentations for a specific audience and with an intended purpose. By definition they must include some combination of the many forms of media available to produce a show. To qualify as multimedia, a show must consist of at least slide projectors, screens, and sound or live action. Their design may range from such a minimal concept to very elaborate stage sets with many screens and truly dazzling visual effects. When appropriate, multimedia utilizes actors, singers, dancers, special lighting effects, and multi-channel sound; it is this integration of rich human and technical resources that signifies multimedia in its truest form.

Multimedia as a photographic art was utilized as early as 1939 in the Kodak exhibit featured at the New York World's Fair—a wraparound slide presentation staged in a circular theater. Multi-projector, multi-image motion pictures were widely staged in commercial theatres in the 1950's. The Montreal World's Fair had dazzling applications of multimedia, which were often designed and produced by photography specialists. Industrial show producers, firms based largely in New York, were using the multimedia concept in the 1960's when they realized that their theatrical presentations could be greatly enhanced by this new technique. Thus, while the art continues to develop as more sophisticated equipment and techniques become available, multimedia shows have been in use for some years.

Types of Multimedia Shows

A Typical Multimedia Show. The minimal multimedia show might be three slide projectors and a single screen with monaural sound, live action, or some other forms of media. A fifteen-projector show is a complicated production. Typically, a multimedia show is built around nine Kodak Ektagraphic slide projectors and three front, or rear, projection screens. (*See:* REAR PROJECTION.) It is

A six-projector multimedia slide show is set up to dissolve images on three sections of a big screen; two projectors are used for each section. Interspersed among the slides are movie clips shown with an arc projector, which is mounted on a swivel to project onto any part of the screen. Two specialists present each program—one narrates and the other operates the equipment. Photos by Keith Boas.

usually designed as follows although there may be exceptions.

The slide projectors are usually mounted in three "towers," each tower consisting of three slide projectors; each projector is set up to project a full image of a standard 35 mm transparency in standard aspect ratio. The three slide projectors in the tower are aligned to cover one third of a wide screen, or an individual screen in a set of three screens. In any case, the array of screen space is equal to a projection area three times as wide as a conventional projection screen. With the three towers it is possible to project images on a single screen, two screens, or all three screens.

In addition to the three towers, multimedia in this configuration uses a dissolve unit for each tower, a programming unit, and usually a four-track stereo tape playback. There are: nine slide projectors, three dissolve units, one programming unit, and the stereo tape deck. Control of the show is either manual—from push buttons on the programming unit—or automatic—from audio pulses laid down on one of the four channels on the audio track.

The key to automatic or manual operation of the multimedia show is the programming unit. Depending upon its capability, it contains either hundreds or thousands of individual instructions to the dissolve units, which will operate the slide projec-

tors. In the multimedia world, each set of instructions is known as a "move." The programming unit on cue instructs the dissolve units. Each dissolve unit in turn signals the set of three slide projectors in the tower that it controls.

Despite the variety and richness possible in multimedia shows, each dissolve unit can instruct the slide projectors in only two ways: (1) projectors can be instructed to advance the slide trays, and (2) dissolve units can control projector lamps at any rate from "off" to "on"; that is, they actuate lamp bulbs instantly, at 2 seconds, 4 seconds, 8 seconds, and so on. The projection bulb brightens, or darkens, at once or at any predetermined rate.

But since one programming unit controls three dissolve units and three dissolve units operate nine slide projectors, even this basic nine-projector array can deliver an astonishing number of effects—effects that are closely analogous to those in motion pictures. Dissolves, fades, double exposures, superimposition, quick cuts, and the illusion of animation are all possible with only conventional slide projectors controlled by dissolve units and a programmer.

Consider a single tower, consisting of three projectors, aimed at a single screen. The dissolve unit is cued by the programming unit to bring one lamp from zero illumination to full intensity. It can do this almost instantly or at any predetermined rate.

The audience will see an image fade in on the screen. This picture can fade out and a second image from the second projector can fade in. By fading one lamp out as another lamp is brought up to full illumination, you get the effect of a lap dissolve. The third projector can fade in or flash on to superimpose yet another image. "Quick cuts" can be achieved by bringing lamps from "off" to full intensity very rapidly; and you can get the illusion of motion—animates—by repeatedly switching rapidly from one image to another.

With three towers, consisting of nine projectors, this typical multimedia setup can do a great deal more. Three projectors, each with a section of an image, can project a mural across all three screens. Two screens can share an image, while a third screen, for example, can show a chart. The combinations in this basic nine-projector configuration are very nearly endless; and additional slide projectors, more screens, ingenious set design, actors, and video projection can be added almost without end. Never-

theless, the basic nine-projector arrangement described here is widely considered to be sufficient in many multimedia presentations.

Multimedia for Speech Support. A large percentage of commercial multimedia production is intended for what the industry and its clients call "speech support." Many companies are finding the combination of live speakers—managers, executives, consultants—and multimedia an excellent way of enlivening and enriching sales and marketing meetings. The same combination—live speakers with multimedia support—is finding increasingly wide use in introducing new products within a company to dealers and to journalists at press meetings and conferences. Stockholders' meetings and annual meetings also make use of live speakers and multimedia.

Speakers using this kind of multimedia often write their own speeches, or have them written either by the multimedia production firm or another outside source. It is the task of the multimedia de-

(Left) The title for a three-screen, three-projector presentation is illustrated here with components grouped logically. (Center left) The word "Promotion" appeared on the left-hand screen (not shown), and was repeated on the central screen (as shown); the text was then added to the right-hand screen. (Below left) The spread of artwork over two screens results in larger overall image size than with a single-screen setup.

Two uses of the three-screen setup are shown here. Series at left illustrates progressive addition of three sections of artwork from right to left. Photos above show the appearance, first, of the artwork background, followed by the artwork plus title overlay.

signer to "visualize" the individual speeches by seeking out key phrases and important concepts within the written speech, and to create suitable ways of utilizing the resources of multimedia to enrich, clarify, and support what the speaker will say.

While each move of multimedia for speech support is programmed before going "on site," the equipment is customarily cued manually; someone backstage signals the programming unit to keep pace with the speaker as he or she speaks to the audience. Each single cue can trigger a very complicated move on the projection screens.

Speech support, by and large, is rear-projected so the audience can have an unimpeded view of the person talking and of the support multimedia material. (Shows are often presented in meeting rooms unsuited for front projection.)

Multimedia Modules. Contrasted with speech-support multimedia—using an in-person speaker, manually cued slides, and other visual support—

multimedia modules are designed to run automatically and to be able to stand alone. Modules are generally short—2 to 4 minutes—but modules up to 10 minutes in length are workable. Modules are comparable to short motion pictures in that they usually have a single theme, a single concept, or one story to present. A taped narration is employed, together with suitable music and sound effects.

Configuration of the sound tracks has yet to be standardized. Some multimedia producers use audio tracks No. 1 and No. 3 for stereo sound; they leave No. 2 clear, and put their control pulses on No. 4. Still others use half-track, reel-to-reel tapes, with monaural music and narration on one half of the tape and programmer pulses on the other half.

DuKane Corporation suggests tracks No. 1 and No. 2 for sound, with No. 3 and No. 4 reserved for control signals. This system requires a four-track playback.

Another setup favored by many multimedia producers uses tracks No. 2 and No. 4, which are the rear tracks in quadraphonic playback, to carry the stereo track for the module. Track No. 3, the right-front, carries the "pulse track"; and track No. 1, the front-left track, carries a monaural "mix" of the sound track.

Proponents of this arrangement point out its advantages: If a quadraphonic tape playback *is* available, the module may be presented with stereo sound from the two rear tracks. If, however, a four-track machine is not available and a conventional two-track player must be used, the multimedia module may be shown with the monaural mix from the left track. In both two-track or four-track machines, the control pulse is to be found on the No. 3 track. In either case, the show runs automatically.

The pulse track, or control track, does automatically what the person backstage does manually for multimedia speech support; the programming unit is triggered to make one move. As previously indicated, one move can be quite complex. The programming unit, under manual or automatic control, makes only one move per cue; however, many projectors are advanced, lighted, or turned off in that one move.

Modules are often featured as an element in meetings that are for the most part multimedia-supported speeches. Modules are used in permanent installations—museums and corporate headquarters—as well as in the multimedia shows that are rapidly becoming a form of paid public entertainment, and in support of Broadway stage shows.

The production of a typical nine-projector multimedia show may be sketched by taking the production from script to its final on-site presentation. For the sake of simplicity, it is assumed that each sequence in preparing the show requires one person; in fact, many multimedia professionals can and do act in several capacities.

Aspects of the Multimedia Show

Although multimedia is considered to be mainly a photographic art, not all of the people involved in producing multimedia shows come to the field by way of photography, motion pictures, or television. While some of them do have experience as photographers, more of them have a background in some aspect of the theater, such as theatrical technicians, stage managers, scenic and lighting designers, actors, and producers. Not least of all are the writers who are a very important part of multimedia productions.

Script Writing. Virtually every multimedia program begins with a script and a writer. This includes fairs and exhibits, motion pictures, and those programs produced by commercial and industrial firms for sales and marketing meetings; new product announcements to employees, dealers and distributors, and the press; and stockholders' meetings. This script is then interpreted by other people.

The Designer. The designer's task is to create the overall "look" of the show. The job requires both artistic creativity and a working knowledge of what can and cannot be done with a multimedia presentation.

This work begins with analysis and translation into visuals of what until now has been only the written word. The designer's end product is the storyboard—the pictorial blueprint of the show. Ideally, the storyboard is cued closely to key words and concepts in the script. In designing, the storyboard shows not only what each image is to be, but it also indicates moves—what is to happen on the screens—and even suggests timings for the moves. The designer also indicates the slides that are to be artwork, the live photography that will be required, and the titles that will be used. The better the storyboard, the more complete a blueprint.

After the storyboard has been approved, it moves along with the show through each stage of production; ideally, the storyboard is updated as the show evolves from concept to the finished production.

The Producer. The many activities of artists and technicians engaged in making a multimedia show are under the direct supervision of the producer, whose role is primarily financial. Rates of pay, costs of services and equipment, and the hiring of specialists are all under the control of the producer. It is the producer's job to see that work is moving forward, and that the show will be produced within the allotted budget. The producer is also the liaison between the client's desires and the creative aspirations of photographers, artists, designers, and others.

Stage and Lighting Design. This element of the multimedia show obviously involves the placement and lighting of podiums for live speakers, the setting of the show, and the kind and number of projection screens. If many screens are involved, or if unusual screen placement or special lighting effects are called for, the sketches and ideas of the stage and lighting designer are given to the designer of the show itself since his or her options would be controlled by the stage setting, lighting, and screen design.

The Job Manager. This person is in charge of all aspects of the production of the transparencies. Among other things, he or she must see that all artwork is completed, approved, and ready for the camera. The job manager's responsibilities also include making sure that photography and graphics—all elements of the show that will become transparencies—are approved and translated into transparencies.

Photography for Multimedia. Photography for multimedia is often the combined work of several people because the typical multimedia show utilizes three rather different kinds of image. There is, typically, live photography of people, products, and locations—the type of work a professional photographer might expect as a routine assignment.

There is also "stand photography"—photography of artwork, graphics, and transparencies themselves on transparency film. Most of this copy work requires a special copy stand equipped with a still camera, and an accurate means of "fielding" or determining the size of the image, and illumination directed from above for flat copy and from below for transparencies.

Finally, there is photography from Kodalith film slides. It is, in fact, a variation on stand photography. Multimedia producers have standardized on such photography for masks, titles, and charts—any image that is not simply a transparency. They argue that the qualities of Kodalith film slides, if correctly exposed and developed for multimedia uses, give an image that is either totally black or totally clear. Using Kodalith film slides in multimedia requires the knack of thinking in reverse; since it is a negative stock, a clear image requires taking a black object to the stand camera and vice versa.

Kodalith film slides for multimedia are the basis for a great deal of imaginative work by artists and designers. The image can be dyed with a number of commercial products from art supply stores. These slides are often tinted with a spectrum of theatrical gels. Interesting effects can be created with colored felt-tip marking pens. Solarization and posterization are achieved with Kodalith film slides by either the photographer or the artist without any need for the photographic laboratory. Unlike other special effects, multimedia effects are usually created mechanically by the artist or designer using slide images and any number of multimedia techniques. (*See:* SPECIAL EFFECTS.)

Registration. Multimedia imposes an unusual discipline on its practitioners; registration of images for this work is extremely critical. The alternatives to accurate registration are projected images that fail to hold their alignment, overlap, and move erratically, and a show that fails to meet the standards set by the designer. Cameras for stand work often have registration pins built into the still camera; and the stand itself has provisions for registering both flat work and transparencies that are to be copied.

The photographer who gets his or her first assignment for a multimedia show should be aware that registration of images is critical. There is another reason for this caution in addition to those previously cited: The finished transparencies for multimedia shows will be mounted in special heat-resist glass-and-plastic slide mounts. These mounts have internal registration pins; and unless the photographic transparency has its frame-line exactly between two sprocket holes of 35 mm film, the transparency will not mount without delicate manipulations. It is a simple enough matter to have a photographic repair shop adjust the film advance in any 35 mm camera for multimedia work; and an examination of a contact sheet from your camera will reveal whether or not this adjustment is necessary. The frame-line should be cleanly between two sprocket holes.

The Light-Box Review. The light box—simply a large illuminated surface that will allow viewing a quantity of slides—is the organizing key to multimedia production. As finished slides begin to accumulate from various sources, they are usually laid out on the light box horizontally according to the screen they will be projected on, and vertically according to moves—the sequence of things that will take place as the slides are to appear. It is very seldom that the producer has all slides ready at one time. Missing slides are represented on the light box by Kodak Ektagraphic write-on slides, known in the industry as "glass." The write-ons can be labeled to indicate which image they are substituting for. The light-box review is often the first opportunity to show clients, designers, and programmers how the

Good planning is necessary for a successful slide show. (Above left) Planning cards are useful to organize ideas in the initial stages. (Above) As work progresses, planning cards are gradually replaced with prints of the photos to be used. (Left) Slide illuminators are useful for final editing of the photos to be used.

multimedia show is going to work. Since large light boxes consume space and can be costly, and a nine-screen multimedia show may call for several thousand slides, mounted slides that have been approved can simply be taped to large sheets of brown paper and stacked flat in preparation for programming.

Mounting. Transparencies for multimedia shows are customarily delivered from the processing laboratory in transparent plastic sleeves, uncut and unmounted. This makes it easier to select transparencies and avoids the unnecessary labor of tearing open cardboard or plastic mounts and remounting images. The mounter is responsible for cleaning the transparencies and cleaning the special heat-resist, pin-registered multimedia mounts. This really requires an air compressor and a cleaning cloth that is antistatic. The mounter also attaches gels to Kodalith film slides and prepares "sandwiches"—mounts that are to contain more than one picture, such as a title superimposed over a conventional transparency.

Programming. At this stage of multimedia production, the producer needs the services of a person—the programmer—and a machine—the programming unit. The programming unit, whether it is digital or punch-tape, records the decisions of the pro-grammer and is capable of playing these decisions back. The programmer is armed with the storyboard —the blueprint of what is to happen on the screen. The programmer also has the slides on light boxes or taped to many sheets of paper. His or her work is to enter each move in the programming unit, and as this is done, to "tray" the appropriate slides for that move. Generally, programming is done to a prerecorded audio track made earlier in the work of producing the show.

Since the typical show discussed here involves nine slide projectors, and since the programming unit offers perhaps 20 or 30 choices for each move, programmers are both highly skilled and, often, highly paid. It goes without saying that the mul-timedia show ready for programming has a better chance of being both successful and on budget.

Programming is usually done with front projec-tion; after approval of the completed show, a show for rear projection goes back to the mounting room to be "cleaned and flopped," that is, reversed and replaced in the slide tray. Because of the thickness of the heat-resist slide mounts, only the Kodak Car-ousel universal slide tray is used in Kodak mul-timedia. Its capacity is limited to 80 slides, and a typical multimedia show will require many changes of slide trays while it is being shown. Considerable ingenuity may be required to prevent tray changes from interrupting the flow of the show.

Taking the Show On Site. It is unusual for a multimedia presentation to be shown to its intended audience at the place it was produced. Most shows are shipped out and reassembled in meeting rooms or auditoriums for meetings and conventions. The multimedia producer and all others concerned should have information about the conditions on site: electrical supply, seating, local audiovisual suppliers, and everything that could work for or against the success of the show. Shipping many pro-jectors, dissolve and programming units, tape decks, and the many, many trays of slides for a typical show should be carefully planned.

In the case of taking a show to a foreign coun-try, an experienced customs broker is almost always essential. The operation of a multimedia presenta-tion on site may involve several of the people who produced the show—the producer, for example, and the programmer who functions on site as a stage

manager responsible for making the show operate as planned. But these functions are beyond the scope of this article.

Multimedia is a rapidly evolving industry; its producers are individualistic and idiosyncratic. There is nothing in the typical multimedia presenta-tion that has been described here that cannot be done in a different format, with different equipment, in different ways.

• *See also:* REAR PROJECTION; SPECIAL EFFECTS.

Further Reading: Amble, Patti. *A Multimedia Presentation: Definitions, History and Survey in Business and Theater Today.* M.A. Thesis. Dallas, TX: Southern Methodist University, 1972; Gordon, Roger L., ed. *The Art of Multi Image.* Abington, PA: Association for Multi Image, 1978; Vaughan, Ted W. *An Educator's Guide to Large Screen/Multiple Image Presentation.* Laramie, WY: University of Wyoming, 1973.

Multiple-Exposure Techniques

Multiple-exposure photographs are those made by giving one sheet of film or one frame of roll film in a camera more than one exposure to different sub-jects, or to the same subject in different poses. The multiple-exposure technique can be distinguished from a multiple-image technique, in which a multi-faceted prism or repeater lens is used to make multi-ple images of the same subject in the same pose on the film in one exposure. Other techniques used to obtain similar effects are multiple printing, sand-wiching, and copying of multiple projected images from a screen.

Controlling Multiple Exposures

With certain exceptions, multiple exposures made with normal exposure-control settings will re-sult in overexposure. If the subject is normal with various tones scattered over the picture area, com-pensation of the exposures must be made. The sum total of the exposures should be equal to the normal exposure. The rule for multiple exposures of this type of subject is to divide the normal exposure by the number of exposures you plan to make. For example, for two exposures, divide the normal expo-sure by two to find the exposure for each image.

With automatic or semi-automatic cameras, or when using an exposure meter to find the exposure, a convenient method is to multiply the film speed by

Multiple exposures made with normal exposure-control settings will be overexposed unless compensation is made. To get the correct exposure, divide the normal exposure by the number of exposures planned for each frame. Photo by Michos Tzovaras for Editorial Photocolor Archives.

the number of exposures. For example, if ASA 200 film is used, and three exposures will create the multiple-exposure image, set the film speed at 600 (3 × 200 = 600).

The major exception to this rule is when a black area is left in the first image, and the second image is exposed in this black area. For example, a fully silhouetted profile portrait exposure can be made that is relatively large on the film. Then a normal head-and-shoulders portrait with a black background can be made with the image smaller and placed within the silhouetted profile. Since both portraits are imaged against black, they both receive full exposure. Other examples of imaging against black

are when a matte box is used to divide a picture area, and when pictures are taken at night. For example, if several bursts of fireworks are to be imaged in different areas of the film against a night sky, normal exposure should be given for each burst.

Another situation involves multiple exposures of the same subject in the same pose, but with changed lighting. Night pictures of buildings can appear as just light rectangles against black if simple night exposures are made. If multiple exposures are made—one at dusk and one or more after dark—the shape of the buildings can be seen against a blue, late-evening sky. The camera should be kept unmoved on a rigid tripod between exposures. The

Multiple-Exposure Techniques

dusk exposure is just enough to create slight detail in the buildings, and should be about one stop less than normal to achieve this. The night exposure of the lighted windows is then superimposed over this, and should be about one-half stop less than normal, because a slight overexposure has already been made.

Camera Techniques

Some 35 mm and medium-format cameras have a special provision for multiple exposures—the shutter can be cocked without moving the film. All view cameras can easily be used for multiple exposures.

Many 35 mm cameras without special cocking provision can be cocked without advancing the film by pressing the rewind button while activating the film-advance lever. If registration of the multiple images is not too critical, a slight creeping of the film will not be too serious. Read the instruction manual for your camera to see if and how multiple exposures can be made with it.

With most cameras, it is necessary to note where the details of the first image are located, in order to place the second image in proper relationship. With view cameras, important details of the first image can be sketched on the ground glass to

When a black area is left in the first image for the exposure of a second image, normal exposures may be used for both images. Here, a matte box was used to create such an effect. Photo courtesy Ambico, Inc.

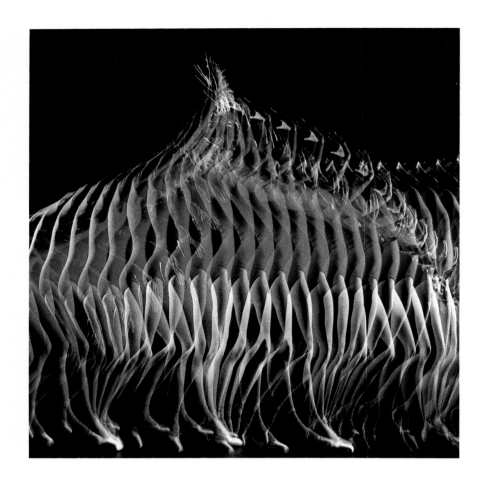

Multiple exposures of a moving figure can be made by firing a series of electronic flashes at desired intervals in a darkened room. The camera shutter remains open until the final exposure is made. Photo by Neil Montanus.

obtain a more exact location. Use the back (shiny side) of the glass, and mark it with a grease pencil, a china-marking pencil, a negative pencil, or a permanent ink felt-tip marker. All of these marks can be cleaned off afterwards with lighter fluid on a cloth or tissue.

For critical control of multiple-exposure composition and registration, particularly in motion-picture work, the use of a matte box is a valuable aid. (*See:* MATTE BOX.)

Electronic Flash. Multiple exposures are often made with the subject in the dark against a black background. The movements of the subject—for example a dancer—are carefully plotted in advance. As each state of movement is reached, electronic flash is fired to capture it. This is repeated until the sequence is completed. (*See:* PAINTING WITH LIGHT.)

Stroboscopic Light. High-speed movement, such as a golfer's swing, can be captured by stroboscopic light. The units operating at 1/1000 of a second will stop most human activities. Speeds of up to 1/100,000 will stop a bullet in flight. Multiple images with stroboscopic light require multiple stroboscopes and automatic triggers for the lights. (*See:* STROBOSCOPIC PHOTOGRAPHY.)

Zooming. Another way of making multiple exposures employs a lens of variable focus—a zoom lens. An initial exposure is made, usually with flash. The focal length is changed and one or more additional exposures are made in sequence. This kind of multiple-exposure technique requires some experimenting and is effective in proportion to the persistence of the photographer.

• *See also:* MATTE BOX; PAINTING WITH LIGHT; STROBOSCOPIC PHOTOGRAPHY; ZOOM LENS.

Multiple Flash

Pictures made with direct, single flash on the camera show very little modeling of the subject (the showing of form by light and shade), and usually show a narrow black shadow line on the background. On the other hand, pictures properly made with multiple flash show good modeling, natural-appearing shadows, and hence a good three-dimensional appearance.

Because flash units are very portable, multiple flash lets you take studio-type lighting with you on location. With extension or slave flash units, you can have two or three light setups wherever you go.

Techniques for Multiple Flash

There are two major ways you can make multiple-flash pictures. One is to use one or more extension flash units wired to your camera. The other is to use slave extension flash units. A slave unit has a small photocell that triggers its own flash when it "sees" the light from the flash triggered by the camera. Any combination of conventional flashbulbs or electronic flash can be used as long as a proper exposure is determined. In this article, you will find guide tables for multiple flash all used at the same distance from the subject, usually used to light large subjects, and for flash used at different distances, used to light these subjects with good modeling.

Wired Extensions. Many conventional flashbulb units have a socket into which you can plug an extension flash unit. Most extension flash units have their own battery power supply, so be sure to maintain battery polarity when you plug in the extension; many sockets will accept the plugs in only one way.

Some electronic flash units allow additional flash heads to be fired from one power pack. If all your flash heads are identical, this arrangement simply divides the light equally among all flash heads attached to the power pack. It does not give more total light than one flash head attached to the power pack, but you do gain flexibility and control.

In any wired extension flash system, all lamps are flashed by the synchronization contacts in the camera shutter. This means synchronization is no problem if the same type of bulb is used in all units.

Slave Extensions. Slave systems do away with the need for extension wires. This one fact makes them much easier to use. The main concern with slave units is getting all the units to flash while the shutter is open. The type of photocell used with electronic flash units has a delay of 1 millisecond or less—so short that it poses no synchronization problems. But the type of photocell circuit usually used with flashbulbs has a delay of 5 to 12 milliseconds between the flash peak at the camera and the flash peak at the slave unit, depending on the distance from the camera. This can sometimes cause problems.

Most flashbulbs reach the peak of brightness about 12 to 20 milliseconds after current is applied. (This includes flashcubes, magicubes, AG-1B, M2B, M3B, 5B, 25B, and most other commonly used bulbs.) You have to allow for this delay, plus the delay of the triggering circuit itself. Keep a copy of the accompanying table taped to your flash unit for reference in order to get proper synchronization.

NOTE: This chart is based on the use of a photocell with about a 1-millisecond delay with electronic-flash slaves and a 5- to 12-millisecond delay with flashbulbs. In any case, check your camera and flash-unit instructions before starting. Pick a system that suits your equipment, and stick to it until you have mastered the technique.

Slaves vs. Wires. Wired systems are easy to synchronize, but their wires are easy to trip over, and in many places, such as on a busy sidewalk, they cannot be used. Slave systems are convenient to use, but the flash units of other photographers may trigger your unit. In sunlight and at great distances, wired systems are best. The maximum distance at which most slave units can be triggered is about 50 feet.

One advantage of a slave system is that *any* kind of on-camera flash can be used to trigger the units. Even a simple box camera with a flash unit can trigger slaves.

If your unit accepts plug-in extensions, you may want extra lamp heads to use with it. If your electronic flash unit accepts more than one flash head, you have another way to take multiple-flash pictures. And if you wish, photocells to trigger electronic units can be bought at electrical supply stores.

Multiple-Flash System	Type of Flash Lamp at Camera	Type of Flash Lamp at Extension	Synchro-nization	Shutter Speed (sec.)	
				Leaf Shutter	**Focal-Plane Shutter**
Wired	Electronic	Electronic	X	Any	Up to 1/50 or 1/60*
	Flashcube, AG-1B, M3B, 5B, 25B	Flashcube, AG-1B, M3B, 5B, 25B	M	Any	—
	Flashcube, AG-1B, M3B	Flashcube, AG-1B, M3B	FP	—	Up to 1/30*
	6B, 26B	6B, 26B	FP	—	Any
Slave	Flashcube, AG-1B, M2B, M3B, 5B, 25B	Flashcube, AG-1B, M2B, M3B, 5B, 25B	X	Up to 1/30	—
	Electronic	Electronic	X	Up to 1/250	Up to 1/50 or 1/60*
	Electronic	Flashcube, AG-1B, M2B, M3B, 5B, 25B	X	Up to 1/30	—
	Flashcube, Magicube, AG-1B, M2B, M3B, 5B, 25B	Electronic	X	Up to 1/30	—
	Flashcube, AG-1B, M3B, 5B, 25B	Flashcube, AG-1B, M3B, 5B, 25B	M	Up to 1/30	—
	Flashcube, Magicube, AG-1B, M2B	Flashcube, AG-1B, M2B	X	Up to 1/30	—

*See the camera instruction manual for shutter speeds that can be used with your camera.

Circuits for building both slave and triggering devices are often published in electronics hobby magazines.

Making Pictures

The following lighting arrangements will help you produce good pictures. Some require a flash unit on the camera. Others call for *no* flash at the camera. So you need an extension cord to connect one flash unit to the camera's flash socket. Flash extension cords can be purchased at most photo supply stores.

Main and Fill Light. The most basic two-light arrangement uses an extension flash as the main light source, and the flash on the camera to fill in the shadows. This arrangement is good for informal portraits and is easy to use for candid shots. Have someone hold the extension flash where it is needed, or simply clamp it to a convenient object such as a

Multiple flash may be used to create a feeling of depth and form. For this photograph, the main light was placed high and to the left of the camera, and slightly forward of the subject. A fill-light was added high and to the camera's right, almost on the same plane as the subject.

Multiple Flash

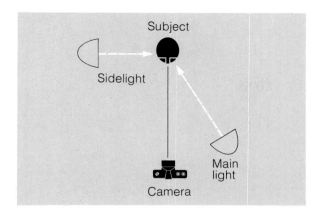

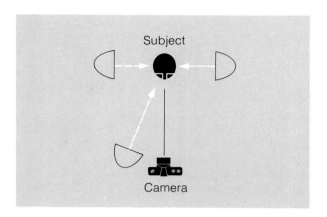

Alternate Positions for Main Light

One flash at the camera serves as a main light, while the second is placed to one side to provide accent highlights. Use of a black background with this setup will avoid shadow problems.

Sidelights Equidistant from Subject

With three flashes, modeling of the subject can be improved. This "Y" lighting setup utilizes two side flashes placed fairly high and equidistant from the subject. The main light at the camera produces the modeling effect.

door or the back of a chair. Any clamping device can be used to hold the extension light; tape can also be used to hold a unit in position. As a variation of the main-and-fill-light arrangement, try placing the main light in one of the alternate positions shown in the accompanying diagram. Or try using bounce flash or bare-bulb flash for the fill light.

Sidelighting. Two sidelights produce interesting crosslighting effects. This arrangement is especially good with dark backgrounds, profile portraits, and edge-lighted glassware. Usually each sidelight is placed the same distance from the subject.

"Y" Lighting. This setup combines the best of the main-and-fill and sidelight arrangements. It requires three flash units. Put a light on each side of the subject, and the main light at the side of the camera about 1½ feet above the subject's eye level. See the accompanying diagram.

Large Subjects. Some subjects are too large to be lighted properly with one bulb. Several units may be necessary to fully illuminate the subject, each light aimed at a different part of the subject. The accompanying diagram shows how a large subject can be illuminated with three units.

Multiple-Flash Exposure. Photographers are sometimes confused by the problem of determining the exposure for more than one lamp, and find it

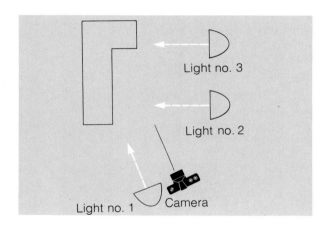

Large subjects are difficult to photograph well with one bulb. Three bulbs may be necessary to fully illuminate the subject, each light aimed at a different part of the subject.

especially difficult to decide what guide numbers to use for several lamps.

The problem is much simpler than it appears at first; it is simply a matter of deciding upon the exposure for a single lamp and then making corrections for the light of the additional lamps. The questions then are how much additional light is obtained and how much allowance must be made for the additional light?

Here is the surprising fact. The change in exposure for additional lamps can be quite small, often much smaller than expected.

Given a single lamp, the guide number formula directly determines the exposure. (*See:* GUIDE NUMBERS.) Now, assume that a second lamp is employed. If it is placed at the camera position, alongside the first lamp, its light merely adds to that of the first lamp, and the result is to double the light. But if the light is doubled, the guide number is multiplied by 1.4, which is equivalent to a single lens stop.

This is the maximum effect that a second lamp can have. If the lamp is placed anywhere else than right next to the first lamp, it will illuminate only part of the subject. Going to the opposite extreme, if the second lamp is placed behind the subject, either to illuminate the hair or to brighten the background, its effect on the exposure of the subject itself will be zero. In this case, use the guide number for the lamp at the camera position and ignore the added lamp altogether.

These are the two extremes; all other cases must lie between them. If a lamp is placed to the side, it will add only to the light on the highlight side of the face, but will put no light on the other half of the subject. Since the exposure must fall between that for two lamps and that for a single lamp, and since it is seldom possible to split lens stops in smaller parts than halves, simply make a half-stop reduction in lens aperture for the added lamp, and the results will be well within the practical latitude of the process.

In the case of black-and-white films, making any compensation for a second lamp is seldom done, unless it is doubling the power of the main lamp. Otherwise, the latitude of the film will handle the matter nicely. With color films, most photographers make several exposures, bracketing a half stop above and below the estimated correct exposure. If the same thing is done, after allowing a half stop for the extra lamp, one of the three exposures will almost certainly be correct.

For more than two lamps, the same method is used, but additional lamps have even less effect on the exposure. Returning to the first example, where two lamps are placed at the camera, the exposure required is cut by a single lens stop. Placing another lamp there will not double the light again (2 + 1 = 3), and the added illumination will be only about a half stop.

Several lights arranged behind the subject provide a rim effect which outlines the baby's form. Aside from the flash, there were no other lights in the area where this picture was taken.

Multiple Flash

Exposure Calculations

When two or more flash sources with the same output (that is, with the same guide number for the film in use) are used at equal distances from a subject, and their outputs overlap, a smaller *f*-stop must be used to adjust for the greater light intensity. The simplest way to do this is to determine a new guide number for the combination of sources, as follows:

$$\begin{matrix} \text{Combined} \\ \text{Guide No.} \end{matrix} = \begin{matrix} \text{Guide No. for} \\ \text{one source} \end{matrix} \times \begin{matrix} \text{Multiple unit} \\ \text{factor (see table)} \end{matrix}$$

Multiple Unit Exposure Factors

No. of flash sources	2	3	4	5	6	7	8
Factor*	1.4	1.7	2	2.2	2.4	2.6	2.8

*The factor is the square root of the number of sources used.

Note that when multiple sources of the same output are used to light a large area without overlapping, exposure should be based on the guide number for a single unit.

When two flash sources are used at different distances from a subject, first use the individual guide numbers and distances to determine the *f*-stop required with each. Then proceed as follows:

Difference between f-stops called for	*Expose at*
2 stops	Smaller of the two (smaller aperture, larger *f*-number)
½ to 1½ stops	½ stop less than the smaller of the two
1 stop	1 stop less than the smaller of the two

Again, if the added lamp or lamps are not exactly coincident with the main light, the effect will be less. As an example, if three lamps are used—one for a main light, one for a side light, and one for a hair light—the hair light may be ignored completely, allow a half stop for the side light, and the exposure will be that for the front lamp, reduced by about a half stop. Or the guide number for the front lamp may be multiplied by 1.2, and the result will be the *f*-stop for the combination.

In short, the whole problem of multiple flash comes down to deciding which is the main lamp, and making a small adjustment for additional units, seldom exceeding a half stop overall.

This leaves a single problem—what occurs when the lamps are at different distances from the subject? Although this seems at first consideration to be more complicated, it actually is not. Again assume that both lamps are at the camera position, but that one is nearer the subject than the other. If the guide number for the nearer of the two lamps is used, it is evident that the other lamp will not even double the light, and the compensation will necessarily be less than one lens stop for the second lamp. In short, the added light will always be less than double, and the compensation for two lamps will be less than a full stop at most, again diminishing as the second lamp is moved from the camera position.

Thus, in a seemingly complicated situation with several lamps all at different distances, all that is necessary is to take the lamp most nearly frontal to the subject (and nearest the subject as well) and calculate the exposure for this lamp. Then the others, being farther from the subject and at angles to it, will contribute little additional light, and a reduction in exposure will usually be no more than a half stop for adequate compensation.

• *See also:* ELECTRONIC FLASH; FLASH PHOTOGRAPHY; GUIDE NUMBERS; MULTIPLE-EXPOSURE TECHNIQUES.

Multiple Printing

There are a great many techniques for combining multiple images or image elements in a single composition. As described in separate articles, collage, montage, combination printing, multiple exposure, and stroboscopic photography all use two or more different images—either the subjects are different, or a single subject has moved or otherwise changed from image to image. While combination printing is making a single print from several negatives, multiple printing uses a single image that is repeatedly printed at different positions within the overall picture area to produce the impression of recorded movement.

Because the attitude or posture of the subject does not change throughout the repeated images, it often appears as if a very high-speed movement has been recorded, especially if the displacement between the images is slight. In other cases, a widely

The feeling of movement in the runners was created by making three different exposures of the negative, moving the easel slightly after each exposure. This color print was made from a black-and-white high contrast negative; different color filters were used for each exposure. Photo by Paul Kuzniar.

separated set of positions produces a stylized impression of movement, or the sense of a stop-motion sequence.

Multiple printing is often combined with other image modifications such as the Sabattier effect, posterization, or tone-line rendition to create an expressive effect.

Techniques

The basic method for multiple printing is simple: The image is shifted between repeated exposures. In contact printing, either the negative or the print paper may be moved. In enlarging, it is usually easier to shift the easel—and there is more latitude for movement in any direction—than it is to shift the negative.

When printing with black-and-white materials, it is a simple matter to place a suitable filter over the printing light so that the image position can be observed as the change is made without further exposing the print. Or, register marks drawn on the baseboard to mark successive positions can be seen by safelight illumination. When printing with pan-

chromatic or color materials, the shifting must be done in complete darkness by feel or by estimate. Alternatively, the print can be removed from the easel and placed in a light-safe location each time so that the image can be shifted with the printing light turned on. This is laborious, but offers a great degree of control. It is a good idea to clip one corner of the print so it can always be returned to the easel in darkness with the same orientation.

Moving the Enlarger Head. Rather than move the negative or the easel, it is possible to move the enlarger head toward or away from the print paper in successive stages; this produces a zoom-like effect. For best results, it is necessary to refocus the image each time the enlarger head is moved, which may be a cumbersome process. In addition, the exposure changes as the lens-to-paper distance changes. Although some of the exposure difference will be covered by the overlapping image areas, tests should be made beforehand to determine proper exposure at the closest, middle, and farthest distances. Compensation for in-between positions should then be easy to estimate.

This multiple-exposure print was made from a single high-contrast negative. After each exposure, the enlarger easel was moved. To achieve the midtones, each exposure was kept extremely short. The original picture, taken on slide film, was printed on line copy film to produce the high contrast negative. Photo by Keith Boas.

To create this zoom-like view of the Empire State Building, the photographer made an exposure on the paper, and then moved the enlarger up and made another exposure. He repeated this many times without moving the paper, but always dodging the main building. Then he dodged the rest of the paper while printing-in the building. Photo by Stanley W. Cowan.

Overlapping Exposures. The overlapping of repeated exposures can be a serious problem if the subject occupies most of the frame, or if the background is significantly dark or detailed. After a few exposures, details in the subject will become obscured. The easiest images to multiple-print are subjects that are clearly defined, those that are reasonably small in the frame, and subjects photographed against a light background. Often, high-contrast duplicates are made in order to simplify a subject for multiple printing. Preliminary exposure tests will improve results significantly.

Expressive Effect. In addition to changing the image position, other factors may be changed between exposures. The most widely used technique is to change primary color filters while multiple-printing a color image. A variety of mattes, masks, texture screens, or other devices can also be used.

• *See also:* COLLAGE; COMBINATION PRINTING; DIRECT POSITIVE PAPER PHOTOGRAPHY; MONTAGE; MULTIPLE-EXPOSURE TECHNIQUES; POSTERIZATION; SABATTIER EFFECT; TONE-LINE PROCESS.

To make this contact print from a black-and-white high-contrast negative, the bottom area was masked out with black paper while the bird was exposed, repeatedly, through the color filters. Then the bird was masked with paper while the bottom half of the negative was exposed once to white light, to produce the black in the print. Photo by Barbara Jean.

Multiple Printing

Murals

Murals, or photomurals, are large prints and transparencies, in either black-and-white or color, made to almost any size. Apart from the many technical uses of large photographic prints, they serve numerous purposes in advertising, display, and interior decoration. In some cases a large picture combines these functions and serves both as a selling aid and as a decoration. A large print has the advantage of being able to display merchandise when it is impractical to show the actual product.

This article deals with making and mounting big black-and-white enlargements and photomurals; it is intended principally as an outline to guide those photographers who have not yet attempted this kind of work. For information on making large color displays, see the article LARGE COLOR PRINTS AND TRANSPARENCIES.

The following definitions of size groups are given so that the references to "big enlargement" and "mural" will be understood:

1. Big enlargement: A large print with a width that is smaller than, or equal to, that of a full-sized roll of photographic paper. The usual photo-paper roll is 40 or 42 inches wide. However, Kodak mural paper is available in rolls 54 inches wide.
2. Mural: A print made of two or more sections that must be spliced together to obtain a final width greater than that of a roll of photographic paper.

If you wish to make a few big prints—say about 30″ × 40″—for your own display or decoration, the

This 40″ × 60″ print is technically a big enlargement, made on a standard 40-inch photo-paper roll. Big prints such as this may be made in most photographic workrooms, although processing may require some improvisation.

equipment found in most photographic workrooms can be used to make them. Some improvisation may, however, be needed to process the prints.

Making murals or enlargements larger than 30″ × 40″ on a commercial scale requires some skill in handling large sheets of wet paper, a specially built enlarger, and all the supporting equipment. Such an installation is necessarily costly, and the expenditure can be justified only if sufficient work is available to keep the equipment in use most of the time. But, you can order these larger-size prints from a specialist and mount them yourself.

Subject Matter

Subject matter should be chosen carefully with due regard to the surroundings in which the picture is to hang. A subject that is suitable for one situation may be incongruous in another. Some pictures continue to be pleasing when viewed constantly. Others seem good on a first viewing, but begin to pall if they must be looked at very often.

Good composition plays an important part in making a constantly pleasing picture. The best way to arrive at this is to make a smaller print—say 11″ × 14″—from the whole negative, and crop this print in several ways until the composition is pleasing. Any further improvements to be made in the final enlargement can be determined at this stage.

Viewing Conditions and Print Density

It is well to remember that very strong light makes a print look weak; by the same token, a print that looks good in strong light may be too dark and muddy in subdued illumination.

Prints used for advertising or for exhibition are often displayed in strong light—commonly, 80 to 120 footcandles. Therefore, prints intended for this purpose should be printed a little darker than normal. On the other hand, large decorative pictures made to be viewed in ordinary room illumination should be lighter in density, because a large, dark mural can be oppressive, whereas a light one gives an impression of space. This effect is valuable for making a room appear larger than it is.

The Negative

For enlarging to high magnifications, an original negative is usually preferable to a reproduced or copy negative. Dense negatives should not be used for this purpose because they are generally grainy, and the long printing exposure required has an adverse effect on print quality. A good negative for enlarging is fairly thin, but full of detail; it prints well on grade No. 2 or 3 paper.

If it is possible to make the negative yourself, use a medium-speed panchromatic film. Such films, correctly exposed and processed, yield negatives of excellent sharpness and fineness of grain.

If you must use a certain picture, and the negative is unsuitable because its size is incompatible with your enlarger or lens, or because of too-high or too-low contrast, it is then necessary to reproduce the original negative in a size or contrast that is more suitable.

Making a New Negative. The following method of making a reproduced negative is recommended because it yields a greater range of tones than does a copy negative from a print.

1. Make sure that the original negative is free from dust or fine lint; the latter is often invisible, but can be removed by gentle blowing, or by the use of dust- and static-eliminating equipment.
2. Use a diffused-light enlarger to make an enlarged positive transparency on Kodak commercial film. An 8″ × 10″ positive is suggested because this size is easy to spot or retouch. The positive should have higher density than one that is used simply for viewing; this is to make sure that all essential highlight detail is recorded on the straight-line part of the characteristic curve of the film. Good tone reproduction is thereby obtained.
3. Retouch or spot the positive.
4. From the positive, make the final negative, by contact, on Kodak commercial film 6127. If necessary, the negative can be reduced to the required size by using an 8″ × 10″ enlarger.
5. Spot the negative.

A more direct method of making an enlarged copy negative from an original negative is to use Kodak professional direct duplicating film (Estar thick base) SO-015. This is an ortho-sensitive, medium-contrast, direct-reversal film for one-step duplication of continuous-tone black-and-white negatives and positives.

Because a duplicate negative made in this manner is, in effect, a print from the original negative, its orientation in the mural enlarger is with the base side toward the paper, rather than the normal emulsion-to-emulsion position.

The Paper

Any good-quality projection-speed paper is suitable for making prints up to about 40″ × 60″. The paper used to make larger sizes, however, must be able to withstand a great deal of handling. Kodak mural paper is manufactured with a tough single-weight base specially designed for this purpose, and the lustre, tweed surface is excellent for finishing and coloring. At the same time, the textured surface tends to minimize objectionable grain.

Kodak mural paper tones well in several toners, but to save unnecessary handling, a one-solution toner is recommended. Water-resistant papers are eminently suitable for making murals. The medium-weight paper base is resin-coated, providing a resistance to water that shortens processing and drying times. The paper base is extremely tough and dimensionally stable as well.

Cutting Unexposed Paper. When large rolls of photographic paper are used instead of sheets, a bench on which to measure and cut the desired length of paper from the roll is required. For rolls of paper 40 or 42 inches wide, the bench should be about 4 feet wide. For rolls of Kodak mural paper 52 inches wide, the bench should be 5 feet wide. It should be long enough to accommodate the greatest length of paper to be processed.

Paper is unrolled with its emulsion side down, and the leading edge is tucked into the beveled edge of the wooden measuring stop. If the wooden stop is equipped with pegs and the bench with holes at measured distances, paper of commonly used lengths can be measured quickly. At the cutting position on the bench, attach a piece of hard maple with two strips of metal, slightly spaced, mounted on it. Under the necessary safelight conditions, a single-edged razor blade, a knife such as a linoleum knife, or a rolling blade cutter can be guided easily to cut the paper in the area between the metal spac-

ers. Allow space for an ample border, up to several inches, around the print image.

The Exposure

The Enlarger. To make big prints you need a rigidly mounted enlarger that has sufficient illumination to provide at least 2 footcandles of light at the easel surface when the lens is at full aperture and the easel is 6 feet away. This measurement should be taken without a negative in the carrier. Tungsten and tungsten-halogen enlarger lamps are suitable sources of illumination if the negative is protected by proper placement of heat-absorbing glass.

You can obtain greater magnification with most vertical enlargers by rotating the head to a horizontal position and projecting the image onto a wall. An alternative is to turn the enlarger head so that the image is projected onto the floor. You can also get greater magnification with a lens of shorter focal length; however, too short a focal length results in unsharp edges and uneven illumination.

When you enlarge to high magnifications, optical deficiencies, mechanical irregularities, and uneven illumination are greatly accentuated; therefore, it is wise to check for these defects before you start to work. Be particularly sure that the enlarger is properly aligned with the easel so that the projected image will be evenly focused and illuminated from edge to edge.

The Lens. An enlarging lens should be of sufficient focal length to cover the negative sharply to the edges. As a general rule, a suitable focal length is equal to the diagonal of the negative, that is to say, the measurement from corner to corner. A lens of longer focal length can be used, but this will increase the lens-to-paper distance.

A good-quality enlarging lens is indispensable to making big enlargements; camera lenses are seldom suitable for this purpose. Specially designed lenses having a "long throw" with optimum sharpness at 50 or more diameters of enlargement are available for making murals and extremely big prints. Whatever lens you use, make sure that it is clean and free from dust, because a good enlargement cannot be made with a dirty lens.

The Easel. It is desirable to have an easel large enough to accommodate the full size of the eventual print, so that the negative does not have to be moved to make successive sectional exposures. A large vacuum easel with multiple channels is most efficient for this purpose. It will hold the photographic paper flat across its entire surface during the exposure and release it instantly, without a mark, when the suction is released. Lacking vacuum equipment, tack the paper to a smooth, flat surface. This can be made from plywood or insulation board. Do not use hardboard, because you cannot stick pins into it. For smaller prints, roll the paper onto a smooth surface that has been treated with Kodaflat clear solution, sold by graphic arts dealers.

Focusing. Focusing often becomes more complicated at high magnifications. Lack of field flatness may make it impossible to obtain critical sharpness over the whole area of the image; in this case, compromise by focusing at a point about one third in from the edge of the picture. Furthermore, with some lenses the focus tends to shift as the aperture is reduced. To overcome this difficulty, you can focus with the lens stopped down to the aperture that you are going to use.

To focus a large picture, turn the safelights off and allow some time for the eyes to become adapted to darkness; the projected image can then be seen clearly, and the enlarger adjusted for the best sharpness. If you can see the negative grain, focus on that.

Procedure. Mask the negative in the negative carrier so that no light surrounds the projected image; such light is reflected by adjacent surfaces and is sufficient to degrade the enlargement by adding fog to the highlights. This effect is more serious with a dense negative that requires a long exposure.

If the enlarger has sufficient light intensity, reduce the lens aperture by 1 to 2 stops. When the exposure is longer than 90 seconds you may have to compromise by using a larger aperture, but in any case, do not use the full aperture of the lens, because enlarger illumination is rarely even with the lens wide open.

Make a test exposure with a strip of paper that includes the edges of the picture. If extra exposure is needed to compensate for uneven negative density, time this extra exposure carefully so that you can repeat it exactly in the final print, or in the succeeding sections if the enlargement is to be made in more than one part. Make as many test exposures as may be necessary to get correct exposure; good print quality depends on this.

You cannot expose all the sections of a mural simultaneously because an overlap of image is necessary for splicing. Mark the negative where you expect the splices to be, and locate the paper on the easel so that the marks and 1½ inches of extra image are included. This method makes sure that enough overlap is available to make splices, and to trim off rough edges and pin marks.

Position the paper on the vacuum easel and turn on the suction, or pin the paper to the wooden easel with enough push-pins to keep the edges flat. Make sure that the paper is quite flat over its entire surface; large bulges may cause unsharp patches and mismatched splices if the print is made in more than one section.

Processing

Big Prints. If you do not have suitably large processing trays, a few big enlargements can be processed in the following way. Soak the print in clean water until the paper is limp. Lay it on a flat surface—plastic material, stainless steel, or hardboard will do. Do not use ordinary wood because it absorbs chemical solutions that may stain the print. Swab or brush the solutions over the print until the process is complete. Remember to rinse both sides of the paper after each step in the process. The rinsing and final washing can be done with the spray from a hose.

An alternative method of processing big enlargements is to roll them through the solutions, using trays that are much narrower than the actual prints. Again, soak the print briefly in clean water, and develop it in diluted developer; in this way, the developing time is extended, and the risk of uneven development is thereby reduced. Remember to keep the exposure at the minimum necessary to make a good print because an overexposed print may not develop evenly by this method.

Narrow, half-rounded trays made specially for processing big enlargements by the rolling method are available from photo dealers. If you prefer, you can make your own half-round trays by cutting an appropriate length of large-diameter PVC drain pipe lengthwise and capping the ends. The waterproofed corrugated cardboard wallpaper troughs available at paint stores are suitable for temporary use as narrow processing trays.

The cleanest and most economical way to process a quantity of big prints up to about 30″ × 40″

is to use a set of trays that are, say, 34″ × 44″. These trays may be made of plastic material or stainless steel. The latter type is more durable, but plastic trays give excellent service if they are used carefully and kept clean.

Processing Murals. To process murals successfully, you need some experience in handling big sheets of wet paper; you also require adequate sinks and trays, and sufficient space to accommodate them.

In general, it is wise to make the sinks as large as space and financial means permit; thus rolling and handling of the prints is reduced to a minimum, and at the same time the efficiency of processing is increased by keeping the prints flat in the trays.

Developing Murals. Suitable developing times and dilutions for Kodak mural paper in Kodak developers are given in the accompanying table. For other papers, see their specific instructions. To complete the processing, follow the steps listed here.

Rinse. Rinse for 5 to 10 seconds in a stop bath.

Fix. Fix with agitation at 18–21 C (65–70 F) in a paper dilution fixing bath. Fix fiber-base papers for 3 to 5 minutes and water-resistant papers for 2 minutes.

Hypo Clearing Agent. Since most big prints and photomurals will be displayed for considerable lengths of time under either artificial or natural light, it is very important that the steps of processing be carried out according to instructions. In particular, fixing chemicals and soluble silver compounds must be thoroughly removed in order to prevent staining and fading of the image. The combination of a washing apparatus that changes water *completely* every 5 minutes and the use of a hypo clear-ing agent will produce prints, even of the largest dimensions, that are free of residual chemicals to a degree almost impossible to obtain by washing them with water alone. For more details on processing for permanence, see the article ARCHIVAL PROCESSING.

NOTE: Do not use conventional paper wash methods with Kodak water-resistant papers. Prolonged fixing and washing should be avoided. Wash prints for 4 minutes *only* in 18–21 C (65–70 F) running water with constant agitation.

Toning. Before toning a print, take into consideration the nature of the subject and the surroundings where the picture is to hang. For example, a snow scene or seascape that is brown-toned might seem unnatural, whereas a leafy autumn scene might be much enhanced by a brown tone. Also, the color of the picture should be harmonious with the color scheme of its surroundings.

To avoid unnecessary handling, a one-solution toner is recommended for toning big enlargements and murals.

Erratic developing and fixing time results in variations in tone that are objectionable when toned prints are displayed side by side, or when several sections of a mural are mounted together. For further details see TONING.

Drying. Large, twin-belt matte driers that can dry any size print are available. When involved in large-scale production of big enlargements, a drier of this kind is a good investment. The alternative is rack-drying. Racks are light, wooden frames with fiber glass, cloth, or plastic screening stretched tightly over them. A wooden stand can be made to

KODAK MURAL PAPER DEVELOPMENT TIME			
Kodak Developer	Dilution	Development Time in Minutes*	
		Recommended	Useful Range
Ektonol	1:1	2	1½–4
Ektonol	1:3	4	3–8
Selectol or D-52	1:1	2	1½–4
Selectol or D-52	1:3	4	3–8
Selectol-Soft	1:1	2	1½–4
Dektol or D-72	1:2	1	¾–2
Dektol or D-72	1:4	2	1½–4

*At a solution temperature of 20 C (68 F).

Murals

hold a number of racks spaced about 5 inches apart to allow ventilation.

Enlargements are laid face downward on the screening after the surplus water has been sponged from both sides of the print. Paper dried in this way stays flat if the relative humidity is not too low—say 50 percent for good drying. Water-resistant papers should be placed with emulsion side up.

Hardening. The gelatin on prints toned in some toners tends to be soft and easily damaged; therefore, when such prints are dried on racks or belt driers, they should be hardened after toning. Otherwise, a pattern of the screening on which they are dried may be transferred to the print surface. The following hardener is recommended for use after toning:

> 1 part Kodak liquid hardener
> 13 parts water

Immerse prints in the hardener for 3 minutes after a thorough rinse in water. After hardening, wash the prints thoroughly before drying.

Drying Water-Resistant Paper Prints. For fast drying, remove the surface water with blotters or a soft, wet viscose sponge or cloth. Do not ferrotype the prints. Prints can be air-dried at room temperature or by circulated warm air. Double-belt drum driers can be used if the drum-surface temperature does not exceed 88 C (190 F). Low drying temperatures will provide maximum dimensional stability.

Mounting Big Enlargements

Dry-Mounting. Enlargements up to 48″ × 96″ can be readily dry-mounted on suitable ¼-inch cardboard, Masonite Panelwood, Fom-Cor mounting board, or plywood with Kodak dry-mounting tissue type 2 if a large mounting press is available. A suitable press, capable of mounting work up to this size in one operation, is manufactured by Seal Incorporated, 550 Spring Street, Naugatuck, Connecticut 06770.

The actual temperature across the heating platen should range from 82–99 C (180–210 F).

The print, the mounting board, and the cover sheet used over the face of the print should be dry to prevent cockling or sticking and possible damage to the print surface. Before sandwiching these components for mounting, it would be wise to briefly preheat them individually in the press, in order to

remove residual moisture. After preheating, place the "sandwich" in the press and close the plates for a second or two several times to drive off any remaining moisture.

Then close the press tightly for approximately 30 to 60 seconds—longer in case of a thick mount. Sufficient time must be allowed for the heat to penetrate the mounting board and effect a proper seal. Yellowing may occur if the mounting time is prolonged.

To prevent warping caused by moisture penetration through the unsealed back of the mount, apply varnish or lacquer to the back surface as soon as possible after mounting. Or, dry-mount a piece of kraft paper to the back surface.

Wet-Mounting. When a large mounting press is unavailable, or when the print is too big to be dry-mounted, you must resort to wet-mounting. This is done by sticking the wet print to a board with a water-soluble adhesive. For many years, paperhanger's paste was used as an adhesive for this purpose. More recently, printer's padding compound has been found eminently suitable as a mountant for big enlargements. This adhesive has a consistency suitable for mounting wet prints, although it can be thinned with water for sizing mounts. It is available from most paper-supply houses.

Tempered hardboard is the most suitable material for wet-mounting. It is relatively nonabsorbent, and can be obtained in the large sizes necessary for mounting big enlargements and murals.

To wet-mount a big print in a single piece, follow this procedure:

1. Prepare the board by sizing both back and front with a 1:1 dilution of padding compound. Allow this to dry. For very large mounts or when extra strength is needed, attach the board to a wooden frame. Nail heads should be countersunk, and the holes filled with a filling compound sanded flush with the board surface. Any joints in the board should also be filled and sanded flush because imperfections in the surface of the mount will be clearly visible on the finished print.
2. Soak the print to be mounted in clean water until it is limp.

3. Lay the print on a flat surface and sponge the surplus water from both sides.

4. Use a paint roller to apply an even coating of full-strength padding compound to the surface of the mount. Make sure that the whole area is covered by adhesive, and wash the roller immediately after use; this adhesive is not readily soluble when it has been allowed to dry.

5. With the help of an assistant, lift the print by the corners and lay it in position on the mount.

6. Use a damp sponge or a flat-blade squeegee to press the print into contact with the mount. Sponge away any traces of adhesive that remain on the print surface. This adhesive is difficult to remove when the print is dry.

7. Trim off the overlapping paper with a sharp blade; alternatively, stick the overlap to the back of the mount. To make a neat job of this, miter the corners of the print where the sides and end overlap on the reverse side of the mount.

8. As the wet-mounted print shrinks, it may warp or bend the mount. To equalize this stress, wet-mount a sheet of paper—photographic paper of the same weight as the print is ideal, but heavy kraft paper will do—on the back of the mount. Since paper does not shrink to the same extent in both dimensions as it dries, make sure that the grain of the backing sheet runs in the same direction as that of the mounted print.

Adhesives for Mounting Water-Resistant Papers. Water-resistant papers can be dry-mounted very successfully by using the new dry-mounting tissues. Because of the resin coating, the pre-soak wet method of mounting does not work.

In addition, some adhesives can be used to mount this type of paper. Among them are some padding compounds used by printers, heat-setting adhesives, rubber cements recommended for photographic papers, contact cements, some glues, and double-faced adhesive tape. It is good practice to experiment first with old prints before trying a new cementing material with good photographs. Kodak publication No. E-67, *Finishing Prints on KODAK Water Resistant Papers,* is kept updated on specific adhesives that have been tested.

With conventional-base papers, some of these adhesives can cause stains. The resin coatings on water-resistant papers are resistant to paper-base absorption adhesives and serve as stain preventatives. However, with rubber cements, including contact cements, it is wise to let the cement dry for the maximum recommended time before placing the print on the mount, to allow as much solvent as possible to evaporate.

Mounting Murals Made on Fiber-Base Papers. Although a mural can be mounted directly onto a wall, you may become tired of the picture, or you may wish to redecorate the room. In any case, removal is difficult; only prolonged soaking and some scraping of the wall will enable you to get the print off. Therefore, it is seldom desirable to mount prints on the wall as you would wallpaper. If you cannot avoid mounting the mural on a plaster or plasterboard wall, follow this procedure:

1. Free the wall surface of old wallpaper and any loose material that may be present. Wash the wall thoroughly.

2. Fill all cracks and indentations with spackling compound, and sand this flush with the wall surface.

3. Since moisture readily penetrates plaster, the wall must be sealed to prevent the mural from lifting. Seal the wall with a liberal coat of print lacquer; when this is dry, apply a second coat.

4. When the lacquer coating is completely dry, apply a sizing coat of soluble gelatin. Sizing the wall in this way facilitates later removal of the mural. Mix the sizing solution according to the following formula.

Gelatin sizing solution

Clear gelatin
  (food quality) . . . .   236.5 g (8 oz)
Water at 38 C
  (100 F) . . . .   1928 millilitres (64 oz)

Use this solution before it cools, because the gelatin solution sets as a jelly.

5. If the mural is a large one, use a plumb line to draw a vertical guide line on the wall. Lay the edge of the first section to the line. This procedure provides an upright picture.

6. Follow the procedure indicated in the section on splicing murals for mounting murals that overlap, but use gelatin sizing solution as the adhesive in this case.

NOTE: Do not use padding compound because this adhesive is not readily soluble once it is dry. Consequently, the mural would be very difficult to remove from the wall.

7. For protection of the mural against dirt and unfavorable atmospheric conditions, spray the picture with matte print lacquer. This provides a washable surface that can be cleaned.

NOTE: If the mural must be detached from the wall, first remove the lacquer coating with lacquer thinner.

A better way to hang a mural is to mount the picture on a board, and then to attach the mount to the wall. A suitable molding can surround the picture as a finishing touch, and at the same time hide the raw edge of the print. Masonite Panelwood, available in sizes up to 48″ × 192″, presents an excellent mounting surface for murals. Border and brace the mounting surface to make it rigid and to prevent its warping. Holes caused by countersunk finishing nails should be filled with a spackling compound and sanded smooth. Mounting a single sheet of paper over a joint between two sheets of hardboard is generally unsatisfactory for permanent installations, because the joint will show up in time as a crack or ridge.

Splicing Murals. If a big picture is made in more than one section, the pieces must be spliced together on the mount. Splices should be so contrived that they are hardly visible. A joint is less obvious if you can arrange it to coincide with a natural line in the picture, such as the horizon or the side of a building.

Two kinds of splice can be made: The feathered edges of two sections can be overlapped, or the trimmed edges butted together. The latter splice is the least obvious, but because part of the print must be kept wet while the area adjacent to the splice dries, this type of joint can only be made if the print is mounted in a horizontal position.

To make overlapped splices, use this procedure:

1. Lay out the various dried sections of the mural on the mounting board so that the sections are roughly in register. Hold the sections in place with weights.

2. Note the amount of overlapping and cut all edges so that the overlap does not exceed 2 or 3 inches.

3. By using pinpricks along the edges to be matched and by noting where the pinpricks fall on the lower sheet, register the first two sheets to be joined. Generally, the left panel is mounted first, with the right panel next. Thus the edge of the right sheet should be placed on top of the left sheet as the sheets are being registered.

4. On the two sheets and on the mounting board, circle the pinpricks with a grease pencil. On the mounting board, draw a grease-pencil line along the pinpricks.

5. On a line ⅜- to ½-inch to the right of the line determined by the pinpricks on the left-hand section, break the emulsion by drawing a very sharp blade along the line. Use a straightedge to guide the blade. Turn the print over and bend the edge along the cut, using the straightedge to guide the bend at exactly the line of the cut.

6. Carefully tear the edge by pulling it toward the print. Some of the paper backing will come off in the tear, producing a feathered edge. Sand this feathered edge with very fine sandpaper so that just a thin amount of paper backing remains at the cut edge. This edge is now extremely delicate, and must be treated with care or it will be damaged.

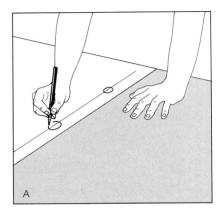
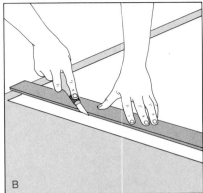
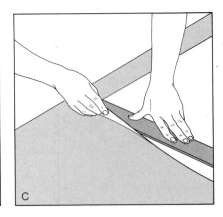

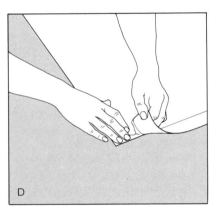
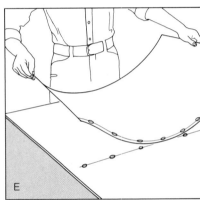
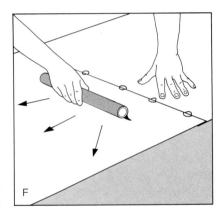

(A) Circle the pinpricks with a grease pencil. (B) Break the emulsion with a sharp blade. (C) Bend the edge along the line of the cut. (D) Tear the edge by pulling toward the print. (E) Align the middle section of the left panel with the pencil line on the mounting board. (F) Align the right-hand section with the left-hand section so that the grease-pencil circles are complete. Squeegee the first section radially from the first area mounted. Again squeegee radially from the first area mounted.

7. Soak the print section in water for 3 to 6 minutes. Unroll the section, emulsion side up, on a clean surface and, with a squeegee, remove excess water. If necessary, the print can be folded like wallpaper ready to be hung.

8. Apply the adhesive, full strength, to the mounting surface.

9. Carefully align a middle section of the left panel with the feathered edge along the grease-pencil line on the mounting board. Spread the feathered edge outward to the borders. Then brush or squeegee the print radially from the first area mounted. Since the wet paper tears easily, it may be necessary for two

people to perform the mounting operation.

10. Miter the corners and overlap the edges onto the glue-covered frame of the mounting board.

11. Remove all traces of adhesive from the emulsion surface, before it dries, by swabbing the print with a wet sponge.

12. Prepare the right-hand section for mounting, but this time cut the edge exactly along the line formed by the pinpricks, leaving "half moons" of the grease-pencil circles, and feather the edge. If any section of this skived edge becomes too thin and exposes the base side of the emulsion, the finished print will appear darker than normal in that area. Carefully cut that area away with a new blade, exposing the normally overlapped part of the left-hand section.

13. Prepare the mounting surface and print backing as shown. Start mounting the right-hand section in a middle section along the feathered edge. Align the right-hand surface so that the edge is exactly along the pinpricks and the "half moons" are completed by the grease-pencil circles of the left-hand section. Again, mount the print along the entire skived edge before brushing it out radially from the middle of the feathered edge. Check the alignment frequently. Sponge the surface to remove any adhesive from the emulsion.

Three or more sections are mounted similarly, with pinpricks to register the sections. Since regular photographic paper expands when wet, the pin markings on the mounting board will fall short of the paper edge as successive sections are laid. Careful alignment of the first section, however, will make sure that horizontal and vertical lines in the picture will be parallel to frame lines. If the print is not exactly in the position desired, lift it from the mount and start again. The size of the frame needed can be determined by adding the amount of expansion to the size of the print when it is dry, or the surplus created by expansion can be trimmed.

After the mural has been mounted, cover it for half an hour with cheesecloth dampened with water.

Finally, after the completed mural is dry, remove any grease-pencil marks by gently rubbing with a soft cloth.

To make a butt joint, follow this procedure:

1. Prepare the mount as previously directed.

2. Register the image where the two prints overlap.

3. Using a steel straightedge as a guide, trim both prints simultaneously with a sharp blade. If the picture is made in more than two sections, trim all edges to be spliced at this stage.

4. Soak the first section for 2 minutes, and then mount it as directed for wet-mounting big enlargements.

5. Soak the second section for 2 minutes, and then mount it beside the first section. Make sure that the edges of the prints butt together, and that the image matches. Mount the succeeding sections, if any, in exactly the same way.

6. Cover the whole area of the picture with a damp cloth, *except for a strip 6 inches wide on either side of the splices.* The uncovered part will dry first; thus, the joints will not be pulled apart as the paper shrinks. When the uncovered parts are dry, remove the cloths and allow the rest of the print to dry normally.

When wet-mounting murals in a very dry location—that is, when the relative humidity is below 25 percent—use ordinary paperhanger's paste as an adhesive instead of padding compound. Otherwise, the print may split due to too rapid drying. As a further precaution against splitting, keep the mural damp by hanging a double sheet of damp muslin over it to prevent the paper from drying out too quickly. If it is not convenient to hang muslin over the mural, dampen it at 20-minute intervals with water mist from a spray gun. Spray once over lightly with the air regulator set at 50 psi and with the largest spray pattern that the gun will yield. Spray from a distance of about 15 inches from the print surface, and set the

Murals are widely used for advertising, interior decoration, and display purposes. Photo by Don McDill.

material control on the spray gun at a low setting so that water does not form droplets or run on the print. Drying should be retarded for about 3 hours by using this procedure.

Splicing Water-Resistant Papers. Large prints and murals on water-resistant papers both feel and handle differently than those made on regular paper. The base material of this paper is actually a sandwich of medium-weight, white paper with a thin, water-resistant polyethylene coating on both sides. To the touch, both sides feel smooth. In fact, the base side of water-resistant paper feels slightly more slick than the emulsion side, when dry. There is little or no curl to the paper, wet or dry, and practically no change in dimension during processing, provided proper processing and washing times have been observed. Reroll exposed and/or processed water-resistant paper to the same configuration as in the original package for optimum size stability.

Because the resin coating on both sides makes overlapped splicing difficult, butt-joining of sections of water-resistant paper murals is recommended. It is not necessary to soak print sections before mounting, or to cover the mounted sections with damp cloth after gluing.

Murals on water-resistant paper cannot be removed from plaster walls by soaking. Therefore, a hardboard base is essential if future print changes are contemplated.

Retouching

It is a good rule to do all the necessary retouching on the negative before making final prints. In particular, be sure to correct any minus-density areas in the negative, such as dust spots, pinholes, or scratches, which would result in unwanted plus-density areas on the print. Although it is possible to etch (to physically remove some of the silver density) on black-and-white prints, it is difficult to do it evenly on the large areas encountered in murals. Adding density by means of neutral dyes or a soft lead pencil is relatively simple; however, dyes fade in time—long before the silver image—and pencil retouching must be over-sprayed with lacquer to keep it from wiping away. (*See:* RETOUCHING.)

Lacquering. If murals are to be permanently displayed, their appearance can be enhanced and protected by coating them with one of a number of lacquers available from photo dealers. These lacquers are made especially for photographic use. By varying the type of lacquer, dilution, and method of application, you can achieve a variety of surfaces ranging from glossy to matte and including stipple and brush effects. However, semimatte (half glossy, half matte) lacquer is most popular. Lacquering helps protect the surface from abrasions, fingerprints, atmospheric contaminants, graffiti, and dirt. You can clean a lacquered print by wiping it with a damp cloth. Even blemishes from ball-point pens and felt-tipped markers can usually be removed with lacquer thinner.

• *See also:* ARCHIVAL PROCESSING; LARGE COLOR PRINTS AND TRANSPARENCIES; RETOUCHING; TONING.

Mutoscope

The mutoscope is a simple motion-picture viewing device, based on the "flip-book" principle. In the mutoscope, paper prints made from frames of a motion-picture negative are fastened to a central hub or drum, and the edges pass under a finger-spring. As the drum is turned, the pictures are released one by one, in rapid succession, and drop out of the way, revealing sequential images, and giving the illusion of a motion picture. Mutoscopes were made as coin-in-the-slot machines for use in amusement parks during the first part of the twentieth century.

Muybridge, Eadweard James

(1830–1904)
American photographer

Although he was born (and died) in England, Muybridge's photographic career flourished in the United States. Coming to San Francisco, California in 1852, he was soon an assistant and then a partner to Carleton Watkins before striking out on his own, first as "Helios Studio" and then as "E. Muybridge, Photographer."

Two internal views of a mutoscope. View at left does not show the image cylinder. View at right, with the image cylinder in place, shows the "flip-book" method of picture viewing. Photo courtesy International Museum of Photography, Rochester, N.Y.

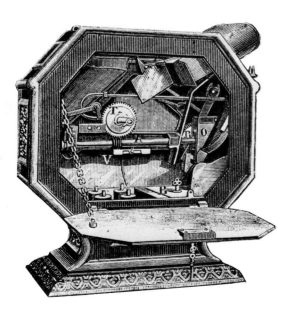 

Analytical Photography

An outstanding photographer of landscapes, nature, and stereo card subjects, Muybridge's greatest achievement was in analytical photography. In the early 1870's, he was hired by Leland Stanford—Governor of California and a leading breeder of race horses—to photograph the gait of a trotting horse. The object was to determine whether at any time all four hooves were off the ground simultaneously.

Muybridge arranged a series of 12, and then 24, cameras side-by-side along the straightaway section of a training race course; the shutters were released in succession by the horse's body breaking a series of threads stretched across the track. The collodion wet plates of the period were too slow for definitive results when Muybridge made his first photographs, but later attempts with gelatin dry plates proved conclusively that there were moments when the horse was completely off the ground.

Projected Images

A colorful personality, Muybridge was a popular lecturer on topics of the day, using lantern slides of his own work for illustrations. This led to his invention of the first projected images of continuous motion. He arranged lantern-slide positives of his trotting-horse sequence around the perimeter of a large glass disk so that they would revolve through the plane of a projector. These, coupled with a slotted shutter plate that revolved in the opposite direction, resulted in a series of images flashed in rapid succession on the screen. When sufficient speed was reached by hand-cranking, persistence of vision in the viewer's eye fused the images to create the illusion of actual movement. The synthesized motion effect was a sensation, and Muybridge enjoyed great success with his *zoogyroscope* and *zoopraxiscope* presentations both in the United States and in Europe.

Muybridge's camera No. 20, which he used for his University of Pennsylvania studies on location. The camera used 3¼" × 4¼" plates; it is believed to have had a 15-inch lens. Photo courtesy International Museum of Photography, Rochester, N.Y.

Muybridge, Eadweard James

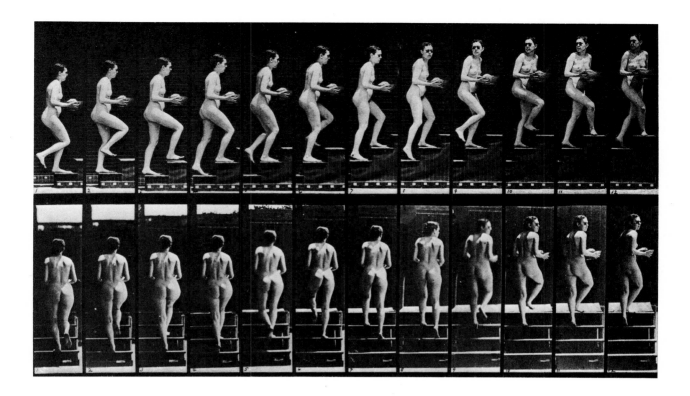

This series, "Woman Ascending Stairs," is from Muybridge's 1887 work "Animal Locomotion."
Side views and rear views have been recorded simultaneously. Other studies also included a
third simultaneous view. Photo courtesy International Museum of Photography, Rochester, N.Y.

Locomotion Studies

The California work led to Muybridge's being hired by the University of Pennsylvania to undertake a mammoth photographic study of human and animal locomotion. In the early 1880's, under his direction, more than 700,000 photographs were made of humans, animals, and birds in motion.

Usually, three camera batteries were employed. Each consisted of 12 separate lens-film compartments, and a thirteenth lens for framing and focusing. One battery was set to photograph the subject broadside against a dark or light background, depending on the subject tonality; another at a three-quarter angle; and the third either directly head-on, or tail-away. A complex electromagnetic system made it possible to operate the individual shutters of the three batteries in unison, at selected speeds and with selected intervals between exposures. Thus,

each action could be recorded in a series of distinct steps from three different viewpoints. A reference grid on the background made it possible to calculate subject speed of movement from the known shutter speeds and intervals between exposures.

The published results of Muybridge's work affected physicians, artists, engineers, therapists, animal trainers, and all others concerned with knowledge of how living beings move. It was a monumental project, financed and published by J. P. Lippincott, that remained unequaled until the invention of high-speed motion-picture analysis of movement. Selections of the work are in print today in *Animal Locomotion* and *Human Locomotion*, published by Dover Books, Inc.

• *See also:* MAREY, ETIENNE JULES; MOTION STUDY; ZOOPRAXISCOPE.

Muybridge, Eadweard James

Nadar (Gaspard Felix Tournachon)

(1820–1910)
French photographer

Nadar probably had the most varied career and the widest variety of talents of any nineteenth-century photographer. At the age of 32 he turned from a shaky existence as a journalist and caricaturist to photography. Within a few years he had established himself as one of the foremost portraitists in Paris. In the course of time, he photographed many notable intellectuals, artists, performers, scientists, politicians, and other celebrities of his period.

A staunch supporter of art as well as photography, he was the first to suggest, in 1856, that photography ought to be included in exhibitions of the Académie des Beaux-Arts. Although this came about in 1859–1860, it was a short-lived acceptance, and soon thereafter even various painting styles were being rejected. In 1874, Nadar turned over his studios to Claude Monet and others for an exhibit of the "Salon des Refusés"; these artists were creating the style of painting that later came to be called Impressionism.

An ardent experimenter and innovator, Nadar took the first photographs underground, in the Paris catacombs in 1859, by the light of a Bunsen generator. He was a pioneer balloonist, and also took the first photographs from a manned, free (untethered) balloon, in the early 1860's.

In 1886, the year of his retirement, he created the first photo-interview with Eugene Chevreul, former president of the Académie Francaise and discoverer of the laws of simultaneous contrast

Nadar, at right, speaks with Eugène Chevreul during the world's first photo-interview, while a stenographer takes notes. On the subject of inventors, Chevreul remarked that they are given to illusions and tend to be boring conversationalists. Photo courtesy International Museum of Photography, Rochester, N.Y.

of colors. It was Chevreul's 100th birthday. Nadar's son and partner, Paul, photographed Chevreul using a camera equipped with the new Eastman-Walker roll-film holder, while Nadar posed questions and a stenographer recorded the answers. The published interview was a journalistic sensation that was soon imitated throughout the world.

• *See also:* HISTORY OF PHOTOGRAPHY.

Nameplates, Photographic

Nameplates fulfill a host of functions in addition to simply identifying objects. They serve as functional dials or as decorative detail. They carry vital information or serve as advertising displays. Letters, numbers, symbols, words, designs, and even continuous-tone images can be photographically reproduced to convey information and instruction.

Conventional, continuous-tone films and papers can be used for making nameplates; or high-contrast graphic arts materials can be used to produce dense, black images against clear or white backgrounds. A simple method for producing attractive photographic nameplates is to make a photographic print combining the desired images, laminate the print, and mount the durable image where it is needed.

Processes

There are a number of special-purpose photographic processes or materials that can be used to produce a variety of useful or highly decorative nameplates. These include the silk-screen process, presensitized metal plates and foils, a photographic emulsion on acrylic plastic base, and a variety of photoresist materials.

In silk-screen printing, an image on high-contrast film is transferred to a special silk-screen film that adheres to the silk screen and serves as a mask during printing. The silk-screen image is printed onto a surface by forcing inks through the screen with a rubber squeegee while the screen is in contact with the receiver. Silk-screen prints look like they have been painted with poster paints. This process is widely used to create designs and lettering on glass, metal, fabric, and paper surfaces.

Presensitized metals, chiefly anodized aluminum, are available under such trade names as Foto-foil, Photo-Aluminum, and Metalphoto. These materials can produce a black or colored image that is extremely durable. The photosensitive surface produces high contrast, but halftone screening can be used to reproduce continuous-tone images.

Kodak Photoplast plates have a high-contrast emulsion on an acrylic plastic base that is shatter-resistant and optically clear. Because the acrylic plastic can easily be machined into almost any configuration, this material is useful for illuminated instrument panels and controls, and for edge-lighted advertising displays.

Photoresists can be coated on metals and other substrates, and exposed, processed, dyed, or etched or plated through to produce a wide variety of nameplates. Metal nameplates are unaffected by weather, shock, abrasion, or moisture. The following details give one method for producing a metal nameplate with the tools normally found in almost any photographic darkroom.

Making a Metal Nameplate

Preparing the Artwork. The first step in making a nameplate is to prepare black-and-white original artwork. Make the artwork reproduction size or larger. You can use paste-up letters or lettering sets such as those used for drafting. Both provide an easy way to achieve good detail and a professional appearance. Art-supply dealers are a good source of this type of material. Use india ink for all hand lettering, designs, borders, and so on.

An original with black letters on a white background will yield nameplates with dark letters on a light background. If you prefer the reverse, an intermediate positive transparency can be made by contact printing. Normally, this is easier than trying to put white artwork on a black background. (See the accompanying diagram.)

Making the Negative. The next step is to copy the original artwork on film so that the size of the resulting negative will be the same as that planned for the nameplate. Use a process camera or a camera with a ground-glass back and a suitable lith film. The subject of copying and the fine points related to it are covered in the article COPYING.

After processing and drying the negative, inspect it by transmitted light, and opaque the pinholes and dust images.

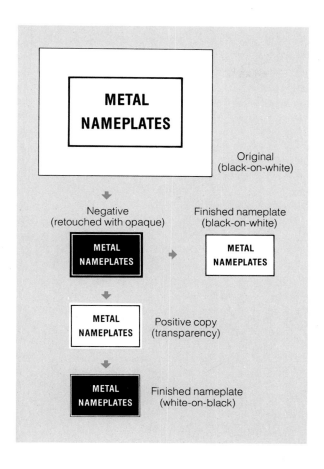

METAL NAMEPLATES

Original
(black-on-white)

Negative
(retouched with opaque)

METAL NAMEPLATES

Finished nameplate
(black-on-white)

METAL NAMEPLATES

METAL NAMEPLATES

Positive copy
(transparency)

METAL NAMEPLATES

Finished nameplate
(white-on-black)

In making a nameplate, black-and-white artwork must first be prepared; then a negative or transparency is made, which yields the finished nameplate.

If you want a reverse nameplate (light letters on a dark background) contact-print the negative onto the same type of film. To retain right-reading copy, print through the film base (emulsion to base).

If several identical nameplates are needed, additional duplicate negatives or transparencies can be gang-printed on the metal sheet.

Preparing the Aluminum Plate. Sheets of anodized aluminum, in a variety of thicknesses and colors, are available from most metal suppliers. You will need aluminum with a smooth surface that has been anodized, dyed, and sealed. The thickness chosen will depend on the end use of the nameplate and how it is to be mounted (adhesive, tape, screws, brads, and so on). Do-it-yourself sheet aluminum, which is available in many hardware and building-supply stores, can be used for some applications, but usually a smoother, more highly polished surface is better. Freshly anodized aluminum is *chemically* clean. Use care to keep it clean until you are ready to coat it with the photoresist.

Safelight Illumination. Gold fluorescent lamps or yellow "anti-bug" incandescent lamps provide a convenient level of illumination that will not appreciably fog photoresist coatings, if they remain in this type of illumination for only a short while. Daylight or white fluorescent, and tungsten lamps should be covered with yellow or orange plastic sheeting.

Most photoresists in liquid form are practically insensitive to light. They become light-sensitive only when coated on a surface and dried. Then they are sensitive to ultraviolet radiation and to a very small segment of the visible spectrum.

Coating and Drying. Make sure that the anodized surface is clean and free of oil, wax, fingerprints, and so on. You can clean it with a lintless rag and resist developer or trichloroethylene. Wipe the surface dry and make sure that it is free of dust. (Dust particles protruding through the resist coating may allow the etching solution to get through and etch the plate where it is not desired.)

Dip the clean sheet in full-strength photoresist and then stand it on edge, with one corner down, to drain and dry. Dry it for 30 to 45 minutes at room temperature; for faster drying, a film-drying cabinet should be used.

Exposure. Be sure that the glass cover on the contact-printing frame is clean. Place the emulsion of the negative or transparency in contact with the dry, resist-coated aluminum sheet in the printing frame. Expose the nameplate for about 5 minutes (overexposure is not critical) with a lamp, such as a 300-watt reflector-photoflood lamp, at about 12 inches. Other photoflood lamps can be used if this type is not available.

Development. The exposed resist will adhere to the nameplate, but the unexposed resist will remain soluble and wash away during processing.

Into a glass, enameled, or stainless-steel tray, pour enough resist developer to cover the plate. Do *not* use a plastic tray. Use tongs (non-plastic) or rubber gloves to avoid skin contact with the devel-

(Left) The negative or transparency of the nameplate to be printed is laid face down on a resist-coated aluminum sheet in a printing frame. The nameplate is then exposed for about five minutes with a photoflood lamp. (Right) The anodized layer is removed from the metal plate with etch solution. When the etching is complete, it is washed thoroughly with water.

oper. Submerge the plate in the developer for 2 minutes, and agitate occasionally by rocking the tray.

Remove the nameplate and spray-wash it immediately—before the developer evaporates. A stream of warm water through a faucet aerator is fine. Air-dry the nameplate for about 30 minutes; for faster drying, use a film-drying cabinet.

Etching. Carefully mix a 5 percent (by weight) solution of sodium hydroxide and water; pour it into a glass, enameled, stainless-steel, or PVC tray. Do not allow the solution to come into contact with the skin.

NOTE: Read the accompanying "Important Safety Precautions" before mixing the etch solution.

With tongs or rubber gloves, place the plate in the etch solution. Gently agitate the solution to help loosen the anodized layer. To check etching prog-

ress, remove the plate from the solution and rinse it with water. If the anodized layer has not been completely removed in the image area, return the plate to the etch solution. When the unprotected (non-resist-coated) area has been etched away, remove the plate, wash it thoroughly with water, and dry it with a soft cloth. To remove the remaining photoresist coating, scrub the plate with a swab dipped in photoresist developer or thinner.

Finishing and Mounting. The nameplate retains a better appearance and is easier to clean if it is sprayed with a transparent plastic coating. Many satisfactory brands of coating are available.

The finished nameplate can be mounted in a number of ways. It can be fastened with screws or brads through small holes, so that it can be removed or changed easily. Adhesive mounting is less evident, and there are several readily available adhesives that will fasten the nameplate securely to a variety of surfaces. Pressure-sensitive, double-sided tape can also be used, and it is easy and convenient, but the mounting is not as permanent as that provided by other methods.

• *See also:* COPYING; LAMINATING; PHOTOFABRICATION; PHOTORESIST; SCREEN PRINTING PROCESS.

Namias, Rodolfo

(1867–1938)
Italian photochemist

Namias worked to improve color images produced by silver-dye mordanting. For black-and-white photography, he formulated the permanganate reducer. In 1922, he produced an improved method for printing photographic images permanently on ceramics. A bichromated gelatin relief image, printed from a negative, was dusted with powdered glaze pigments; the resulting colors were then fused to the surface during glaze firing. He founded the noted Italian photographic publication *Il Progresso Fotografico.*

Natural Light

Broadly speaking, natural light is merely daylight (distinguished from "available light," which may be either daylight or artificial light) as it exists at a given place and time.

While there is considerable variation in natural light in different places and at different times of day, for any one general situation, daylight is a remarkably constant thing. This is why it is possible to secure a high percentage of good exposures without a meter when photographing outdoors. Over many years, photographers have gathered data that provide good camera settings outdoors, and these have been published in the form of tables and charts.

Exposure Calculation

For purposes of exposure calculation, natural light falls into a few broad classes, and exposures for each class will usually be found on the instruction sheet that is packed with any given film.

All of these are based on a single bit of mental arithmetic that can be done by anyone in seconds. The rule is: For daylight exposure on a bright, sunny day, with the subject illuminated by full sunlight (no overhead shade), the exposure for a film of any speed will be:

$$\frac{1}{ASA} \text{ at } f/16$$

Thus, for example, the basic outdoor exposure for a film of ASA 100 (daylight) is simply 1/100 sec. at $f/16$; for an ASA 50 film, the exposure is 1/50 sec. at $f/16$; for an ASA 200 film, it will be 1/200 sec. at $f/16$, and so on. This formula is for bright sunlight, with the subject in the open. Most other situa-

EXPOSURE CALCULATION

Bright or Hazy Sun, Distinct Shadows		Cloudy Bright, No Shadows	Heavy Overcast	Open Shade
On light sand or snow	Average subjects			
f/22	f/16	f/8	f/5.6	f/5.6

tions can be classified according to the accompanying table, with the shutter speed set at 1/ASA.

It is necessary, however, to understand exactly what is meant by each of these situations:

Bright or Hazy Sun. The sun is shining between 10 A.M. and 4 P.M. and the sky is clear or faintly hazy. The key is that objects cast distinct shadows.

Cloudy Bright. The day is overcast and quite bright, but with enough cloudiness so that an object does not cast a distinct shadow. The subject matter is in the open—not shaded by anything overhead.

Heavy Overcast. It is a dull, gloomy day with heavy clouds, but the subject is not shaded.

Open Shade. This situation refers to pictures made on bright or hazy sunny days, where the subject is shaded from direct sun. The subject is, however, illuminated by a large area of clear sky overhead; for example, pictures taken on the shady side of a house. This situation does not include pictures taken under trees or on porches.

It is not possible to establish a rule of thumb for exposures of subjects in full shade, that is, with neither sunlight nor clear skylight illumination; an exposure meter must be used in such situations.

Natural Light with Color Films

The foregoing exposure recommendations apply both to black-and-white and to color films. Daylight, however, changes color in various situations, and this must be taken into account.

Color films for daylight are usually balanced for a mixture of direct sunlight and blue skylight, and produce their best color rendition when used in this situation. In mixed light of this sort, it is not quite technically correct to give a color-temperature value to the light. However, in a practical sense, it is common to say that standard daylight has a color temperature of about 5500 K, and that daylight color

Open shade is the lighting condition in which the subject is shaded from the sun by a large object that is nearby but not overhanging. A meter should be used for correct exposure. Photo by Frank Cowan.

Natural Light

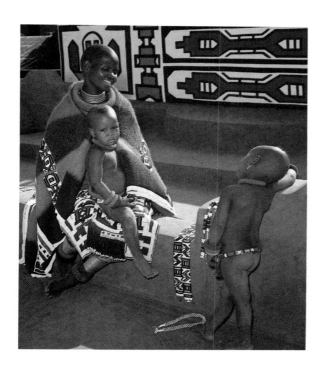

(Left) In bright or hazy sun, objects cast distinct shadows. To avoid harsh shadows and strong contrast, exposure may be increased by one or two stops, depending upon the position of the sun in relation to the subject. Photo by Norm Kerr. (Right) On heavily overcast days, when the sun's position cannot be located, acceptable pictures are possible with an exposure of about three stops more than for bright sunlight. Photo by Esther Henderson.

Cloudy bright days, either completely overcast or with scattered clouds, require exposures of about two stops more than for bright sunlight. On such days, the sun's disk is obscured, but a bright area in the clouds will reveal its location. Photo by Bob Clemens.

Natural Light

film is balanced for this color temperature. (*See:* COLOR TEMPERATURE.)

Daylight between 10 A.M. and 4 P.M. will usually produce the most natural color balance when pictures are taken on daylight-balanced films. At times earlier or later than these, the light gets progressively yellower and redder; pictures taken very early in the morning or approaching sunset will have a typically reddish color. In some cases, this is desirable, and no correction is necessary.

If, however, you wish to make pictures of subjects in early or late illumination and do not want a sunrise or sunset color effect, correction can be made with a filter. Such a filter will be bluish in color, but because the light changes rapidly in color during the early or late hours, it is not possible to specify a particular filter for this situation. In all likelihood, a bluish light-balancing filter will be required; it may be anything from an 80C filter to an 80B filter, depending upon just how reddish-yellow the light is. Only trial and error can teach you how to make this correction, and if a picture is critical, it will be necessary to make a quick series of exposures using different filters. Do not forget to make allowance for the filter in setting the exposure; an 80C filter will require 1 stop additional exposure, while an 80B filter will require 1⅔ stops of additional exposure. Lighter colored bluish filters in the 82, 82A, and 82B series can be used with the 80B and 80C filters to fine-tune the color balance.

Color pictures on hazy and overcast days, on the other hand, will tend to be bluish in color. Most of this is due to excess ultraviolet radiation, and can be partially corrected by the use of a Kodak skylight filter, which is colorless or faintly pink. Since it absorbs only ultraviolet radiation, no increase in exposure is needed. However, an 81C yellowish color-conversion filter may give a more fully corrected color balance when the sky is overcast.

The skylight filter is required only with daylight-balanced films; if you are using a tungsten-type film with a conversion filter, no additional filtering will be necessary, because the conversion filter also absorbs ultraviolet radiation completely.

Open shade is very bluish in color, and may be said to have a color temperature of from 8000 K (hazy sky) up to 20,000 K. A skylight filter gives a partial correction, but an 81EF filter will give much more natural color balance for hazy blue skylight,

while an 85C filter will give better color balance for open shade subjects when the sky is deep blue. The addition of a No. 81 or 81A filter (yellowish in color) to either an 81EF or an 85C filter warms up the color balance even more.

• *See also:* AVAILABLE-LIGHT PHOTOGRAPHY; COLOR PHOTOGRAPHY; COLOR TEMPERATURE; LANDSCAPE PHOTOGRAPHY; LIGHTING; NATURE PHOTOGRAPHY.

Nature Photography

Many pictures show natural features of the geology, the plants, and the animals that make up the earth and its inhabitants. These may be pictorial, as well as showing specific aspects of nature. The primary function of a nature photograph is to show the essence or behavior of the natural environment, the flora and fauna that inhabit its atmosphere, waters, and land.

Some types of subjects, such as microorganisms, require equipment that must be used in the laboratory—but most subjects produce the most honest pictures if they are taken in the subjects' own habitats. Pictures taken in a zoo may be difficult to tell from those taken in the wild. The zoo picture, how-

Animals photographed in the zoo, rather than in the wild, may nevertheless appear quite natural. Photo by Mike Keza for Editorial Photocolor Archives.

Natural Light

ever, is not as honest as the one taken in the natural habitat. Some competitions for nature photography have categories for both types of pictures.

Elsewhere in this Encyclopedia, there are articles that cover specific nature subjects in detail. These are listed at the end of this article. The purpose of this article is to summarize the equipment and techniques commonly used in the practice of nature photography.

The general heading "Nature Photography" includes photography of microorganisms a fraction of a millimetre long, and 50-ton whales as well. It includes mineral specimens that do not move at all, and high-speed creatures than can require a truckload of gear to photograph well. Most subjects fall between these two extremes, and an active photographer can take many types of nature pictures without special equipment.

There are many things to photograph if you develop an awareness of the living things around you. Especially when you learn to "look small," you will realize there are enough subjects to last a lifetime. Everyone at first looks for the bigger things—hawks, deer, moose—and is disappointed if they are not immediately found. But the seasoned nature photographer looks closer and finds warblers, voles, shrews, frogs, snakes, insects of all kinds, flowers, and fungi—the possibilities are endless.

Lichens and mosses, in random bursts of color on stone, make excellent small nature subjects, abundant and easily accessible. Photo by Robert Walch.

This tiny salamander discovered in a puddle on a country road was photographed with a close-up lens. Sidelighting produces a translucent effect which enhances the delicacy of the subject. Photo by Michael Winter.

Cameras and Lenses

The scope of the equipment you have available —or are willing to lug into the field—largely determines what sort of subjects you can photograph. The average-size birds and mammals, turtles, and so forth, can be photographed successfully with common, everyday cameras—even simple cameras—although there are some special techniques involved.

Single-Lens Reflex Camera. The common 35 mm single-lens reflex camera is an excellent camera for nearly all types of nature photography. It will accept extension tubes or bellows for extreme close-up pictures of insects and small flowers, and it will accept telephoto lenses for pictures of timid and wary wild animals. Many single-lens reflex cameras will also accept motor drives, and adapters for attachment to microscopes and telescopes. More types of lenses are available for this type of camera than any other, and more films, both black-and-white and color, are made in the 35 mm size than in any other size. For almost all types of nature photography, the single-lens reflex camera is the best choice.

In nature photography, the "normal" 50 mm lens may be the least used focal length of all. But every 35 mm camera seems to come equipped with one, and it is useful for some nature scenics because it is usually fast enough to be helpful in low-light situations. More often you will use a wide-angle or a telephoto lens.

Wide-Angle Lens. The wide-angle lenses are good for sunsets, pictures taken of a forest from inside a forest, or the recording of some small object

Sunsets are best photographed with a wide-angle lens, which can encompass the sweep of the sky and clouds. Photo by Michael Fairchild.

or creature close-up, with a sweeping wide-angle view of its habitat in the same picture. Many wide-angle lenses focus fairly close, too, and can double as near-macro lenses.

Macro Lens. For any great amount of close-up photography—insects, flowers, gem specimens, and so forth—a serious photographer should have a macro lens. For close-ups of living creatures, a 100 mm macro lens is much better than a 50 mm lens. You can get a life-size image with either, but you do not have to get as close to the subject with the 100 mm lens. There are other focal lengths as well.

Telephoto Lens. Telephoto lenses are the real workhorses of wildlife photography. With the vast majority of wild subjects, you cannot get close enough with a normal lens, and the telephoto lens

For photographing small creatures, a long-focal-length lens allows the user to make life-size images without the need to approach the subject too closely. Photo by Michael Fairchild.

These two photographs show the advantage of using a telephoto lens for distant and/or dangerous subjects. While slow shutter speeds are a disadvantage of long telephoto lenses, these napping lions in a Kenya game preserve made ideal subjects. Photos by R.J. Morris for Editorial Photocolor Archives.

lets you take close-up pictures from a distance. This is such a decided advantage that photographers use long telephoto lenses to photograph birds, mammals, reptiles, amphibians, insects, and even flowers that grow high off the ground or out in a muddy swamp.

The average field photographer usually carries a 200 mm or 300 mm lens, and a few put up with the vagaries of the 400 mm; this is about the limit for field work. Two of the limitations of most extremely long-focal-length telephoto lenses are their slow speeds—which is a disadvantage when you want to use a fast shutter speed or when the subject is in the shade—and their inability to focus close enough for many subjects. Some have modified close-up lenses to permit focusing as close as 20 feet.

Zoom Lens. Zoom lenses are very convenient to use, and modern ones, "computer designed," are effectively about as sharp as a single-focal-length lens. Certainly a zoom would be a good choice if a lot of hiking is planned. The disadvantages are high cost, and the fact that the lens is nearly always as big as and heavier than a comparable telephoto lens of its longest focal length, no matter what focal length you are actually using. Zoom lenses also nearly always have a higher flare level than telephoto lenses, which lowers the contrast of the pictures taken with them.

Films

Most present-day nature photographers shoot in color and use slide films. There are quite a few to choose from, and they all differ in terms of sharpness and acutance, color saturation, color contrast, and film speed. A common choice is to use Kodachrome film for those situations where there is enough light to use a moderate-speed film, and to use Ektachrome 200 or 400 film for situations where the light level is low, or where you need to use a very fast shutter speed.

Color negative films are the best choice if you know for sure you will want prints as the end result. Of course, it is possible to get slides from both types of color films, and prints from both types as well; but, generally speaking, the best slides come from slide films, and the least expensive prints from negative films. Prints made from slide film may be just a bit sharper, however, and highlight tones may be "muddy" from tone compression because prints from slides are essentially copy prints.

With few exceptions, the sharpest, finest grain pictures result from using the slowest films available, in either black-and-white or color, except when use of a slower film causes camera or subject movement.

Exposure Meters

Exposure meters and techniques used in nature photography do not vary greatly from those used in

Under the adverse lighting conditions of overcast or rainy days, a high-speed, daylight film will produce good results. Pictures made under such conditions may have a characteristic bluish color which can add mood. Proper exposure must be determined with a meter. Photo by Lee Howick.

ordinary photography, except that there may be more unusual subjects or lighting situations.

Most single-lens reflex cameras have built-in exposure meters, nearly all of which have full-field or "averaging" coverage. These provide accurate exposures for most subjects. However, it is important to remember that the meter does not, and cannot, know what you consider most important in a scene. Many serious photographers prefer to use a separate "spot" type meter and do their own averaging if necessary.

Motor Drives

The motor-driven camera is very useful in many nature photography situations. With this equipment, you can stay hidden, and take a whole roll of pictures moving your finger once for each exposure. And, many times you will have only a second or two to get all the pictures you are going to get; with a motor drive, this can be four or five different exposures instead of one or two at the most. Running deer, flying birds, swimming beaver or muskrat, even a bird at a nest or feeder—all are good subjects for a series of pictures.

Accessories

With the never-ending and ever-changing situations encountered in nature photography, it is wise to carry a few accessories to be prepared for the unexpected. Small electronic flash units will let you take many shots you would otherwise miss, and they are lightweight and inexpensive, as well. A 3-foot sync-cord extension is a good accessory, too, in addition to lens caps for the front and back of each lens, and a body cap for a second camera body, if you carry one. Other accessories that you may need include folded plastic bags for use during a shower, a small pair of vise-grip pliers, and a "clampod" device which will allow you to make a camera support from nearby trees or fences.

An air-type cable release with 30 or 40 feet of vinyl tubing will allow you to attempt simple remote-control pictures of any birds' nests you find. You can set out bait for a chipmunk, squirrel, or woodchuck, with the camera aimed at the bait, and trip the shutter from a position that will not frighten your subject. With flowers and many other small subjects, it helps greatly to reflect some light onto their shaded sides. A reflector with aluminum foil on one side and diffuse white on the other will do this nicely. Another choice is a piece of aluminized fabric, gold or silver, or even one of each.

Carrying and Caring for Camera Equipment

The nature photographer has some unique problems, one of which is figuring out how to carry all camera gear on a lengthy hike. A gadget bag can be unwieldy and uncomfortable, and is usually unsuitable for carrying the equipment necessary for nature photography. Gear made for hiking, backpacking, and cross-country skiing is usually better; it is light and durable, easy to wear, and comfortable as well. The "fanny-pack" that straps around the waist is especially good; the big ones will hold two cameras and three lenses, and the smaller ones will hold all the film, filters, and miscellaneous equipment you will usually need to carry. Two fanny-packs can be worn at once, stacked one atop the other. Also good are little zippered belt pouches, each large enough for a 100 mm or 200 mm lens or a pair of binoculars. Backpacks are good for extended hikes with a lot of gear, but getting at a particular piece of equipment can be a slow and inconvenient process.

Keeping your equipment dry and functional can be difficult when caught by a sudden shower or dust storm, but preplanning is the key. Some fairly large plastic bags, folded up and secured with rubber bands, will keep water and dust at bay; a large ear syringe can be used to blow dust off lenses and out of nooks and crannies. Pipe cleaners are also useful in camera cleaning. A small pack of lens tissue—kept dry in a plastic bag—is good for the cleaning of lenses and filters. If a camera gets wet from either fresh or salt water, *do not* try to dry it out if you will be home in a day or two. Instead, keep the camera submerged in fresh water, in a bucket or plastic bag, and take it to a repair facility. It is the combination of air and water that causes the rusting.

Preparing for Field Work

Going into the field on a photography trip need not be a chore, nor hard work. So instead of trying to be prepared for everything you will possibly meet, take along enough equipment to handle the things you expect to meet and like to photograph (and perhaps a telephoto lens for the unexpected). If the subjects are flowers and insects—which always seem to go together—take along a camera with a macro lens, or a normal lens and extension tubes, a bellows, or supplementary lenses. You should also have a reflector and a small electronic flash unit. A square yard or so of dark-green or light-blue cloth is often good to use as an out-of-focus background, especially if the natural background is a fence, road, dump, or other distraction. A piece of heavy fabric or rubber to kneel on is a big convenience, as is a tripod, but it is a little cumbersome to carry. For birds and mammals, telephoto lenses are needed, as is bait, whenever you think it will attract your subjects. For snakes and amphibians, you will need a snake-hook and a sweep net. For mineral specimens, a geologist's pick and some collecting bags will be useful.

The major thing to consider when packing for a day's trip is to take along enough things to keep yourself comfortable. Always try to be prepared for weather conditions you are likely to encounter—heat, cold, wet, and insects are the main things to think about. If the trip spans early morning and late afternoon, perhaps you will need an extra jacket or sweater. A hat of some sort offers protection from sun or cold, and a pair of gloves has a considerable warming effect on the whole body. Sunglasses can provide additional comfort, and in summer, insect repellent can provide great relief. In extremes, you may even have to wear a headnet of mosquito netting. A tube of suntan cream is a good idea, with a pack of tissues to keep your equipment clean.

Stalking Techniques

Once in the field and properly equipped, you must get reasonably close to a wild creature before you can get good frame-filling pictures. Telephoto lenses are a great help, and useful for large and small creatures alike, but there is nearly always some stalking involved. The whole key is to move slowly enough so that your quarry is not alarmed—99 percent of the time it will see you first, but if it decides you are not dangerous, it may not move off. Make slow motions, and wear darkish neutral-color clothing. Camouflage suits made for duck hunters seem to work. The techniques of stalking are about the same for all wild creatures, but the size of your subject and the length of your telephoto lens dictate how close you must get. With deer or moose, it may be 100 to 200 feet; with robin-size birds, 10 to 20 feet; and with singing toads or butterflies, perhaps 8 to 15 feet. With the latter, wind direction is of little importance, and you can circle to get the lighting you want. With most mammals, wind direction is very important, and you have to accept whatever lighting exists. Try for an upwind approach, keeping behind bushes or trees if possible, and in whatever shadows you can find. Walk at an angle facing slightly away from the animal, as though you were going somewhere else, and step sideways toward it, stopping and crouching if it shows signs of alarm. Practice stalking creatures every chance you get; the more you do this, the better you will become at it. Above all, move *slowly* and *smoothly;* you will soon learn what provides the best method with any wild animal.

Blinds

Stalking is one way of getting close enough for good pictures; the use of a blind is another. A blind (in England, a "hide") is any structure or object that covers and conceals a photographer so that wildlife doesn't know he or she is there. Blinds work beautifully in bird photography, and are more fully discussed in the article BIRDS, PHOTOGRAPHY OF. You can often work almost eye to eye with a nesting bird,

and get a whole series of excellent pictures. With mammals, blinds are less often successful, but worth a try if you can locate yourself downwind of a well-used game trail or waterhole. Consider using an automobile as a blind; many wild creatures are used to seeing them, and you can often drive along slowly and get quite close. With a sunroof or convertible, you can sidle along under a bird in a tree or on a wire and get good pictures. This technique is seldom used, but it is a good one to remember.

(Above) Before attempting close-up photography by remote control, a dummy camera such as this may be gradually moved closer to the nest over a period of several hours or days, so the bird can become familiar with the photo equipment. (Left) This upland plover was photographed during the nesting season. This is the best period to photograph birds, as their natural instinct to protect their eggs often overcomes their fear of the photographer. Photos by Richard D. Robinson, FRPS.

By using this blind, the scene of action can be watched through a pair of binoculars from 30 to 40 feet away, and the shutter can be released at the desired moment.

Remote Control

If for any reason you cannot get yourself *and* your camera close enough, you can often get just the camera within range, and set it off by remote control. There is no way to change focus or aim after the camera is set up, and this technique is best for creatures that have a favorite perch, respond to bait or a feeder, or use well-defined trails. Then watch and wait, and make the exposure when the animal is in the right place.

With both blinds and remote-control work, use a telephoto lens. This avoids placing the blind or camera too close to the nest; it is easy to cause a parent bird to desert a nest. This is totally unnecessary, and ruins everything. *The health and welfare of the wildlife subjects should always come first.*

In its simplest form, a remote control for a camera is simply a spool of black thread and a few rubber bands, paper clips, and strips of wood. These are attached to the camera so that pulling a thread trips the shutter. Thus, you are free to go about other tasks, and pull the thread whenever the field of view looks interesting. A refinement is to stretch the thread across a game trail, or tie it to a bait, and

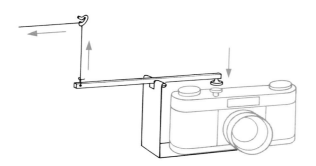

If the camera has a plunger-type release (downward action), the end of the lever to which the string is attached should be pulled upward. A properly positioned screw-eye will ensure that the pull is in the proper direction.

A telephoto lens will make it easy to keep a safe distance between photographer and subject— for the health and welfare of both. This family of Canada geese was photographed with a 135 mm lens. Photo by Richard D. Robinson, FRPS.

When photographing dangerous or timid animals, a pressure mat covered with a few leaves can be placed in a baited area. When the animal steps on the mat, an electric circuit is closed, and the shutter is automatically released.

let the animal take its own picture. With flash, a simple camera trap like this becomes a 24-hour affair, and you can successfully photograph many kinds of animals, including deer, bear, raccoon, fox, vulture, coyote, and beaver. Put a plastic bag over the camera when you leave it, cut a hole for the lens, and tape or tie the bag down so it will not flap.

Air-Release. A more refined way to set off a remote camera is to use an air-release. It is similar to that used by the old-time portrait photographer — a rubber bulb, some tubing, and a piston/cylinder on the shutter. The modern air-release is a regular rubber bulb, 40 or 50 feet of vinyl tubing (do not use rubber; it stretches), and a piston that actuates a cable release screwed into the camera. The tubing can be led through a window or under a door with care. Another method is to use an electric solenoid, and a wire and push-button to set it off. This takes a fairly large solenoid, which must be designed to fit the cable release, as well as batteries; so it takes considerable preparation.

Motor Drive with Remote Control. With all these, though, you can only take one picture, and then must go to the camera to rewind it for another exposure. This naturally frightens off all the wildlife within view, and slows things down a lot. The answer—readily available, but a bit expensive—is a motor drive for your camera. This includes a built-in solenoid, so all that is needed is wire and a switch. With this arrangement, you can set up the camera, go away 100 feet or more, and take up to 36 exposures without going near the camera again. Lots of wild creatures, especially birds, get used to the camera's noise and will not go very far between exposures. Some of the braver birds may even stay on the feeder or perch when the camera goes off.

Flash. When a camera setup is left for a long time, natural lighting conditions are likely to change. An alternative is to use flash, and for this use it is best to employ a flash unit that runs on house current or a high-voltage battery pack. These

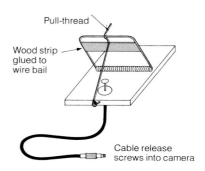

Pull-thread

Wood strip glued to wire bail

Cable release screws into camera

A simple tripping device can be made with a mousetrap and a camera set up some distance away. When the subject is in camera position and the string is pulled, the wood strip strikes the cable release button, snapping the picture.

An ideal way to photograph birds in flight is through the use of a photoelectric trip. A beam of light is directed across a game trail at a photoelectric cell. A change in light striking the cell closes an electric circuit and activates the camera solenoid, thus tripping the shutter.

will both be silent, whereas most low-voltage battery units whine and beep, which will frighten off some creatures. Try to avoid strong daylight; cameras with focal-plane shutters require the use of 1/60 or 1/125 sec. with flash, and you will get a smeared daylight "ghost image" at these slow speeds with a sharp flash image superimposed on it.

Radio Control. A motorized camera can be effectively used in a camera-trap setup, but trigger switches are complicated, and it is risky to leave this equipment unattended. On the other hand, this is an excellent rig for a backyard bird feeder or mammal bait station. One further refinement to consider is to use a radio control to avoid stringing long wires. The outfits made for model airplanes work very well, if they are of the *superheterodyne* type. The *super-regenerative* circuits can be set off by passing taxis and various amateur-radio transmitters, and you will waste film photographing empty perches.

• *See also:* Animal and Pet Photography; Astrophotography; Birds, Photography of; Camera and Lens Care; Close-Up Photography; Flower Photography; Insect Photography; Landscape Photography; Telephotography; Underwater Photography; Zoo Photography.

Further Reading: Bauer, Erwin and Peggy. *Outdoor Photographer's Digest.* Chicago, IL: Follet Publishing Co., 1975; Bennett, E. *Nature Photography Simplified.* Englewood Cliffs, NJ: Prentice-Hall, Inc., 1975. Editors of Time-Life Books. *Nature Photography.* New York, NY: Time-Life Books, 1971; Hosking, Eric J. *Wildlife Photography.* New York, NY: Praeger, 1974; Nuridsany and Pérennou. *Photographing Nature.* New York, NY: Oxford University Press, 1976.

 Negatives

A negative is a photographic film or plate in which subject tones (and colors) have been reversed so that light tones are dark and dark tones are light. In color negatives, both tones and colors are negative. Negative colors are the complementary colors of the originals. This reversal is readily apparent in a black-and-white negative; it is less easily discernible in a color negative for two reasons: (1) The human eye is not accustomed to recognizing cyan, magenta, and yellow as the opposites (complementaries) of

Negative colors are complementaries of the originals. However, the overall orange tone usually obscures the actual dye colors. Photo by Albert Gommi.

red, green, and blue, respectively. (2) Residual color couplers, which help balance the printing characteristics of a color negative, produce an overall orange-tan color that obscures the actual colors of the dyes in the negative.

The earliest experimenters in photography did not recognize the potential of the negative image and considered its production a mistake or a failure. William Henry Fox Talbot was the first to appreciate that the negative was an intermediate step to the final correct-tonality, or positive image, and that it made possible an unlimited number of copies from a single camera exposure.

Character of a Negative

A negative is the joint product of exposure and development. The exposure registers a latent image in the emulsion, and the development makes the image visible (fixing, washing, and drying are also necessary steps in making a usable negative). The character of a negative is determined by its densities, the deposits of silver or dyes that modulate printing light so as to expose print material in a manner that produces an acceptable positive, or normal-tonality, image.

The difference between the maximum and the minimum densities in a negative defines the overall contrast as indicated by the density range. The degree of difference between intermediate densities determines the local contrast of the negative. The basic overall density of a negative is determined by exposure, since a certain minimum is required for all subject brightnesses to affect the emulsion to a developable degree. Contrast for a given film is primarily a matter of development, for in sufficiently exposed areas (middle and high brightnesses) there is enough latent-image halide to produce increasing density with increased development.

The visual impression called graininess is a secondary negative characteristic in a positive. It is a product of the inherent grain size of the emulsion, and the density produced in any given area by the combined effect of exposure and development. As a rule, increased density produces increased graininess.

Underexposure and Overexposure

For any subject, the optimum negative is produced by sufficient exposure to record dark (shadow) area details as printable densities, coupled with development that does not produce unprintable (too heavy, or thick) densities in bright (highlight) areas. Underexposure of a film produces thin densities and low density range. If the contrast grade of the printing paper is chosen to compensate for the negative contrast, upper tones may achieve nearly normal contrast in the print, but the shadow details will be lost.

Overexposure produces high density, increased density range, and increased graininess when the negative is given normal development. Reduced development may keep the contrast within a printable range, and if the overexposure is not too great, it will keep the graininess at a moderate level.

Unblemished Negatives

Because they are master records from which duplicates (prints) are made, negatives are very valuable photographic images. Unfortunately, they are made, by necessity, of fragile material; a slight amount of damage to a negative is far more apparent than the same degree of damage to a print. Although retouching can change some details in a negative and can sometimes repair the effects of damage, the quality obtainable from an unblemished original cannot be matched.

Special-Purpose Negatives

Special-purpose negatives include internegatives, made from color transparencies to facilitate making prints; duplicate negatives, made from prints or other negatives to protect an original from excessive handling; color-separation negatives, which are black-and-white records made through red, green, and blue filters for use in various color-reproduction processes; and screened negatives, made through halftone-dot or line screens for photomechanical production.

Sabattier Effect

Negative tonalities are sometimes used as the print image for expressive effect. Negative prints are usually produced by printing from a positive rather than a negative image, or by causing a tonal reversal during positive processing—usually by flashing the image with white light. Such flashed images are usually only partially reversed; this is called the Sabattier effect.

Neutral Density Filters

A neutral density (ND) filter is one that reduces the amount of light transmitted by a known amount, but does not change the color or spectral distribution of the light.

Uses

Neutral density filters have many uses in practical photography. They are used with miniature cameras and color films, where the light is too strong for correct exposure and a small aperture cannot be used. This is often the case with motion-picture cameras, which have fixed shutter speeds, usually from 1/30 to 1/50 sec. Professional camera operators often prefer to use large apertures for minimum depth of field, thus keeping background objects out of focus and unobtrusive. In addition, they often desire to make all shots in a given film at one aperture to avoid differences in lens performance at different apertures.

Density Values

Neutral density filters are classified according to the amount of light they absorb; this is generally given in terms of diffuse density.

Density values are logarithmic, and as a quick rule of thumb, one may remember that a density of 0.3 will transmit half the incident light (the logarithm of 2 is 0.3), and each additional 0.3 will subtract half the remainder. Then, a density of 1.0 will transmit just $\frac{1}{10}$ of the incident light, a density of 2.0 will transmit $\frac{1}{100}$ of the incident light, and a density of 3.0 will transmit $\frac{1}{1000}$ of the incident light.

The accompanying table gives transmission and exposure data for densities from 0.1 to 4.0. To arrive at other values, it is only necessary to remember that *adding* density values is equivalent to multiplying the percentages of transmission. Thus, for example, suppose a neutral filter has a density of 1.3—this is equivalent to a density of 1.0 plus a density of 0.3. And since a density of 1.0 transmits 10 percent (or 0.10) and a density of 0.3 transmits 50 percent (or 0.50), the combined transmission is $0.1 \times 0.5 = 0.05$ or 5 percent. The transmission of any other density is found in the same way.

	NEUTRAL DENSITY VERSUS TRANSMISSION		
Neutral Density	Transmission (percent)	Filter Factor	Exposure Increase (lens stops)
0.1	80	1 ¼	⅓
0.2	63	1 ½	⅔
0.3	50	2	1
0.4	40	2 ½	1 ⅓
0.5	32	3	1 ⅔
0.6	25	4	2
0.7	20	5	2 ⅓
0.8	16	6	2 ⅔
0.9	13	8	3
1.0	10	10	3 ⅓
2.0	1	100	6 ⅔
3.0	0.1	1000	10
4.0	0.01	10,000	13 ⅓

Combining Filters

Kodak Wratten neutral density filters No. 96 consist of colloidal carbon plus suitable dyes dispersed in gelatin. They are available in the densities noted in the accompanying table. Other densities can be produced by combining filters. These neutral density filters have very little scattering effect on the incident light; thus, they are suitable for use over the camera lens or in other image-forming beams.

Neutral filters can, of course, be used in combination with color filters, where desired. Often, an outdoor scene is photographed at a large aperture, and the density of the neutral filter is simply added to that of the color filter to determine the correct exposure.

For critical work, it is often not desirable to use several filters in combination; a number of special filters are available that combine a color filter and a neutral density filter in one single filter.

COMBINATION FILTERS

Kodak Wratten Filter No.	Composition
For Black-and-White Photography	
3N5	Wratten no. 3 + 0.5 ND
8N5	Wratten no. 8 + 0.5 ND
For Color Photography	
85N3	Wratten no. 85 + 0.3 ND
85N6	Wratten no. 85 + 0.6 ND
85N9	Wratten no. 85 + 0.9 ND
85BN3	Wratten no. 85B + 0.3 ND
85BN6	Wratten no. 85B + 0.6 ND

Gelatin filters are easily damaged by heat, and are not usually suitable for use over a light source, although they may be so used for short periods. Where great stability to heat is required, certain neutral filters of thin, evaporated metal layers (frequently Inconel) are available on either a glass or a quartz base; the latter is especially useful where ultraviolet radiation must be transmitted. These are very stable, and can be used with high-power beams, including lasers.

Home-Made Neutral Devices

Simple and inexpensive neutral devices, such as filters, step tablets, and wedges, can be made with flashed and developed photographic films; the silver image is quite neutral and stable. Because of the scattering by the silver grains, however, such filters cannot be used in image-forming beams. They are, however, used as reference densities in color separation and similar work.

Special-Purpose ND Filters

Other special-purpose neutral density filters are available for specific spectral ranges or with balanced response throughout the ultraviolet, visible, and infrared wavelengths. Polarizing screens are reasonably neutral, although the approximation of neutrality changes with crossed polarizers as they are rotated with respect to each other. Simple wire screening serves as a neutral attenuator when placed in a light beam; screening causes diffraction effects when placed in an image-forming beam. Several manufacturers make neutral glass filters for such applications as microscopy.

• *See also:* FILTERS; WEDGE SPECTROGRAM.

Newspaper Techniques

On the big-city newspaper, the mechanical and photographic processes used to produce the medium are usually the province of printing craftsmen. On the small-town daily or weekly paper, especially that produced by offset lithography, the photographic techniques involve most of the production staff and even much of the editorial staff. Such techniques include phototypesetting, halftone preparation, making screened paper prints, making halftone prints from color originals, doing paste-ups, making line negatives, and platemaking.

Phototypesetting

There are several reasons for the abrupt growth of phototypesetting. The introduction of low-priced, high-speed typesetters brought phototypesetting within the range of the smaller newspaper publishers. The same low-cost phototypesetters are capable of speeds up to and above 50 newspaper lines per minute, compared with 5 to 15 newspaper lines for hot-metal and early phototypesetting equipment.

Phototypesetting equipment accepts a wide variety of photographic materials as output. For newspaper work, typesetters generally choose paper over film because of its lower cost and its compatibility with paste-up procedures. However, with the advent of the video-display terminals and their ability to store and turn out errorless output tape, phototypesetting films are more feasible than ever before for newspaper work. See the article PHOTOTYPESETTING for more details of the process.

Halftone Copy

Although a newspaper plant normally has little or no control over the quality of most photographic illustrations from outside suppliers (particularly national advertisers and wirephotos), the reproduction quality of halftone illustrations could be greatly enhanced if the original art were made with newspaper publishing specifications in mind.

Contrast. Contrasty glossy photographs, while easy to make and appealing to view, may not be easy to reproduce with the more limited tone-reproduction capabilities of high-speed web presses, newspaper inks, and newsprint.

The most accurate tone reproduction would occur if the original photograph were similar in density range to the maximum *practical* printing-ink density range on press. This density can be measured with a standard reflection densitometer that is "zeroed" to the whiteness of the newsprint; density readings of printing inks should be taken from the deep shadow areas of halftones rather than from bold type.

Once the maximum printing density is established—barring any changes in inks or press conditions—original-art photographs should be made as closely as possible to that specification.

Sharpness and Detail. Fairly coarse contact-screen rulings are used for newspaper halftones (from 55 and 65 lines per inch for some letterpress printing, on up to 100 and 120 lines per inch for some offset lithographic printing).

Coarse screen rulings tend to literally "screen out" or obscure fine detail. Loss of detail is magnified even more if the original photograph is unsharp or if the photograph is so small that enlargement of the image will also enlarge imperfections and grain patterns.

Sizing. Although process cameras have almost unlimited size-changing versatility for newspaper

Coarse screen rulings are used for newspaper halftones. Photo below has been reproduced with a typical 55-line newspaper screen; note loss of fine detail compared with 150-line screened photo above.

work, photographs made to final reproduction size reduce labor. The smaller the number of enlargements and reductions made, the less chance there is for error. Besides, composition is a natural 1:1 design, whether hot type or cold type is used. Compatibility of line art to halftone art is greater if both follow a 1:1 sizing ratio.

Making Screened Paper Prints

There are many methods for making screened paper prints from continuous-tone originals. Following are three of these methods.

One Photographic Step. A quick, easy method is to make halftone exposures (main and flash) through a contact screen onto a diffusion-transfer intermediate. Place the exposed negative emulsion-to-emulsion with receiver paper, and process the two sheets together in a diffusion-transfer processor. The result is a semipermanent, high-quality, halftone positive print. This method utilizes only one photographic step—a positive screened paper print made directly from the continuous-tone copy.

Film Negative and Paper Positive. Using continuous-tone reflection prints for copy, a process camera, and a contact screen, make a halftone negative on a lith film. Process the film according to instructions supplied with the film. The result is a halftone negative. From the halftone negative, make a contact print onto a high-contrast photographic paper, using a vacuum printing frame and a point-source exposing light. After processing and drying the paper, paste the print on the mechanical.

Halftone Positive Print. Using a continuous-tone negative in a condenser enlarger, an open-faced vacuum frame (no glass or acetate overlay), and a contact screen, make halftone main and flash exposures to a sheet of high-contrast photomechanical paper. (Because the original copy is a negative, the main exposure controls shadow dot size while the flash exposure controls the highlight dot size.)

Process the paper according to instructions supplied with it. This procedure results in a halftone positive print. When dried, the print is pasted up on a mechanical.

Making Halftone Prints from Color Originals

To make *good* halftone paper prints from color originals, first make a halftone negative and then contact-print the negative onto paper for paste-up. The quality of the results depends on the types of materials used.

Although a panchromatic film gives the best results when making black-and-white reproductions from color originals, it must be handled and processed in total darkness or under the low illumination of a dark green safelight. With a panchromatic film, the normal work flow of the black-and-white camera operation is interrupted; the tendency, therefore, is to use orthochromatic film in spite of the better quality available with panchromatic film.

Paste-Up

Paste-up copy includes type and line, or halftone paper prints (components or elements) that are waxed, glued, or otherwise adhered to a layout sheet or mechanical.

In the past, component elements of the mechanical were permanently stuck to the mechanical with glue or paste. The expression "paste-up" will probably live on forever, but in reality, "wax-up" might be more appropriate today. Glue, paste, and rubber cement have given way to wax and other resin adhesives. Instead of applying the adhesive by hand, the paste-up element is run through a waxing machine (or touched with a hand waxer) to apply the adhesive to the back of the element. The element can be stuck and unstuck as often as needed without ruining either the element or the layout sheet. For repositioning, the element is simply lifted and relocated—recoating is not necessary.

Generally, the elements of the newspaper page are positioned onto layout sheets gridded by squares (or layout lines) of camera-invisible, light blue ink or pencil.

Still another method for laying out a mechanical on paper without grid patterns is to draw or compose the grid on the glass of a light table (or a backlit makeup table). Then place the layout sheet on the glass and "project" the grid through the base of the paper. The problem with this system is that the grid is gone once the mechanical leaves the makeup table.

Making Line Negatives

Making line negatives from paste-up copy is often taken for granted in discussions of graphic arts photography. In newspaper work, however, line

(Top) A dummy paste-up of type and line copy is prepared on a layout sheet. The resulting mechanical is called "camera-ready copy." (Bottom) A line negative made from the mechanical is inspected for sharpness of fine lines and halftone reproductions.

tone dots; reproducing these fine images requires critical focusing of the process camera.

On a negative, line widths that are thicker than the original (indicating underexposure) or thinner than the original (indicating overexposure) are sometimes falsely attributed to film variations or processing inconsistencies. Often, these variations in character weight on a negative can be traced to poorly aligned camera lights. The smaller and more widely spaced the camera lights, the more difficult it is to cover the camera film plane with even illumination. The larger the copy, the more likely it is you will see the effect of improper illumination in the line negative—sometimes called "hot spots" and "cold spots," or areas of plus density and minus density, respectively.

Lithographic Platemaking

While lithographic platemaking is generally beyond the scope of this discussion, an understanding of the methods may help to improve the preparation stages. Modern presensitized lithographic printing plates have a light-sensitive coating on a grained aluminum substrate. The plates are exposed (usually to ultraviolet radiation) through the line negative, which is held in close contact with the plate in a

A lithographic plate, made from a line negative, is processed to make image areas ink-receptive.

photography is far too important to be neglected. Of primary concern are *time,* both in the mechanical acts of making the exposures and in postexposure handwork; *simplicity* in developing a system that will yield the best results with repeatability; and *accuracy* in getting the best possible results from the copy at hand. Normally, no time is allotted for remaking negatives; therefore, line exposures must be right the first time.

Making a line negative of a paste-up mechanical involves reproduction of fine lines, serifs, and half-vacuum frame. Processing the plate makes the image areas ink receptive and the non-image areas water receptive.

Color Reproduction

Because of faster, easier, and more economical methods of reproducing color, and because of its tremendous appeal, modern newspapers utilize both editorial and advertising color much more today than they did just a few years ago.

Color originals usually come into the newspaper either as transparencies or as reflection prints; prints are sometimes accompanied by color negatives. The type (transparency, print, or negative) and size (enlargement, reduction, or same-size) of the color original, as well as the equipment used, determine the method of reproduction.

Transparencies (slides), for instance, are reproducible by any of three methods: (1) direct-screen color separation, (2) indirect color separation, or (3) color-separation prints with pan-sensitive photographic paper. Use the reproduction method for which you are already set up. (Reflection prints cannot be reproduced in an enlarger).

If a change in size is required between the original and the reproduction, contact-printing frames must be automatically ruled out for all phases of the processes, although most color-correcting *masks* are made by contact. If the original is to the final size, it is not necessary to tie up enlargers or cameras; use the contact frame.

These methods have several characteristics in common: They all require that at least *three* separations—color records of the three primary printing colors (cyan, magenta, and yellow)—be made from the original copy. They all require basically the same color filters for making the separations—the filters varying from technique to technique. They all require photographic *masking* to compensate for deficiencies in printing inks. And they all require that the three separations be *screened* at different screen-ruling angles.

Direct-Screen Color Separation. Undoubtedly the most popular method for newspaper color separation, the direct-screen method, uses two color-correcting masks and three (or four) *halftone* separation negatives made on panchromatic lith film.

An automatic film processor greatly aids the darkroom handling and processing of panchromatic emulsions. A big reason for the tremendous growth of newspaper color is the development and perfection of the direct-screen enlarger. The direct-screen enlarger incorporates high-intensity xenon light sources that reduce long exposure times to reasonable lengths (less than 30 seconds in most cases). The quality obtainable with the direct-screen method is excellent.

Indirect Color Separation. The indirect method of color separation is less widely used in newspaper production because it is time-consuming and ties up page-production equipment. Despite its drawbacks for newspaper work, indirect color separation has greater flexibility for color correction and color control than any other system. It allows color correction to take place in any one (or all) of four different production phases of the indirect process. The quality obtainable with this method is excellent.

Color-Separation Prints with Pan-Sensitive Photographic Paper. For color-separation prints, the separated color impressions are made on pan-sensitive photographic paper instead of film. The separation prints are then screened, just as any other continuous-tone prints are screened for black-and-white printing—except that each one is angled differently to prevent moiré or severe rosette patterns when the three halftone separations are registered together for the printing process.

Aside from the separations being made on photographic paper, a major difference between this and other color-reproduction techniques is the type of newspaper department responsible for actually making the separations. Although the photoengravers and offset cameramen could make the separations along with their other work, the press photographers would have greater access to, and greater familiarity with, the materials and equipment necessary for using the separation-print technique. The screening of the separation prints would, of course, be left with the process cameramen. For most applications, the quality obtainable with this method is quite good.

• *See also:* Color Separation Photography; Graphic Arts Photography; Halftone; Photomechanical Reproduction Methods; Phototypesetting.

Further Reading: Burden, J. *Graphic Reproduction Photography.* New York, NY: Hastings House, 1972; Eastman Kodak Co. *Halftone Methods for the Graphic Arts.* Rochester, NY; Eastman Kodak Co., 1974; Wallis, F. G. and R. V. Cannon. *Letterpress Platemaking.* Elmsford, NY; Pergamon Press, Inc., 1969.

News Photography

Although the term *news photography* applies equally to still photography done for newspapers and magazines, and motion-picture photography for television or film documentaries, this article relates only still techniques that will be of most use to the practical photographer. News photography is a specialized form of journalism that uses pictures either to accompany a news item or to tell a story without words.

The news photographer of today is an educated photojournalist with a searching and perceptive eye for meaningful pictures. In addition to taking pictures in sports arenas, music halls, state capitols, and the streets of the city, the news photographer seeks depth by picturing scientific laboratories, industries, hospitals, and many worlds inaccessible to the "man on the street".

The news photographer must be familiar with equipment and technique. Moreover, he or she should bring to every assignment an awareness of each facet of the story being covered; be quick to seize the threads of the spontaneous interaction of a fast-breaking news event; and be able to capture the essence in a strongly composed, information-packed photograph that tells the whole story in one powerful, succinct visual statement.

Photojournalism

The birth and subsequent tremendous popularity of *Life* magazine and its many imitators started a new wave of appreciation for photographic journalism. The reading public quickly came to recognize and appreciate good photographs.

The photo essay was born, and with it, a new breed of photographer. As television became more popular and took more of the advertising dollar, picture magazines started to disappear. But television continued the process of educating the public to camera journalism, and the newspapers responded by increasing their coverage of news events in photographs. A glance at the range of the news events covered in a large metropolitan daily or a small-town weekly shows the scope of the present-day photographer on assignment.

The Newspaper

The daily newspaper covers international, national, and metropolitan news events. These are further fragmented into sections dealing with sports, the home, fashion, business, family, food, the arts, politics, society, personality, science, and medicine. The Sunday edition covers all of these, and may add travel, a magazine section, a book-review section, real estate, and a number of local sections.

The Staff. Besides the full-time staff photographers, many newspapers use a number of free-lance photographers on a fairly regular basis for remote or less pressing assignments. Some of the larger papers also have photographers available in various cities to handle jobs in any part of the country where news is being generated. Additionally, electronic transmission services maintain a steady flow of photographs from news agencies around the world.

When there is a catastrophic event—a disastrous fire, an explosion, a plane crash—both amateur and professional photographers who have been at the site bring in their undeveloped film. The film is processed and compared to pictures from staff photographers and the wire services covering the same scene; the best photographs, no matter who took them, are selected for use in the paper. A free-lance photographer may receive payment varying from $25 to $150 for a picture. The payment depends on the importance of the event, whether it appears on the first page or inside the paper, and the amount of play it receives. For truly spectacular once-in-a-lifetime photographs, newspapers may pay much higher rewards.

Equipment

The news photographer's basic equipment usually includes two 35 mm single-lens reflex camera bodies, an extreme wide-angle lens (perhaps a 20 mm), a moderate wide-angle lens (either 28 or 35 mm), a normal (50 mm) lens, a medium telephoto lens (usually 85 or 100 mm), and a medium-long telephoto lens (180 or 200 mm). The photographer also may use a motor winder or motor drive, depending on personal needs; an electronic flash unit of the "potato masher" or more compact variety; a separate hand-held exposure meter; and an assortment of filters. Many photographers work with two camera cases: one for assignments requiring just the cameras with lenses mounted (frequently 35 mm

The photography staff of any good-sized newspaper is generally large, and may be augmented by freelance photographers and out-of-town regular staff members. The equipment they use in their daily work is extensive; even more specialized pieces are usually furnished by the newspaper "pool" or rented for the occasion. Photo by Arthur Rothstein.

and 85 mm), the flash unit, and a few rolls of film; and another larger case for assignments requiring a more complete range of equipment.

In addition, a newspaper may supply photographers with a "pool" of equipment, including a great many lenses of specialized types. For example, there might be telephoto lenses of 300, 400, 500, 600, and 1000 mm focal lengths. Also included could be macro lenses for extreme close-up photography, "perspective-control" lenses for architectural photography, and wide-angle lenses as short as 15 mm. An assortment of tripods and tilt heads of various dimensions would be available. Super-wide cameras that give coverage to 140 degrees, $2\frac{1}{4}'' \times 2\frac{1}{4}''$ format cameras, and $4'' \times 5''$ format cameras might complete the equipment stocked.

When it is necessary to use even more specialized equipment, such as $8'' \times 10''$ view cameras, high-speed Hulcher motorized cameras, and the like, they may be rented when needed for a particular assignment.

In addition to the usual photographic equipment, each photographer will usually carry an assortment of preferred equipment or accessories. A photographer who likes to photograph architecture may carry perspective correcting lenses for 35 mm camera, or a large-format camera and lenses in the car. A sports photographer will have a larger complement of telephoto lenses. One who does much portrait work will have more extensive lighting equipment.

The Assignment

When on an assignment, the photographer has the responsibility of gathering together the important elements of a story and recording them. Like a written feature, a photographic feature must have a good beginning, usually a striking opening picture. This may be a general view or a close-up of some important element of the story that makes a vital and telling point. This may be followed or surrounded by a series of photographs that tell the story in pictures, and it may be concluded with one photograph that sums up. Since the flow of news on any given day might restrict the number of pictures that can be used, it is important to have one photograph in the set that tells the whole story, if it should be necessary to use only one.

At the Office

Working with the staff photographer is a picture editor or editors. Also working closely with the photographer is the assignment editor. Arriving before the first photographer, the assignment editor assembles editorial requests, determines picture needs, and schedules photographers to handle assignments. Where necessary, the staff photographers are contacted and assigned to cover breaking news events on their way to the office.

In addition to hard-news events, sports, and other routinely covered stories, are the subjects that comprise the feature sections of the paper. Stories may be developed by a reporter who requires photos

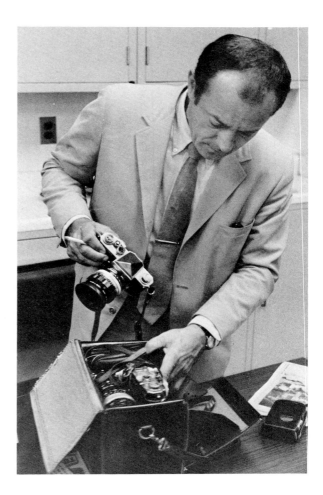

(Top left) Before leaving on his assignment, the news photographer discusses details with his editor. (Right) He checks his equipment before going out. Any special requirements should be noted and provided for in advance. (Bottom left) On assignment—a protest demonstration— the photographer works quickly to gather and record important elements of the story. Photos by Nick De Sciose.

to complete the presentation. Or a reporter-photographer team may develop a story together. An experienced photographer, especially one who can develop a story line, may be asked to work on a feature assignment alone.

When deadlines are not pressing, photographers are frequently given some latitude to come up with original picture ideas or to deal in a new way with the usual "theme" pictures—weather, summer, snow, animals, children. Such "enterprise" photography can provide story leads for reporters, feature

pictures that can be dropped into a "hole" in the page makeup, or a complete picture story. Many photographers try out a picture idea and convince the picture editor to give them an assignment to complete a picture story.

On the Road

Assignments may be grouped by proximity so that the photographer can get from one event to the next easily, or by the photographer's interests and ability. Most photographers will handle routine assignments, such as press conferences, store openings, and parades, easily and competently. Sports, portraiture, fashion, architecture, or aerial photography may call upon special talents or understanding of the subject. The photographer is usually "on call" to be diverted to any fast-breaking news event.

All photographers carry their equipment with them when commuting to and from work, ready to take on an assignment or to get an "enterprise" shot. In fact, the most dedicated news photographers are rarely far separated from a camera of some sort, whether they are on vacation, going to the opera, or mountain climbing. Photographic opportunities do not always correlate with the time of day or the specific assignment.

Taking the Picture

Lenses. Many news jobs can be handled with just two lenses: a 35 mm wide-angle lens and an 85 mm medium telephoto lens. Should it be necessary to use only one lens, the 35 mm wide-angle lens is the choice for most jobs. This lens has the same angle of view as the 5-inch lens, which was used for years as the standard for news photography with a 4" × 5" Speed Graphic camera.

However, if the assignment is a sports event, a trade show, or a political convention, there is no way to cover it without a large selection of lenses. The photographer's vantage point may be situated anywhere from 50 to 200 feet away from the action. In extreme cases, a 600 or 1000 mm lens may be needed to get adequate image size. Before the start of the event, photographers are often allowed to roam freely, getting "color" shots or intimate close-ups of participants. In such situations, the photographer is often working as close as a few feet; it is here that the 35 and 85 mm lenses are most useful. Medium telephotos may have the "reach" needed with the lens speed that is vital for low-light conditions. An extreme wide-angle lens can provide a panorama of the whole event.

Sports assignments usually call for high-speed motor drives and long lenses. The zoom lens has become a favorite with some photographers for certain sports. The ability to compose the picture by zooming the lens is invaluable. The problem with zooms, however, is that they are usually slower than single prime lenses, and in very fast-moving sports such as ice hockey and basketball, it is all but impossible to zoom, focus, and shoot. To get good sports photographs consistently, the photographer must understand the sport, know when and where peak action occurs, and anticipate the action.

Lighting. Light is the photographer's tool. Where possible, the news photographer will make the best use of the light available at the scene. This

Long lenses and cameras coupled to high-speed motor drives are most effective for sports assignments. The photographer must understand the sport and learn to recognize where and when the peak action will occur. Photo by Paul Bereswill.

usually provides the most natural appearance for the photographs. Often the photographer cannot, or must not, be intrusive with the use of a flash. However, he or she must use all of the tools available to get the best possible photographs—technically and esthetically. Where flash is allowed and can provide useful main or supplemental light, it should be used.

Push Processing Film. Although many photographers advocate routine "push" processing of films, this method should be used only where circumstances make it necessary. Pushing the film compromises image quality. Modern high-speed black-and-white films such as Kodak Tri-X film or Ilford HP-5 film can be exposed with a higher index, 800 or 1250, and developed accordingly.

Flash. For many new photographers, the creative use of flash photography is a lost art. Nevertheless, the experienced photographer knows that flash can be used as fill for sunlit portraits, as a bounce light to give a natural, diffuse lighting effect, and to give direct, action-stopping light for sports, dance, or nighttime events. While every news photographer should have a compact electronic flash in the equipment bag at all times, larger units, multiple units, slave flash, or studio units may all be needed on occasion. The photographer should understand the use of all of them.

News Photography Subjects

Hard-News Events. The hard-news event such as a fire, a riot, or a shoot-out may call for long lenses, because police security lines usually keep even the news photographer at a distance from the scene of the action. As the event develops, one of the rapid-fire electronic flash units capable of keeping pace with a motor drive is a great boon. When covering a situation of this kind, it is best to take only the equipment that will fit comfortably in one bag.

The Press Conference. To get interesting photographs at a press conference is a difficult assignment for the news photographer. There is usually a well-known personality standing in front of a battery of microphones, and the television lighting is flat and uninteresting. A trick in covering this sort of static setup is arriving early and leaving late. Often the subject is far more at ease before the television lights and the recorders go on. After the press conference is over, the lights are turned off, and the reporters are leaving, the subject is once again in a more relaxed frame of mind and will often fall into more interesting poses.

Hard-news events, in which the action is totally unpredictable, require cameras equipped with motor drives and fast film. This harrowing portrayal of a Vietnamese family fleeing an attack on their village won the 1966 Pulitzer Prize; it is one of a series of photos taken on a roll of Kodak Tri-X film. The photographer, Kyoichi Sawada, was killed in Cambodia in 1970. Photo © United Press International.

The most interesting press conference photographs are usually taken either before or after the conference itself, when the subject is more relaxed and less conscious of the lights and cameras. This photograph of Casey Stengel was made under just such conditions. Photo by Jim Peppler.

The slower pace of a leisurely feature assignment gives the photographer more time to study his subject and think about how best to employ photographic technique. For this photograph of the artist John Marin, a wide-angle lens was used in order to present the subject in relation to his environment. Photo by Arthur Rothstein.

News Photography

The Leisurely Assignment. When that rare leisurely feature assignment comes along, the news photographer enjoys the change of pace from the hurried look through the lens that is required of most news assignments. The perspective of the subject can be studied through different lenses; the photographer can wait for the sun to move around to a more advantageous position; and the subject can be given the full time, thought, and creative abilities of the photographer.

Hazardous Assignments. Much more common are the assignments in dangerous areas. It is not a wise idea to point a camera at a group of people who obviously do not want their picture taken, but when it is necessary, there are ways of doing it. For example, the "right-angle mirror," shaped like a lens, enables the photographer to point the camera at right angles to the subject while taking a picture. Concealed cameras and miniature cameras that fit into the palm of the hand are also possible solutions to difficult and dangerous assignments.

Architectural Subjects. Architectural photographs for the home, real estate, or business sections

of newspapers present their own special problems. Buildings should have straight lines. This calls for the use of specialized, perspective-control lenses on 35 mm cameras. These are usually found in two focal lengths, 28 mm and 35 mm, and they enable the photographer to keep the camera parallel to the building, while raising the lens to include the top of the structure without the keystoning distortion common to tilted cameras. The view camera or sheet-film press camera with rising front is still best for this application. The extreme wide-angle lenses for 35 mm cameras are worth mentioning for their ability to "stretch" space. Tilting an extreme-wide-angle lens will result in extreme distortion; keeping it level will often enable the photographer to show interiors that would simply be impossible to photograph with any other lens.

Perennials. No rundown on news assignments would be complete without the inclusion of the

(Below) Hazardous assignments, where the subjects are angry and are not likely to welcome photographers, should be approached with caution. While some photographers move right in, others will take more prudent approaches. Photo by Jim Peppler. (Right) Photographs of architectural subjects may require special equipment to avoid extreme distortion. However, some distortion may have dramatic appeal, as demonstrated by this photo taken with a wide-angle lens. Photo by Arthur Rothstein.

perennials—assignments that come around year after year—the annual St. Patrick's Day parade, the first day of spring, July 4th, Christmas, the first snowfall, the first heavy rainstorm or windstorm, the hottest day of the year, the Easter parade, the Veteran's Day parade, and the coldest day of the year. These regular events challenge the experienced news photographer to come up with fresh new interpretations year after year.

"Cream-Puff" Assignments. Unusual opportunities do occur for the news photographer. These may include the coverage of a story or personality in another country, photographing a popular sports event or a major concert—events that might not ordinarily be experienced. These can be enjoyed while they are being photographed.

Processing the Film

Many daily newspapers are now equipped with automatic processors. Such a machine can develop a roll of 35 mm film in 5 minutes, producing a dry negative ready for printing.

For a large number of photographers, processing their own film is still a very necessary part of

(Above right) Pictures of "perennial" subjects, such as the opening each winter of outdoor ice-skating rinks, are always required for the feature pages. The photographer is allowed considerable freedom of expression in this area, and he or she should enjoy the challenge of finding new interpretations of old themes. Photo by Paul Bereswill. (Right) Circuses, concerts, special sports events—so-called "cream puff" assignments—are also part of the news photographer's job. Here, electronic flash captures a critical moment in a circus trapeze act. Photo by Arthur Rothstein.

News Photography

Top row: (Left) Once the photographer returns to the office, his film is processed in the newspaper's photo lab. (Right) The negatives are checked for quality before printing. Bottom row: (Left) After contact sheets are made, the photographer and the writer with whom he has been working examine the prints with an illuminated magnifier. Photos by Arthur Rothstein. (Right) Enlargements are made of selected prints. Photo by Si Solow.

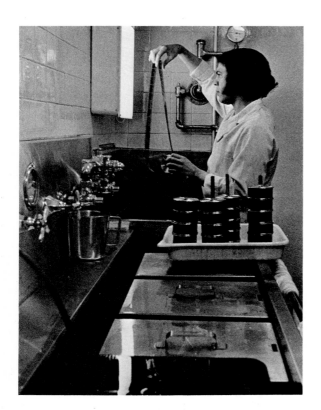

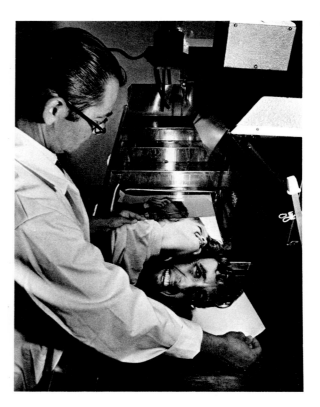

News Photography

their art. With 35 mm films, processing on spiral reels in small tanks by time and temperature is most common. When the film is dry, the photographer inspects it over a light box. Where there is time, a contact proof sheet will be made, and the picture choice made from that. The photographer may forward only the selected enlargements to the picture editor, or may submit the contact sheet as well for the editor's assessment.

The photographer may do the film development and printmaking, or a lab person may do all or part of the job. When the printing is being done by a lab worker, the photographer usually uses the contact sheet to give instructions. Cropping, burning-in, dodging, or other print manipulations will be marked. Many newspapers file all negatives, and the proof sheet marked with a file number is a handy retrieval aid.

Editing the Pictures

Editing pictures is a team effort. The photographer starts with the making of the pictures. Selecting lenses, vantage point, vertical or horizontal format, and composition—all are the photographer's editing tools. In the darkroom, the photographer may have further opportunity to edit by selecting frames, determining cropping, and manipulating printing. The picture editor must decide how and where the picture will appear. The editor may require a particular format to fit a page layout. Time and space may cause the editor to run the picture smaller or to delete it completely. Many good photographs are not used simply because there is no room.

Picture Captions

The photographer prepares caption material for the selected photographs. This information accompanies the photographs as a separate sheet or even attached to the back of the photograph. Caption sheets are often filed with the negatives for possible future use.

• *See also:* AVAILABLE-LIGHT PHOTOGRAPHY; FLASH PHOTOGRAPHY; NEWSPAPER TECHNIQUES; PHOTOJOURNALISM.

Further Reading: Capa, Cornell, ed. *Concerned Photographer 2.* New York, NY: Viking Press, Inc., 1972; Doherty, R.N. *Social Documentary Photography in the U.S.A.* Garden City, NY: Amphoto, 1976; Fox, Rodney and Robert Kerns. *Creative News Photography.* Ames, IA: Iowa State University Press, 1961; Hurley, Gerald. D. and Angus McDougall. *Visual Impact in Print.* Chicago, IL: Visual Impact Publishers, Communicators, 1975; Magmer, James. *Photograph Plus Printed Word.* Troy, MI: Midwest Publications, Co., Inc. 1969.

(Left) Enlarged prints are cropped for best composition. (Below) A rough layout is prepared. Photographer and writer check photos against layout to see if their selection can be improved. Photos by Arthur Rothstein.

Newton's Rings

Patterns of light that are seen when two transparent surfaces are nearly but not quite in contact, are known as Newton's rings. These rings are caused by interference between light rays reflected by the two surfaces, and are most evident when the separation between the two surfaces is nearly equal to, or only slightly greater than, the wavelength of light.

Newton's rings often form between the base side of a film negative and the glass of a negative carrier in an enlarger; they produce a pattern of dark and light bands on a black-and-white print, or colored bands on a color print. Likewise, these rings often appear in glass-mounted transparencies when the base side of the negative is pressed against one of the cover glasses.

There are several methods of eliminating Newton's rings. One way is to separate the base side of the negative or transparency from the glass by a paper or foil mask. Another method is to use finely ground glass as a cover, but it must be much finer than the usual camera ground glass if it is to produce an effect that is not grainy in the print. In enlarging, the simplest and most effective means to eliminate the problem is to use a glassless negative carrier.

Newton's rings are used in lens manufacture to test the accuracy of polished lens surfaces. A master test glass is carefully placed on the lens surface and illuminated with a monochromatic light source that makes dark and light rings clearly visible. Measurements made this way readily measure the accuracy of lens surfaces in millionths of an inch.

Nickel-Cadmium Battery

The nickel-cadmium (NiCad) battery is a type of rechargeable battery using nickel and cadmium electrodes and an alkaline electrolyte that is sealed in the battery case so there is no danger of leakage. This is possible because no gas is emitted when the battery is charged. It is also preferable to the older type of storage battery, such as the lead-acid type, because it does not lose its power when allowed to remain in a discharged state for extended periods of time.

Photographic equipment made for use with nickel-cadmium batteries usually has a built-in charger, or one supplied as an accessory. Nickel-cadmium batteries are also made in sizes corresponding to those of dry cells. They may be substituted for the latter, but in this case, must be removed from the equipment for recharging. However, since the voltage of nickel-cadmium cells is lower than that of dry cells (1.3 volts for NiCad versus 1.5 volts for dry cells), the equipment may have slightly less output when used with rechargeable batteries.

A new type of nickel-cadmium battery is capable of very fast recharging, and is useful when there is not time for a full recharge on normal cells. Some photographers, however, carry extra batteries that are fully charged for emergency, and many flash units can also be run on dry cells when the nickel-cadmium battery is run down.

Niépce, Joseph Nicéphore

(1765–1833)
French engineer; one of the inventors of photography

Niépce was the first to record images in a camera, probably as early as 1816. He first obtained negative images on paper sensitized with silver chloride, and was partially successful in fixing them using nitric acid. Niépce was aware of the possibility of printing his paper negatives, but was unsuccessful at first. He then successfully attempted to make positive, permanent images.

Niépce used pewter plates in his lithography business, and used various light-sensitive varnishes and pitches as a coating on the metal to record the image. His first success, 1826-27 was with bitumen of Judea coated on a pewter plate. It took 8 hours of exposure to differentially harden the coating, which was washed in oil of lavender diluted with white petroleum. The exposed areas were hardened and did not dissolve; unexposed areas remained soluble and were removed. Because the bitumen coating was a tan color on a dark pewter, this formed a positive, permanent image.

Later, in 1829, Niépce tried using a silver plate, coated as before. After the exposure and oil wash,

Niépce's 1826–27 heliograph, so called because it was obtained by the action of sunlight, was made on a pewter plate coated with a solution of bitumen of Judea. The process required eight hours of exposure. This view from Niépce's window of the courtyard of the family farmhouse is believed to be the first image ever recorded in a camera. Photo courtesy University of Texas at Austin.

the silver was treated to iodine fumes, which blackened it. He apparently did not realize that the blackening effect was the result of exposure on light-sensitive silver iodide.

In 1826, Niépce was introduced to Louis Jacques Mandé Daguerre by a Parisian optician who was supplying both workers with lenses and other equipment. They formed a partnership to develop a photographic process in December 1829. Daguerre's use of silver plates was probably suggested by Niépce. He also successfully made bitumen photographs on glass—probably the first glass negatives.

Niépce died in 1833 without ever seeing the success of the process he started. His son Isidore inherited the partnership with Daguerre, which continued through Daguerre's announcement of the daguerreotype process, and he shared in half of the profits.

• *See also:* DAGUERRE, LOUIS JACQUES MANDÉ; HISTORY OF PHOTOGRAPHY.

Night Photography

You will probably take your first night pictures with whatever equipment you already own. Any adjustable camera can be used successfully for night photography. Their compact size combined with the large selection of fast films and large-aperture lenses available have made 35 mm cameras the favorites of professional photographers specializing in available- or low-light shooting.

The primary criterion in choosing a lens for night photography is its speed. A lens is said to be "fast" or "slow" depending on the size of its maximum aperture. Lenses are available with settings of $f/1.8$, $f/1.4$, or even $f/1$, but they are expensive. A more reasonably priced $f/2$ or $f/2.8$ lens, used with fast films, should be sufficient for night and available-light shots.

For full coverage of almost any shooting situation, your kit should include moderate wide-angle and telephoto lenses in addition to a normal lens.

Exposure Meters

The light meter is the most important accessory, for the quality of the camera, lens, or enlarger does not matter if the film is under- or overexposed. Until

Look for bodies of water to form reflections of night lights. Exposure should be determined with an exposure meter, depending upon how much shadow detail is desired. Photo by Don McDill.

the advent of the cadmium sulfide cell, most night exposures (except under bright light conditions) were made by trial and error and, finally, by experienced guesswork. Even now, although there are meters that read "by the light of the moon," experience still plays a part in the determination of many "available-darkness" shots.

Metering Methods. For medium to well-lit street shots at night, a good CdS meter will determine the settings. If you want detail in the shadows, meter a dark area or take a reading from your hand and shoot at two, three, and four times more than the indicated exposure.

For bright neon lights, moving lights at fairs, and so forth, a good starting point would be $f/2.8$ at 1/30 to 1/250 sec., for films with EI 400. Pointing the exposure meter at the bright lights will only give an inflated reading. Exposure meters were not designed to read light sources. They read the light reflected by the subject or light falling on the subject.

Colors and patterns created by large neon signs and their reflections on other shiny surfaces create vivid pictures. Exposure meters are not useful for such pictures; instead, try using a wide aperture and bracketed shutter speeds. Photo by Robert Walch.

Tripods will not be needed for brightly lighted scenes such as this. Some blur in the picture adds to the feeling of "action" suggested by the neon signs themselves. Photo by Robert Walch.

Night Photography

Distant scenes at night usually require time exposures. (*See:* Available-Light Photography and Existing-Light Photography.)

Be sure to check the film ASA rating each time before you use the meter. If you plan to take many shots in a given area, take all necessary readings first to free yourself for picture-taking. Avoid having to go back for readings in darker or lighter areas. With an incident-light meter, do not forget to compensate for a very light or dark subject. With a reflected-light meter, measure for the important tones you want in the final picture. Then select the *f*-stop/shutter-speed combination that will interpret the subject the way you wish to represent it.

Tripods

For very low-light scenes that require a slow shutter or a time exposure, a tripod is a must.

The heavier the camera, the sturdier the tripod should be to provide complete immobility during exposure. Tripods have telescoping legs that are adjusted to the height of the subject, and are collapsible for easy carrying. The addition of a sturdy, movable center post saves raising and lowering the legs with every change of camera height. If you want to adjust the camera angle, you need an adjustable top or pan head. Look for one that swivels completely around, has a lock, tilts up and down, and has a movable base plate that flips sideways and will lock tightly when you want to change from horizontal to vertical framing.

To avoid camera shake on a tripod when depressing the shutter release at slow speeds, use a cable release; this screws into a cable-release socket in the camera.

Miscellaneous Equipment

A well-organized camera bag can greatly simplify photographing at night. To cut down on confusion, pack only those things you have a real expectation of using. Segregate color and black-and-white film for quick, correct reloading. Pack special items such as cable releases and special-effects filters in specific locations in the case for handy access. Replace them in their proper places after use for quick re-access.

Do not overlook the one ingredient that night shooting lacks—plentiful light. A small penlight or pocket flashlight will provide enough illumination for reading meters, camera settings, and film data sheets even on the darkest nights.

Dealing with Light at Night

The biggest problem in photographing at night is the wide variety of light sources that must be dealt with. Outdoors in daylight, problems concern themselves with sun and shade—but outdoors in the evening, you will be confronted with moonlight, fluorescent, incandescent, neon, street lights, and many other types of light.

Since many night pictures contain strong light sources, unusual mood shots can be created by throwing the camera out of focus to obtain abstract light shapes and by using diffusion screens or diffraction gratings in front of the lens to break up the light source into interesting patterns. Or, by holding one or two pieces of wire screen or nylon stocking in front of the lens, you can create a "star" around the light. As you experiment with these techniques, you will discover many other ways of dealing with light at night.

Extreme Contrast

Very often in available-light night photography, you will run into situations in which the separation between shadow and highlight areas is so great that it is extremely difficult to reproduce both equally well. These are situations of extreme contrast.

In order to obtain a usable photograph under such conditions, you will have to decide exactly what you want in your reproduction of the scene. You can decide, for example, that either the highlight or shadow area is more important, and expose for that area alone. The result can be a very dramatic photograph. Or, you may decide that it is important to have detail in both the highlight and shadow areas. In this case, you can expose for the shadows; open up one or two stops, and then underdevelop to retain some gradation and detail in the highlights. By this technique, you will gain a compromise between high and low tonal values, though it is impossible to completely reproduce the entire range of shadow-to-light values. Such extreme ranges are beyond the film's ability.

Another way of handling extreme contrast in addition to the overexpose-underdevelop method is to use a soft-working developer, such as Kodak Microdol-X or Kodak developer D-23. With these developers, emulsion speed is maintained without blocking the highlights. Then print on a normal contrast paper.

When shooting color, the extremes of night lighting play an important role. Color film lacks the contrast latitude of black-and-white film, so exposure should be made for correct detail in the highlight areas. Otherwise, highlights will be washed out.

"Scapes"

"Scapes" are among the most popular of all photographic subjects—even at night. Seascapes, landscapes, and cityscapes all offer many exciting picture subjects at night when they appear in completely different moods than by day.

Many photographers tend to set their cameras at infinity and use a small lens opening to get depth of field—but often these pictures are unexciting and unimaginative. Why not experiment with different *f*-stops? And instead of attempting to capture the entire scene, spend a little time searching out an unusual angle from which to take your picture, or concentrate on a small segment of the total scene that seems to have a special meaning to you? Then isolate it through selective focus with the background or foreground thrown out of focus by a large lens opening.

The easiest time to take these pictures is at dusk, just after the sun has gone down. This will allow you to work at faster shutter speeds and to register more detail and separation between sky and foreground.

If the sky does not register dark enough to appear as night in your first print, burn-in this area after you have given the rest of the print the proper amount of exposure.

Seascapes. The romance and mystery of the sea has captured man's imagination for centuries. Here

Situations of extreme contrast, where it is impossible to reproduce both highlight and shadow equally well, may result in dramatic photographs. In this photograph, only the highlights were exposed for. Photo by Ed Knapp.

Time exposures help record more detail after the sun goes down. Just after sunset, the sky may still retain its colors, adding great drama to the picture. Photo by Ray Atkeson.

is one of the most exciting areas of scenic photography, for the seas, rivers, and other large bodies of water reflect a myriad of moods. Sunsets, twilight, night, and pseudo-night shots perhaps best reflect to the viewer the mystery of the sea.

Water acts as a strong reflector. Thus, there are many unusual patterns of light to be caught at any hour, from reflections, to moonlight, to dancing sunlight underexposed to create an unusual night effect. Exposures made with apertures from $f/11$ to $f/22$ tend to change bright light reflections on water into diamond-shaped, and other unusual patterns.

True night shots of the sea are best undertaken during a full moon. The time exposures make a tripod or other firm camera support a must. The motion of the waves can be used to lend a note of liveliness if you include some static element such as rocks, driftwood, or shoreline in the foreground.

Landscapes. Perhaps the most important element in landscape photography is design, for without a good sense of design, the most unusual and beautiful landscapes will be boring when ineptly captured on film. You cannot, of course, rearrange your subject matter when dealing with scapes, but you can interpret nature in your own way through choice of angle of view, lens, lighting, or through film choice and method of printing.

Different weather conditions, such as rain, snow, fog, and mist, will help to capture unusual moods in landscapes. To strengthen your creative eye, choose a landscape near you and photograph it over a period of time under these many varying conditions. This will help you to know what to look for in future situations.

Night and pseudo-night photographs necessarily sacrifice the fine detail and texture that can hold interest in your daytime landscapes. Try to pick out interesting masses and shapes to include in the composition. The eerie silhouette of a single tree against the moon and sky, or a bare foreground branch with the moon behind it out of focus, will maintain interest by their strong design.

Cityscapes. A third exciting subject is the cityscape, as revealed in its patterns and design. This subject never seems to lose its power over photographers. In fact, if a guess could be ventured as to which night subject has been photographed more than any other, it would no doubt prove to be the city.

The magic seems to lie in the fact that each city has its own personality, and this personality seems to exert itself most at night. Trying to capture the personality on film is a challenge to a photographer.

Floodlit Landmarks

Many cities floodlight their most famous landmarks, buildings, and monuments at night. These prove to be ideal subjects for night photography, and

Floodlit landmarks are ideal subjects for night photography. Unless a view camera is used, choose a distant enough viewpoint to avoid severe, upward camera tilt and the distortion that will result.

Night Photography

there is no reason to settle for a standard, commercial picture postcard to document your travels, when you can quite easily take a personal souvenir of your own.

Unless you own a view camera—the architectural photographer's standard tool—with its perspective-correcting adjustments, you should choose a distant enough viewpoint to avoid severe, upward camera tilt and resulting distortion. For natural-looking results, plus a large image size, shoot from a distance, and use a moderate telephoto lens or crop the normal lens negative when printing.

When shooting a building, study it from a variety of viewpoints. The main facade will doubtlessly be well lit and easily photographed. But shot head-on, the building may well appear very flat and lack detail. If you shoot from a corner angle, you will achieve dimension by including the bright facade and a less well-illuminated side. You will also pick up shadow detail on any facade embellishment.

Light and Light Patterns

Moving and stationary lights give a special mood to the night. A time exposure of moving lights will register as a light streak and paint its way across the film in many interesting patterns. To liven up night scenics, include a street with the lights of moving cars. For variation, shoot first in a standing position, crouching to the level of the car lights, and then from a higher point of view.

Streaks of light from moving vehicles, obtained by making time exposures, add interest and vitality to night photographs. Photo by Peter Gales.

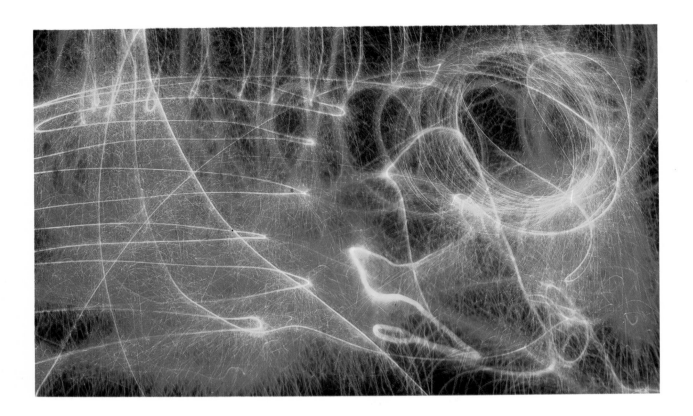

The moving water of public fountains is an example of another form of moving lights. By exposing at a medium or slow shutter speed, the main subject will be recognizable, but the bright water within the picture will create semi-abstract patterns.

Or, you may move the lights yourself for a more abstract approach. Make an exposure of a scene including lights to establish the basic forms. Then, move the camera while the lens is still open (on "T"). Another way to do this is to move the camera throughout the entire exposure. There is no real control in "painting with lights." You can only control the amount of light reaching the film.

A filter-like attachment, called a diffusion screen, will produce soft halos around bright light sources in a picture. A diffraction grating, window screen, or piece of stretched nylon stocking held in front of the camera during exposure will create a star pattern around lights. With the addition of more layers, the star effect is increased by four points for each layer. If you use more than one, increase the original exposure by one third for each additional layer.

Pseudo-Night Pictures

Some of the most dramatic night pictures are created under bright sunlight—a technique long employed by low-budget moviemakers. The trick is in underexposing. The most startling effects come from shooting directly toward or into the sun, with a backlighted effect for trees, boats, animals, or people in the foreground. Water that is backlighted turns

into dancing diamond-like patterns, and all other foreground objects become dark silhouettes.

Because of the intensity of light, it is preferable to use a slow film for pseudo-night shots. For example, Kodak Panatomic-X film, rated at EI 40, will often be exposed at *f*/22 at 1/1000 sec. The brighter the light, particularly when shooting into the sun, the higher the camera settings will be. Take a reflected-light reading from the brightest light source in the composition. No other areas matter because they will all become silhouettes. In addition to the meter reading, also bracket several stops less or several speeds faster. You may have to underexpose as much as eight to ten stops for the really stark effects. A neutral density filter can be used to cut down light coming into the camera without disturbing color or

tonal balance in the picture. These filters come in densities demanding up to a 16× increase in exposure, and allow for pseudo-night shots even on high-speed films.

You can also use a red filter if you are caught with high-speed black-and-white film in your camera, and a marvelous pseudo-night subject presents itself. A medium red filter (Wratten A) has a filter factor of 8, which reduces exposure the equivalent of three stops. The effect of this underexposure will be a thin negative, similar to those taken at night. Very often, pseudo-night pictures are most effectively printed on high-contrast papers. Experiment to discover your personal preference.

For color pseudo-night shots, a gross underexposure shot directly into the sun will produce a basi-

(Above) Many sports events take place at night, and the opportunity should not be missed to capture them on film. Bright stadium lights usually provide enough illumination for photographing at speeds fast enough to stop most action. Photo by Paul Bereswill.

(Left) Available light from a source behind the camera created this black-and-white composition.

Night Photography

cally black-and-white picture. A blue filter used with color film will yield cool, seemingly moonlit results.
• *See also:* AVAILABLE-LIGHT PHOTOGRAPHY; EXISTING-LIGHT PHOTOGRAPHY; FILTERS; LANDSCAPE PHOTOGRAPHY.

Further Reading: Gregory, Tappan. *Nature Photography at Night.* Denver, CO: Denver Museum of Natural History, 1952; Hepworth, T. C. *Evening Work for Amateur Photographers.* New York, NY: Arno Press, repr. of 1890 ed.

Nitric Acid

Rarely used in photography, nitric acid (aquafortis) is regularly used for the preparation of silver nitrate in film manufacture. It was occasionally used as a preservative for pyro, in the silver bath of the wet-collodion process, and in some tray cleaners.
Formula: HNO_3
Molecular Weight: 63.02

It is a heavy, transparent or slightly yellowish liquid.

DANGER: Nitric acid emits irritating fumes and is highly corrosive. It will burn skin if spilled upon it, and is intensely poisonous. It reacts violently with alcohol and forms explosive compounds with many other materials.

6-Nitrobenzimidazole Nitrate

An antifoggant used in developers and prebaths, also known as Kodak anti-fog no. 2.
Formula: $C_7H_6N_3O_2.HNO_3$
Molecular Weight: 210

This antifoggant is made up of colorless crystals or white powder that is soluble in water.
• *See also:* ANTIFOGGANT.

Non-Silver Processes

While the overwhelming majority of current commercially successful photographic processes use silver halides, there are many processes—some old, some quite new—that use other light-sensitive materials. As yet, none of the materials has the sensitivity or the amplification capability of silver halides, so these processes are presently useful primarily for printing and copying procedures.

There are several classes of materials that can be used for non-silver photographic processes. One includes the salts of metals other than silver. It has been shown that some salts of iron, lead, and platinum are also light-sensitive to some extent, and many processes have used these materials.

Another class of light-sensitive materials is sensitized colloids, which are selectively hardened by the action of light. A third class comprises dyestuffs or dye intermediates, which are bleached by exposure to radiant energy.

In addition, there are a number of other experimental and commercially available processes that combine light sensitivity with unique methods of image formation. These processes combine the effect of light or other radiation, heat, pressure, internal chemical reaction, and electrical energy to record the image, amplify the effects of radiation, and fix the image produced. Such processes or materials include electrophotography, photoresists, and vesicular imaging.

Metallic Processes

One of the oldest types of non-silver processes is based on the use of light-sensitive iron salts; such processes include blueprint, cyanotype, and others. The kallitype process uses the light-sensitive iron salt as a catalyst, with the final image produced in silver. Platinum and palladium printing are variations of the kallitype process with the final image produced in platinum or palladium metal.

Lead salts are used primarily in combination with other light-sensitive materials.

Light-Sensitive Colloids

In 1824, Joseph Nicéphore Niépce discovered that an asphaltic material known as "bitumen of Judea" was light-sensitive. If exposed to strong light, it became insoluble in certain oils. More recent processes depended upon the fact that colloids, such as albumin and gelatin, can be sensitized with a bichromate that, with exposure to light, makes the colloid insoluble in water. Processes based on variations of this basic mechanism include carbon and carbro printing, oil and bromoil processes, and gum-bichromate printing.

Light-Sensitive Dyes

Certain dyes and dye intermediates, such as diazo dyes, are light-sensitive and can be used as the basis for printing processes. Several current processes use azo dye-producing systems to provide direct positive images, most frequently with ammonia-fume development. Other processes use diazo compounds alone or in combination with metal salts to produce negative images.

Other Non-Silver Processes

Most modern office copiers are electrophotographic. They use an electrically charged surface as an image receptor. Exposure to light modifies the charge so that powdered pigment adheres to produce a transferable image.

Photoresists work primarily on the ability of ultraviolet radiation or light to cause changes in polymers that affect their solubility.

Photopolymers form the basis for a wide range of commercial processes for printing plates, electronics manufacture, and image-transfer systems.

Vesicular imaging consists in the process of generating a gas upon exposure and development (frequently by heat) to produce an image of minute bubbles encapsulated in an emulsion. The bubble image can be designed either to reflect or refract light so that the image appears as either negative or positive, depending upon the viewing method or support material.
• *See also:* BLUEPRINT PROCESS; BROMOIL PROCESS; CARBON AND CARBRO PRINTING; CYANOTYPE; ELECTROPHOTOGRAPHY; GUM-BICHROMATE PRINTING; KALLITYPE; PHOTOFABRICATION; PHOTORESIST; PLATINUM PRINT PROCESS; XEROGRAPHY.

  Notch Codes

Sheet films are identified by a series of notches in one narrow end. The notches serve two purposes: (1) identification of the type of film, and (2) location of the emulsion side of the film.

When a sheet film is held with the narrow end upward so that the notches are in the upper right-hand corner, the emulsion is on the upper surface of the film, facing the photographer. This makes it easy to identify the emulsion side in complete darkness when loading film holders or handling film for other purposes.

A notch code in the upper right-hand corner of sheet film makes it easy to identify the emulsion side of the film in complete darkness.

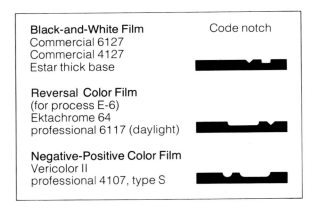

Notch codes for several Kodak sheet films are shown here.

The accompanying illustrations show the notch codes used for several Kodak sheet films. Other manufacturers use similar distinctive notching, located at the same place on the film edge.
• *See also:* FILMS AND PLATES.

Numerical Aperture

In photography, the aperture of a lens is usually given in terms of the f-stop, that is, the ratio of diameter of the entrance pupil to the focal length. In microscopy, however, the f-stop is not a useful measure for several reasons; and instead, a figure called "numerical aperture" (abbreviated NA) is used. This measure is defined in terms of the angle between the most extreme ray entering the lens from the object side and the axis of the lens system. If the angle is represented by α, then the NA is:

$$N \sin \alpha$$

where: N is the refractive index of the medium in which the object lies. Where both object and image are in air, $N = 1$, and the NA is simply equal to the sine of the angle of the entering ray.

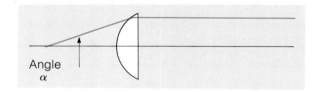

Numerical aperture is equal to the sine of the angle (α) of the most extreme ray entering the lens.

Because the basic formula contains the refractive index of the medium in which the object lies, it is possible to determine an NA for a lens when used in water, or in oil, as is frequently done in biological work.

There is, of course, a relationship between the NA and the f-number of a lens, provided both object and image are in air. In this case, the relationship is as follows:

$$f\text{-stop} = \frac{1}{2\ NA}$$

Thus, a microscope objective normally having an NA of 0.25, when used in air has an f-stop of:

$$\frac{1}{2 \times 0.25} = f/2$$

NUMERICAL APERTURE IN RELATIONSHIP TO f-NUMBER

Numerical Aperture	f-Number
0.0175	f/28.7
0.0349	f/14.3
0.0523	f/9.55
0.0698	f/7.15
0.0872	f/5.74
0.1737	f/2.88
0.2588	f/1.93
0.3420	f/1.46
0.4226	f/1.18
0.5000	f/1.00
0.5736	f/0.872
0.6428	f/0.778
0.7071	f/0.707
0.7660	f/0.653
0.8192	f/0.610
0.8660	f/0.577
0.9063	f/0.552
0.9397	f/0.532
0.9659	f/0.518
0.9848	f/0.508
0.9962	f/0.502
1.0000	f/0.500

It is possible to make a table relating the NA to the f-stop, remembering always that both object and image must be in air.

If the NA $= N \sin \alpha$ and the f-stop $= 1/2$ NA, then the f-stop can be directly given as:

$$\frac{1}{2N \sin \alpha}$$

This leads to the conclusion that since the sine of an angle can never exceed 1.0 and the refractive index of air is 1.0, then the maximum aperture any lens system used in air can have is:

$$\frac{1}{2 \times 1 \times 1} = f/0.5$$

This does not hold true in the case of microscope objectives used with the object immersed in oil. Such liquid media may have refractive indexes as high as 1.5; in this case the maximum NA possible is 1.5 $\sin \alpha = 1.5$, and the corresponding f-stop would be $f/0.33$, a value that is quite impossible for camera lenses.

• *See also:* f-Number; f-Stop; Photomicrography.

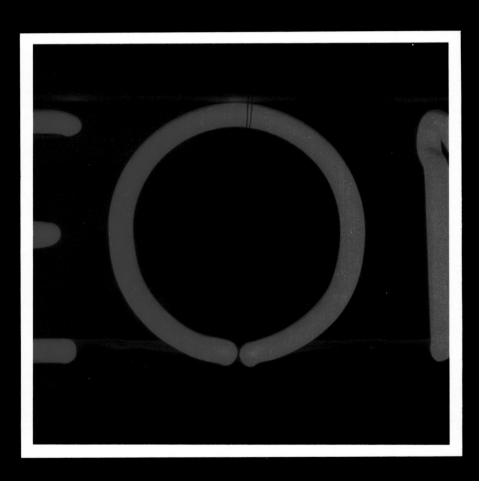

Optics

Optics is a branch of physical science that deals with light, its propagation, and its interaction with matter. This includes reflection, refraction, and absorption in optical devices containing lenses, mirrors, prisms, and so on. It is also concerned with the physiological aspects of sight. For convenience in this Encyclopedia, the nature and basic behavior of light are covered in the article LIGHT. The aspects of light that have to do with sight are included in the articles COLOR THEORY and VISION. The article LENSES includes information about the manufacture and use of camera lenses. This article starts where the article LIGHT leaves off, and develops the optical concepts of importance to photography.

The Nature of a Photographic Subject

A viewer sees, and a camera takes pictures of various subjects in a scene. In order for either to be possible, there must be light. Light is a form of energy that radiates from a source, travels in straight lines to the subjects, and reflects off the subjects in many ways. Some of the light comes from each point in the subject in straight lines to the viewpoint or camera position. Some subjects emit light (lamps, stars, the sun), and some subjects direct light to the camera by scattering (the sky). But most subjects are seen and photographed by the light they reflect.

Each point on a reflection-type subject acts as a secondary radiating source of light, modifying the incident light according to the type of reflector it is. If it is a specular reflector, it reflects the incident rays according to the law of reflection; if it is a diffuse reflector, it reflects the rays in all directions. When the subject is typical, its reflectivity is semi-specular, and it reflects some light specularly and some diffusely. If it has high reflectivity, it reflects much of the incident light and is a light-toned subject; if it has low reflectivity, it absorbs much of the light, reflects little, and is a dark-toned subject. If its reflectivity is selective, it reflects chromatically and appears colored. If its reflectivity is non-selective, it reflects achromatically and appears neutral (white, gray, black).

If a subject point receives direct illumination from the source (is in direct light), the incident light on it will be higher, so that the amount of light reflected (not the percentage) will be higher than if it is shadowed and receives only indirect light reflected from other subjects or from the sky (scattered light).

Some of the light from each subject point is reflected in the direction of the viewpoint. An eye placed at the viewpoint sees the subject by the use of this light. Strictly speaking, the eye does not see the subject itself; it sees the light being reflected from the subject and forms it into an image on the retina. A camera at the same viewpoint forms an image on the film, and this image is formed from the light reflected from all the subject points.

Image Formation with a Pinhole

Nearly all of optics is involved with various ways of forming images. The simplest way to illustrate the basic formation of an image is with a pinhole camera. The pinhole camera is aimed at a subject. Those rays of light being reflected by each subject point in the exact direction of the pinhole all enter the pinhole and continue in their straight-line direction and illuminate the film.

Each ray of light is characteristic of the subject reflectivity. If the subject is light and directly illuminated, the light rays from the subject point, to the pinhole, to the film will have relatively high brightness. If the subject is red (a selective, chromatic reflection), the ray will have more light with wavelengths between 600 and 700 nm than it will have light of shorter wavelengths. By the geometry of straight lines, the film will have an image on it that has the visual aspects of the subject. It will be light where the subject is light, dark where the subject is dark, and colored where the subject is colored, because the light being reflected from each subject point has these characteristics, and it is the summation of the light from all the subject points that creates the optical image.

If the film is moved closer to the pinhole, each subject image on the film gets smaller; if the film is

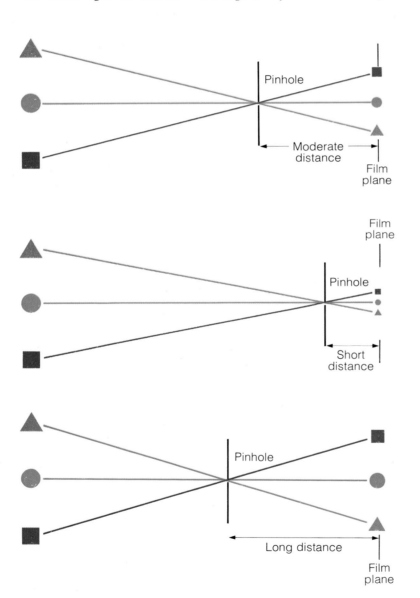

(Top) If the film is held at a moderate distance from the pinhole, the images will be medium-sized. (Center) Images formed by a pinhole will be smaller if the film is moved closer to the pinhole. (Bottom) If the film is moved farther from the pinhole, the subject images will be larger.

moved farther from the pinhole, each subject image gets larger. Considered geometrically, a pinhole that has a diameter just large enough to let single rays of light come through would create a perfectly sharp image of all subjects, regardless of their distance away. In practice, a pinhole that small would create an image so dim that it would take a long time to expose. Further, an extremely fine pinhole causes considerable diffraction of light, so that in practice, a pinhole produces a less-than-sharp image. If the pinhole is made larger to brighten the image for shorter exposure times and to reduce the effects of diffraction, the image loses sharpness because the larger pinhole lets in more rays of light from each subject point, and these rays overlap with adjoining points, thus reducing the sharpness. The practical answer in image formation is to use a lens to form the image rather than a pinhole.

The Lens

When a ray of light enters through the polished surface of a piece of glass at an angle, it is bent at an angle toward the normal—the perpendicular at that point on the surface. This is *refraction,* and it occurs because the light travels slower in the glass than it does in air. The exact angle can be computed using Snell's law:

$$\sin I' = \frac{\sin I}{N}$$

where: angle *I'* is the refracted angle, angle *I* is the incident angle, and *N* is the index of refraction of the glass.

If the glass has plane parallel surfaces, as plate glass does, the ray comes out of the other side of the glass going in the same direction it entered the glass, but displaced somewhat. If, however, the sides of the glass are plane but not parallel, they intersect in a line. Glass so shaped is called a prism.

If a ray of light enters one surface of a prism, it bends toward the normal. Then when it leaves the other side, it is bent again, but away from the normal to the second surface. Because the normal of the second glass surface is angled in reference to the normal of the first surface, a prism makes the light bend twice in the same direction. If two such prisms are placed base to base, the two parallel

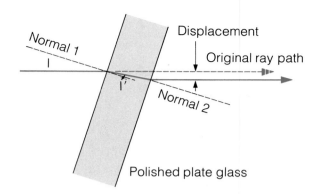

Refraction occurs as a ray of light enters a piece of polished plate glass and is bent at an angle toward the normal. Angle *I'* is the refracted angle and angle *I* is the incident angle.

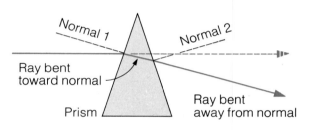

A prism makes the light bend twice in the same direction, because the normal of the second glass surface is angled in reference to the normal of the first surface.

rays of light will intersect. If other pairs of rays of light are put through the prism, each pair intersects at a different distance from the prism. If a number of prisms are made, and the unused parts are tacked up, the angles on the prisms can be changed so that all the rays intersect at a common point on the line where the bases meet. If the number of faces are increased to an infinite number, the prism faces blend to form curves that are arcs of circles, and a cylindrical lens is formed. A cylindrical lens forms an image that is a straight line from parallel rays of light. If the two cylindrical surfaces are replaced with spherical surfaces, a spherical lens is formed. A spherical lens forms an image that is a point from parallel

(Top) If two prisms are placed base to base, two entering parallel rays of light equidistant from the bases will intersect after passing through the prisms. Rays at other distances from the base will not intersect at the same point. (Center) If segments of prisms are stacked up, the angles can be changed so that all rays intersect at a point where the bases meet. (Bottom) By increasing the number of prism faces to an infinite number, they blend to form arcs of circles. These can be the cross section of a cylindrical lens or a spherical lens.

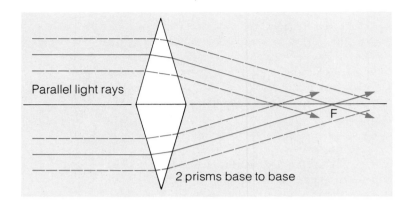

Parallel light rays

F

2 prisms base to base

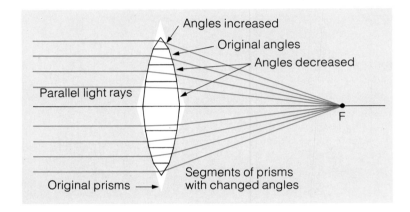

Angles increased

Original angles

Angles decreased

Parallel light rays

F

Original prisms

Segments of prisms with changed angles

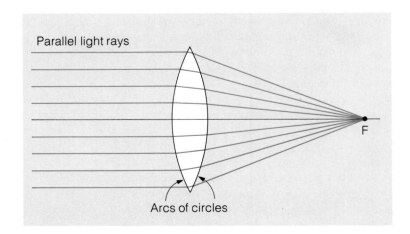

Parallel light rays

F

Arcs of circles

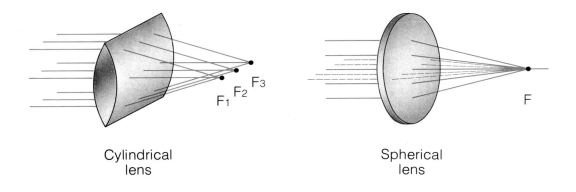

Cylindrical
lens

Spherical
lens

In a cylindrical lens, light parallel to the lens axis forms a line *image. In a spherical lens, light parallel to the lens axis forms a* point *image.*

rays of light. The word *lens,* without adjectives, almost always refers to a spherical lens.

There are three types of spherical lens surfaces. A curve that is like the surface of a section of a ball is a *convex* surface; it curves outward from the lens edges to the center of the lens. A surface that curves inward from the edges to the center—that is hollow like a cave—is a *concave* surface. A lens can also have a flat or *plane* surface.

A circle size is defined by its radius. The curvature of a spherical surface is defined by its radius of curvature. If the radius of curvature is short compared to the lens diameter, the curve is strong. When the radius of curvature is long compared to the lens diameter, the curve is weak. A plane surface is very weak; its radius of curvature is infinitely long.

The spherical lens forming a point image is a biconvex lens; both surfaces are convex spherical curves. It is also called a positive lens—thicker in the middle than at the edges. Positive lenses form real images that can be used to expose film. If a ground glass is placed in the position of a real image, the image can be seen. Sometimes positive lenses are called *crown* lenses because they are usually made of crown glass.

A *negative lens* is thinner in the middle than it is at the edges. This type of lens does not form real images; it forms virtual images. A virtual image is one that can be seen by looking through the lens, but cannot be focused on a ground glass or film.

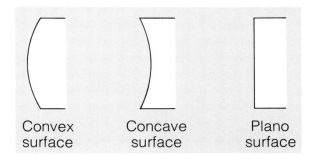

Convex
surface

Concave
surface

Plano
surface

The three types of spherical lens surface are: convex, concave, and plano.

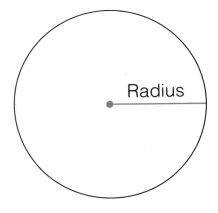

Radius

The size of a circle, or the curvature of a lens, is defined by its radius.

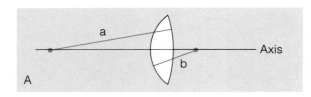

A

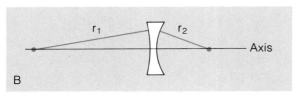

B

(A) The curvature of a spherical surface is weak if the radius of curvature is long compared to the lens diameter. (B) The curve is strong if the radius of curvature is short compared to the lens diameter.

A negative lens forms virtual images rather than real images; it is thinner in the middle than it is at the edges. The radii of curvature are designated as r_1 and r_2.

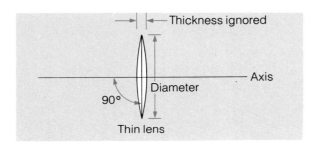

A positive thin lens has a diameter and a circumference. It also has an axis that passes through the center of the lens and is perpendicular to the planes formed by the intersections of the two polished curves and the lens edge.

Characteristics of Thin Lenses

In discussing the characteristics of lenses, the concept of a *thin* lens is normally used. A thin lens is a lens whose thickness is ignored for purposes of illustration. The characteristics of real lenses are quite similar, but with minor modifications. A positive thin lens has several important characteristics. Being round, it has a diameter and a circumference. It also has an axis, which is the line connecting its two centers of curvature. The axis therefore passes through the center of the lens and is perpendicular to the planes formed by the intersections of the two curves and the lens edge.

Focal Length. When light from a point at a great distance reaches the lens, its rays are essentially parallel. If the lens is placed so that its axis is parallel to the light rays, the lens bends the light rays to form an image point, also on the axis. The distance between the lens and this image point is the *focal length* of the lens. If the curves are weak, the focal length of the lens will be relatively long. If the curves are strong, the focal length will be relatively short. If the index of refraction is high, the focal length will be shorter than if the index of refraction is low.

Light rays from a point at a great distance reaching the lens are essentially parallel. The lens bends the light rays to form an image point, or focal point, on the axis if the lens is placed with its axis parallel to the light rays. The focal length of the lens is the distance between the lens and this focal point.

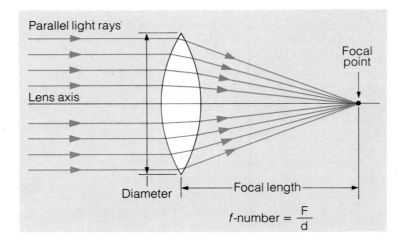

$$f\text{-number} = \frac{F}{d}$$

Optics

An equation that can be used to find the focal length of a lens is:

$$\frac{1}{F} = (n - 1) \left(\frac{1}{r_1} - \frac{1}{r_2}\right)$$

where: F is the focal length, n the index of refraction, and r_1 and r_2 the radii of curvature.

Example: n = 1.5, r_1 = 50 mm, and r_2 = 100 mm.

$$\frac{1}{F} = (1.5 - 1) \left(\frac{1}{50} - \frac{1}{100}\right)$$

$$\frac{1}{F} = 0.5 \times \left(\frac{1}{50} + \frac{1}{100}\right) = \frac{0.5 \times 3}{100} = \frac{1.5}{100}$$

$$1.5F = 100$$
$$F = 67 \text{ mm}$$

f-Numbers. The speed of a lens is given in values called f-numbers. The f-number is equal to the focal length divided by the diameter. The f is written as an italicized, lower-case letter. (In scientific optics, the letter N is often used to designate the speed of a lens. The value of N is the reciprocal of the f-number, and is shown as $N = 1:f$.)

Example: A lens has a diameter of 1 inch and a focal length of 4 inches; therefore, it has a speed of $f/4$.

Camera lenses are rated by speed: The lower the f-number, the greater the speed and the faster the lens. Camera lenses have adjustable diaphragms that *stop down* the lens. That is, they change the working lens speed. The lens speed is based on its maximum aperture—in the example above, $f/4$.

If the diaphragm is changed to have an opening of ½ inch, the working aperture becomes:

$$\frac{4''}{0.5''} = f/8$$

Although f-numbers are continuously variable, diaphragm settings are always based on an agreed upon series of f-numbers:

$$f/1.0, f/1.4, f/2.0, f/2.8, f/4.0, f/5.6,$$
$$f/8, f/11, f/16, f/22, f/32, f/45, f/64$$

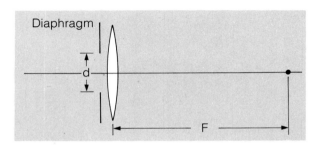

The lower the f-number of a lens, the greater the speed and the faster the lens. The f-number is equal to the focal length of the lens (F) divided by the diameter (d) of the lens. It is possible to stop down the lens if it has an adjustable diaphragm. Therefore, when the diaphragm is changed, the working aperture changes accordingly.

Because the diaphragm is usually placed or *stopped* at these f-numbers, they are called *stops*. Each f-number in the above list is one stop from the next, and each *stop* lets in half as much light as the next lower f-number and two times as much light as the next higher f-number. Therefore, $f/1.4$ lets in twice as much light as $f/2.0$, and four times as much as $f/2.8$; $f/1.0$ lets in 4096 times as much light as $f/64$.

In the f-number series, every other number is twice or half. The series is called a $\sqrt{2}$ series, because a lower number in the series is multiplied by 1.414, the square root of 2, to get the next number. Half of the f-numbers are rounded off—1.4, 2.8, and so on—while the other half are whole numbers—1.0, 2.0, 4.0, and so on.

Focusing. When the light from a subject at a great distance is focused by a lens, the entering light is parallel and it is imaged at a distance from the lens equal to the focal length. Lenses also focus light from objects at closer distances, but the images of close objects are formed at distances from the lens that are greater than the focal length. The closer the object is to the lens, the greater will be the distance between the lens and the image. The accompanying illustration shows the position of four objects: one at a great distance (infinity), and three at various close distances.

The mathematical equation that can be used to calculate the *image distance* (distance between the

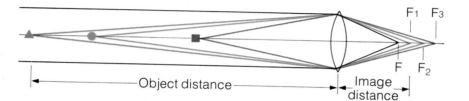

Parallel light rays

Object distance — Image distance

The closer an object is to a lens, the greater the distance is between the lens and the image. When the object distance and the focal length are known, the image distance can be calculated.

lens and the image), when the object distance (subject distance) and focal length are known, is:

$$\frac{1}{F} = \frac{1}{u} + \frac{1}{v}$$

where: F is the focal length, u is the object distance, and v is the image distance. All the values must be in the same units—metres, millimetres, feet, inches, and so on.

Example: $F = 100$ mm, $u = 1000$ mm

$$\frac{1}{100} = \frac{1}{1000} + \frac{1}{v}$$

$$\frac{1}{v} = \frac{1}{100} - \frac{1}{1000} = \frac{9}{1000}$$

$$v = \frac{1000}{9} = 111 \text{ mm (image distance)}$$

When the object distance is infinity,

$\frac{1}{u}$ becomes $\frac{1}{\infty}$, which is zero,

so that the image distance is the same as the focal length. When the object distance is twice the focal length, the image distance is also twice the focal length. In this special case, image size equals object size.

Example: $\frac{1}{100} = \frac{1}{200} + \frac{1}{v}$,

$$\frac{1}{v} = \frac{2}{200} - \frac{1}{200} = \frac{1}{200}$$

$$v = \frac{200}{1} = 200 \text{ (image distance)}$$

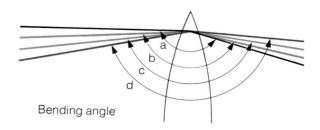

Bending angle

The bending angle for the annular zone of the lens is the angle that the light from the distant object makes with its original path after being bent. If the bending angle of the light path from each distance is measured, it will be the same angle in the same zone.

Bending Power. The accompanying illustration, showing objects at various distances being focused, can be used to show the concept of bending power. The light is being bent only at the periphery of the lens. The angle that the light from the distant object makes with its original path after being bent is the bending angle for that annular zone of the lens. If the bending angle of the light path from each subject is measured, it will be the same angle. In other words, this zone of the lens has a constant bending power.

The bending is greatest at the periphery of the lens. Light coming along the axis is not bent at all. Each concentric circular zone of the lens has a different bending power, but all parts of the circle forming that zone have the same bending power. This is how the lens brings all light reaching it from each subject point to the same point on the image plane.

1814

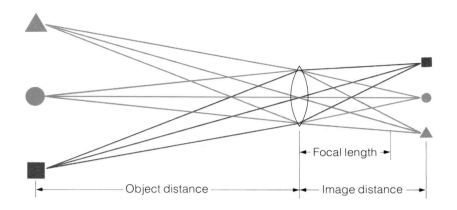

When objects at a close distance from the lens are at different angles from the axis, the light rays from each object point focus in a different position on the film, forming the image.

Focal length

Object distance

Image distance

Image Formation. Up to this point, only objects on the lens axis have been used as examples. In real images, all objects are imaged from points off the axis, except for the one point in the exact center in the picture.

It is relatively easy to understand the image formation by a pinhole, which was discussed earlier. The illustrations on p. 1808 show three colored objects at different distances from the pinhole. Since light travels in straight lines, the light from each point in the objects travels in a straight line and passes through the pinhole to the film. Since each object point is at a different angle to the pinhole, each point is imaged at a different point on the film. The image on the film is made up of light coming from all the subject points, each being positioned by the geometry of the straight-line travel of light.

Image formation by a lens is similar, but slightly more complex. Light rays come from each subject point and radiate in many directions. Those rays that strike the lens from a close subject form a cone—shown in the accompanying diagram as a triangle, which is a cross section of the cone. The ray at the center of the cone passes through the center of the lens without bending, in the same way as the pinhole ray. The other rays that form the cone are bent by the bending power of the lens, so that they fall through the same point on the film as the ray that passed through the center of the lens. The rays from each subject point focus in a different position on the film in the same manner, creating the image. The drawing shows only the outer rays and the central ray of the cone. In reality, the cone from each subject point is full of light rays, each bent to come to focus to form the optical image.

In the article LIGHT, the nature of emitted, transmitted, and reflected light was discussed. Various subjects send different mixes of light to the lens to be imaged. When the subject point is neutral in color, the light coming to the lens is achromatic—an even mix of all colors of light. The image point formed by this light is neutral. If the intensity of the image-forming light is high compared to the other light, the subject is strong, and the light forming the image from that point is strong, or high in intensity. If the subject reflection is colored, the light coming to the lens is chromatic, and it forms a colored image point.

Because of the nature of the light coming from the subject, the image formed by the lens is achromatic or chromatic in various colors, and is light or dark—in other words, the image has the visual characteristics or aspects of the subject. This can easily be seen by looking at the ground glass of a camera. In addition, the image is upside down, as the diagram shows, and is laterally reversed on the surface of the film as well.

When the objects are at a great distance from the lens, the light rays from each point are parallel; the lens bends them to form an image of the point. Furthermore, in a real optical image formed of subjects at different distances from the lens, the focal points are at different distances behind the lens. If the film is placed behind the lens at a distance equal to the focal length, distant objects will be in focus but close objects will not be in

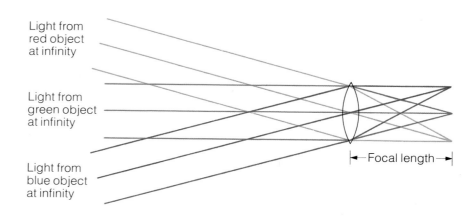

(Right) When objects are at a great distance from the lens, the light rays from each subject point are parallel to other light rays from the same point, but they are not parallel to light rays from other subject points. The image formed by all subject points at a great distance is at a focal-length distance from the lens. (Below) Out-of-focus circles on the film are called circles of confusion. When the circles are so small that they cannot be distinguished by the eye from points in the print or slide, they form acceptably sharp pictures.

Light from red object at infinity

Light from green object at infinity

Light from blue object at infinity

←—Focal length—→

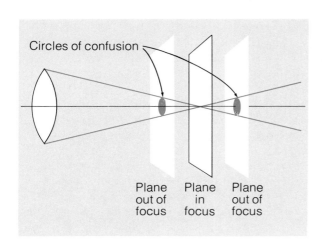

Circles of confusion

Plane out of focus

Plane in focus

Plane out of focus

than the focus distance form circles of confusion. The range of distances at the image plane in which the circles of confusion are acceptably small is called the *depth of focus*.

Depth of Focus. The size of the "just acceptable" circles of confusion depends on the format size. It has been found by experience that the diameter of the just acceptable circle of confusion is about 1/1000 of the focal length of the lens normal for the format, which is equal to the diagonal of the format.

The accompanying table gives the diameters of the circles of confusion normally considered just acceptable. Somewhat smaller circles are used for critical work.

focus. Subjects will be imaged as overlapping circles on the film, rather than as points. Their images will not be sharp; they will be out of focus.

Circles of Confusion. Each out-of-focus circle on the film is called a *circle of confusion*. Because the cone angle becomes greater at wider apertures, the circles of confusion are larger. Stopping the diaphragm down makes the circles of confusion smaller. When they are so small that they can no longer be distinguished by the eye from points in the final print or projected slide, they form acceptably sharp pictures.

When the lens is focused on objects at a certain distance, objects both closer and farther

DIAMETERS OF JUST ACCEPTABLE CIRCLES OF CONFUSION

Format	Diameter	
	Millimetres	Inches
Super 8 cine	0.0165	0.00065
16 mm and 35 mm cine	0.025	0.0010
110 roll	0.03	0.0012
35 mm 126 roll	0.05	0.002
2¼″ X 2¼″	0.08	0.003
2¼″ X 2¾″	0.10	0.004
4 X 5	0.16	0.006
5 X 7	0.22	0.009
8 X 10	0.33	0.013

Optics

Depth of focus is a factor that is of more interest to the camera manufacturer than to the photographer. It is the distance that the film can be away from the optical image of the lens and still produce acceptably sharp images.

The depth of focus varies with a number of factors: the f-number, magnification (which depends on the lens focal length and the distance the lens is focused on), and the diameter of the circle of confusion. Depth of focus is calculated with the following equation:

$$d = c - N \left(\frac{u}{u - f} \right)$$

where: d is the depth at either side of focus, c is the diameter of the circle of confusion, N is the f-number, u is the subject distance, and F is the focal length of the lens.

Depth of Field. The depth of field is the range of distances from the camera that subjects will be imaged with acceptable sharpness, that is, within the depth of focus. Another way to define acceptable sharpness is to relate it to the size of the circles of confusion. Depth of field can be directly related to depth of focus by using the following equation:

$$\text{Depth of Field} = \frac{d}{m^2}$$

It is more useful to know the near limit and far limit of the depth of field for a given set of conditions. When a lens is focused on infinity, the near limit of the depth of field is called the hyperfocal distance. If the lens is focused on the hyperfocal distance, objects at infinity will be in focus, and objects at a distance of one-half the hyperfocal distance will be in focus. This will be the near limit. The hyperfocal distance changes with the variables mentioned above. The following equation can be used to find the hyperfocal distance for a given set of variables:

$$H = \frac{F^2}{f \times c}$$

where: F is the focal length squared, f is the f-number, and c is the diameter of the circle of confusion; F and c values must be in the same units.

Example: F=100 mm, f=8,
c=0.10 mm (0.004 inches)

$$H = \frac{100^2}{8 \times 0.1} = \frac{10,000}{0.8} = 12,500 \text{ mm}$$

or 12.5 metres—about 41 feet. If the lens is focused for a distance of 41 feet, objects from 20.5 feet to infinity will be acceptably sharp.

To find the near and far limits to the depth of field, the hyperfocal distance is found, and the following equations used:

$$\text{Near Limit} = \frac{H \times u}{H + (u - F)}$$

$$\text{Far Limit} = \frac{H \times u}{H - (u - F)}$$

If the above $f/8$ lens is focused at 3 metres, the near limit (NL) and far limit (FL) are:

$$NL = \frac{12,500 \times 3000}{12,500 + (3000 - 100)} =$$

$$\frac{37,500,000}{15,400} = 2435 \text{ mm} = 2.44 \text{ m}$$

$$FL = \frac{37,500,000}{12,500 - 2,900} =$$

$$\frac{37,500,000}{9,600} = 3906 \text{ mm} = 3.91 \text{ m}$$

Many camera lenses have depth-of-field scales marked on them. Many tables are printed showing the depth of field of various focal length lenses at different f-numbers focused at different distances. The KODAK Professional Photoguide has three dials by which depth of field for most cameras larger than 35 mm can be found: one for telephoto lenses, one for normal lenses, and one for wide-angle lenses.

Image Size and Magnification. It is often important to know what the image size is going to be of an object of a given size at a given distance from a lens of a given focal length. The ratio of the image size (I) divided by the object size (O) is called the magnification (m).

$$m = \frac{I}{O}$$

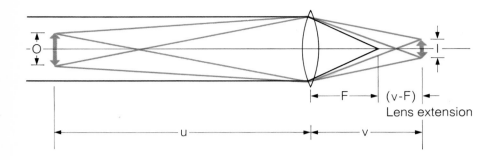

Magnification is the ratio of the image size (I) divided by the object size (O). Magnification is also equal to the ratio of the image distance (v) divided by the object distance (u). The lens is moved to a distance greater than the focal length—the lens extension—when it is focused on an object close to the camera. The lens extension is equal to the ratio of the image distance (r) minus the focal length (F).

The magnification is also equal to the ratio of the image distance divided by the object distance.

$$m = \frac{v}{u}$$

When a lens is focused on an object close to the camera, the lens is moved to a distance greater than the focal length. This amount of movement is called the lens extension.

$$\text{Lens Extension} = v - F \quad \text{and}$$

$$\text{Magnification} = \frac{v - F}{F}$$

Also, when the object distance is known:

$$m = \frac{F}{u - F}$$

This last equation is quite useful.

Example: If a lens focal length is 100 mm, and a 400-mm-long object is 3000 mm from the lens, the image size is found by:

$$m = \frac{100}{3000 - 100} = \frac{100}{2900} = 0.0345$$

The magnification multiplied by the object size gives the image size: $m \times O = I$

400 mm × 0.0345 = 13.8 mm image size

Objects at great distances are said to have an infinity focus. However, when calculating magnification and image size, there is no infinity on earth objects—only in the skies. The infinity for focusing purposes may be 100 feet, but for calculating image size, even distances as great as 100 miles must be used (to find the image size of mountains, for instance).

Magnification values for nearly all camera uses are less than one, while for enlarging they are always greater than one.

From the formulas for magnification, it can be seen that image size is directly affected by the focal length; at great distances it is directly proportional to the focal length.

The accompanying illustration shows three lenses imaging the same object at the same distance. When the focal length is half normal, the image height (h_i) is half normal; when the focal length is twice normal, the image height is twice normal.

The term magnification is also used to relate the image size formed by lenses of focal lengths other than normal. The magnification of the normal lens is said to be 1×, while shorter-focal-length lenses have a magnification factor of less than one, and lenses with focal lengths greater than the normal focal length have magnification factors greater than one.

Magnification Factor =

$$\frac{\text{Focal Length of Lens}}{\text{Focal Length of Normal Lens}}$$

There is yet a third way that the term magnification is used. Often lenses are held close to the eye, to be used as magnifying glasses. How much greater the image appears than the object is in the magnification, and it can be found by the following equation:

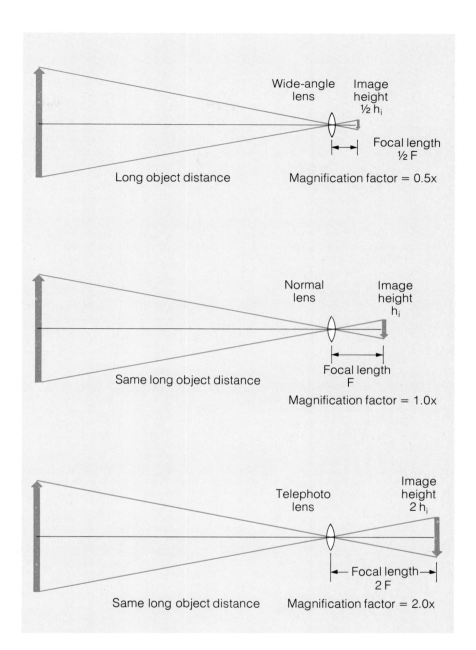

At long object distances, the image size is directly proportional to the lens focal length. When the focal length (F) is half normal, the image height (h_i) is also half normal; when the focal length is twice normal, the image height is twice normal. The magnification factor of a normal lens is 1 $\times$. Shorter-focal-length lenses have magnification factors less than 1, while longer-focal-length lenses have magnification factors greater than 1.

$$\text{Magnification} = \frac{10''}{\substack{\text{focal length} \\ \text{(inches)}}} \text{ or } \frac{250 \text{ mm}}{\substack{\text{focal length} \\ \text{(mm)}}}$$

A magnifying glass with a 2-inch focal length will have a magnification factor of

$$\frac{10''}{2''} = 5\times$$

Things viewed with this lens will look five times larger. It can be called a 5$\times$ magnifying lens.

Real lenses work on the same principles as thin lenses, but are somewhat more complex. They are made of a variety of types of glass and plastic, and have an almost infinite variety of shapes and sizes although all are of seven basic shapes. They do not produce perfect images, but have aberrations.

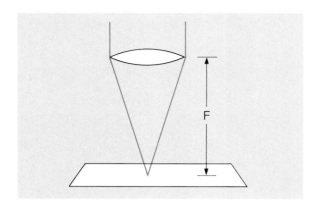

Lenses are often used to magnify objects. The magnification factor depends upon the focal length of the lens.

Most lenses are not simple lenses, but are compound lenses made up of a number of elements in order to reduce the aberrations to tolerable levels. (*See:* ABERRATION.)

Optical Glass and Plastic

In the article LIGHT, the two optical characteristics of transparent matter were discussed: index of refraction and dispersion. It is the refraction that gives the lens its power, and it is dispersion that permits a prism to spread light out into a spectrum.

In real compound lenses, a number of different glass materials with different indexes of refraction and dispersion are required. Fortunately, lens designers have many different optical glasses to choose from and a few transparent plastics from which lenses can be made.

Glass Constituents. Basic glass, like that used to make windows, drinking glasses, bottles, and the myriad of things we use in everyday life, is made of

Flint glass, which results from lead oxides being added to crown glass, has a high index of refraction and dispersion. Barium glasses have high refractive indexes, but relatively low dispersions. Rare-earth glasses have exceedingly high refractive indexes. The index of refraction and dispersion choice is very limited in clear plastic materials.

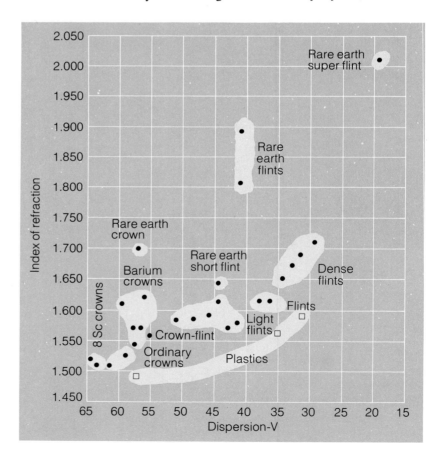

two main constituents: soda ash and sand. A stabilizing ingredient is usually added.

Soda ash is a commercial form of the sodium carbonate used as a photographic chemical. Sand is usually a mixture of a number of rock materials: silicon dioxide, sodium oxide, calcium oxide, magnesium oxide, and so on. The prime sand ingredient is the silicon dioxide. Glass made from soda ash and silica (silicon dioxide) is soluble. Other oxides such as those of calcium, magnesium, barium, and lead are often added, or are present in the sand, to make the glass insoluble or to change its optical characteristics.

Making Optical Glass. The ingredients are heated in crucibles to temperatures in the 1300 to 1540 C (2400 to 2800 F) range. When white hot, they are stirred continuously to thoroughly mix the ingredients. Some glass is allowed to cool slowly in the crucible, and the crucible and glass are then broken into pieces. Slabs are cut with diamond saws from the bigger pieces. Scrap may be remelted with the next batch, unless it is glass that was near the edges of a clay crucible, in which case it is scrapped because of contamination.

Much optical glass is now made in large tanks from which it is extruded onto beds of long rollers that roll the hot glass out to large-sized sheets. These sheets are cut to sizes that can be handled and sold to lens manufacturers as rolled glass. The same furnaces are also used to supply cast blanks for large-sized lenses.

The clay crucibles in which much optical glass has been made contaminate some of the glass, making it useless. In recent years, crucibles made of platinum have been widely used for making glass. Platinum is a non-contaminating metal that retains its strength at the high glass-melting temperatures. Since it is also a precious metal, single crucibles contain tens of thousands of dollars worth of platinum.

Borosilicates added to the basic glass mix give a variety of different refractive indexes and dispersions. Lead oxides added to the basic crown glass change it to a flint glass, which has a high index of refraction and high dispersion. In Germany in 1888, Shott and Abbe offered a series of barium glasses that had high refractive indexes, but relatively low dispersions compared to the indexes of refraction.

In the 1930's, Kodak introduced the rare-earth glasses, which have exceedingly high refractive indexes. Their basic ingredient is boric acid; there is no sand or soda ash in them. Combined with the boric acid are various hydrates and oxides of rare elements, such as thorium and lanthanium, which give the rare-earth glasses their high refractive index.

Many transparent minerals are in the form of crystals, in which the molecules form regular patterns. Most jewels, such as diamonds, and crystalline salts, such as the silver halides, have this pattern. Glass, however, is an uncrystallized mixture and is said to have a *vitreous* condition. This condition is identified as one that does not have a fixed melting point, but goes slowly through a taffy-like stage before becoming a liquid. Vitreous materials are brittle at normal temperatures and tend to chip or flake in curves, resembling a conch shell. They also have the same refracting power in all directions, which crystalline materials do not.

Optical Plastic. There are a few clear plastic materials that are used to make inexpensive lenses. The index of refraction and dispersion choice is very limited in these materials. Polymethyl methacrylate, styrene, and copolymer styrene-acrylonitrile plastics are the mostly commonly used. The manufacturing of lenses from optical glass and plastics is described in the article LENSES.

Real Lenses

Lens Shapes. The thin lens used as a basic example up to this point is a positive biconvex lens. Real positive and negative lenses are made in many shapes to satisfy the requirements of the lens designer in making real photographic lenses, both single and compound. The accompanying illustration shows all the possible shapes achievable by combining convex, concave, and plane surfaces. All the shapes, and variations of them, are used in real lenses.

Where the Light Really Bends. In the discussion of the thin lens, the bending of light by refraction was assumed to be in a plane at the center of the lens. When lens elements are put together to form a compound "thick" lens, it is important to know exactly where the light does bend.

Each ray, except those perpendicular to a surface, actually bends at every glass surface

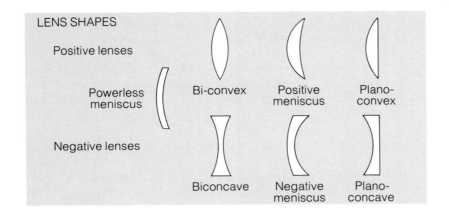

LENS SHAPES

Positive lenses

Powerless meniscus — Bi-convex — Positive meniscus — Plano-convex

Negative lenses

Biconcave — Negative meniscus — Plano-concave

(Left) Shown here are combinations of convex, concave, and plano curves to achieve varying shapes in real lenses.

(Right) Light rays, except those perpendicular to the surface of the lens, bend at every glass surface within the lens. A series of rays entering from each side of the lens intersect at certain points with the final bent rays. The two planes from all the intersections of light rays passing through a lens are known as the first principal plane (P_1) and the second principal plane (P_2). The intersections of P_1 and P_2 are called the front nodal point (N_1) and the rear nodal point (N_2).

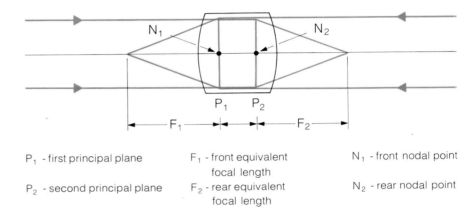

P_1 - first principal plane

P_2 - second principal plane

F_1 - front equivalent focal length

F_2 - rear equivalent focal length

N_1 - front nodal point

N_2 - rear nodal point

within the lens. For the purposes of explaining how the entire lens bends light, it can be assumed that the lens bends light in two principal planes. If a light ray parallel to the axis is drawn through the lens and its final path to the image point on the axis is drawn, then two paths intersect. The accompanying illustration shows a series of rays coming from each side of the lens, and their intersections with the final bent rays. The two planes found from all the intersections are called the *principal planes* of the lens, and the intersections of the principal planes with the lens axis are called the *principal points*.

The principal plane for light coming from the subject to the lens is called the *second principal plane* (P_2), while light put backwards through the lens forms the *first principal plane* (P_1). In normal lenses, both planes will be located within the thickness of the lens. In telephoto lenses, P_2 and N_2 will be located in front of the lens and in front of P_1

and N_1. In reverse-telephoto wide-angle lenses, P_2 and N_2 will be located outside the lens, between the lens and focal plane. Although the bending surfaces of the lens are called planes, they are usually curved, and are a section of a sphere, centered at the focal point.

When a lens is in air, as is the case with most lenses, the principal points coincide with two points called the nodal points. Technically, the nodal points are a pair of points on the lens axis such that any ray, other than an axial ray, that is directed toward the first nodal point emerges from the second nodal point at the same slope at which it entered.

The distance from the second nodal point, N_2, to the focal plane is the equivalent focal length, which is the focal length printed on the lens, and the focal length used in the equations given earlier for thin lenses. The distance from the center of the rear lens surface to the focal plane is the back focal

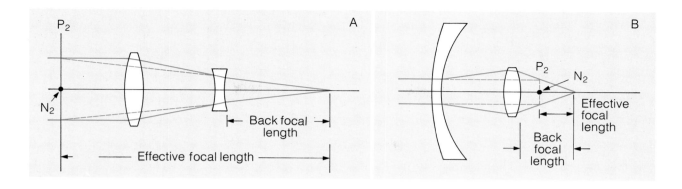

Both planes and points are located within the thickness of a normal lens. (A) In telephoto lenses, P_2 and N_2 are located in front of the lens. (B) In reverse-telephoto wide-angle lenses, P_2 and N_2 are located between the lens and the focal plane.

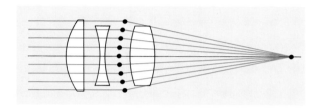

length, or back focus of the lens. Although it is rarely used, the distance from the first principal plane to the front focal point is the front equivalent focal length.

In the equations involving focal length, object distances, and image distances, where thick lenses are involved, the object distance is measured to the front nodal point and the image distance and focal length are measured from the rear nodal point.

Images of Real Lenses. It is assumed in the discussion of thin lenses that light rays from each subject point form a corresponding point in the image. Unfortunately, real lenses form only approximations of points due to the nature of these lenses. The inherent deviations from perfect image-point formation are called aberrations. The entire effort of lens designers in designing real lenses is to reduce the effects of the aberrations to tolerable levels. (*See:* LENSES.) Aberrations are discussed in in the article ABERRATION.

The image plane should be flat and lie in the film plane. Real lenses suffer from field curva-

Spherical Principal Plane

(Left) The bending surfaces of the lens (planes) are a section of a sphere, centered at the focal point.

ture—the focus of rays coming through the lens at an angle tend to focus closer to the lens than do the axial rays.

There are really two image planes formed by rays coming through different areas of the real lens. This effect is called astigmatism. Astigmatism, in addition to causing two focal planes, tends to image each subject point as two lines. The lines imaged in one focal plane are at right angles to the lines imaged in the other focal plane. If the film is placed between the two planes, the object point is imaged as a small diamond-shaped patch. The lens designer tries to get these two planes as flat as possible, as close together as possible, and have the imaged lines as short as possible, so that the image of a point will be as nearly a point in the image as possible. Astigmatism does not occur in the axial region; it is only found in the field.

Light coming through the real lens, parallel to the axis and near the axis, comes to focus at a different point than light parallel to the axis but at a distance from the axis near the rim of the lens aperture. This is *spherical aberration*. The same effect, but with rays that are at an angle to the axis, is called *coma*, because points are imaged in comet shapes.

Dispersion causes light of different colors to focus at different distances from the lens. This is

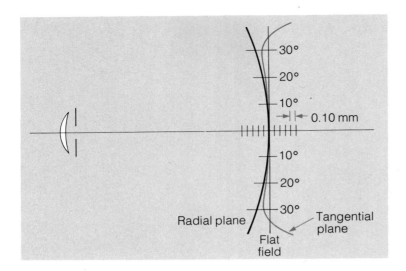

Radial plane

Tangential plane

Flat field

0.10 mm

Rays coming through a real lens at an angle tend to focus closer to the lens than do the axial rays. This is known as field curvature.

longitudinal chromatic aberration. Since the lens has different focal lengths for light of different colors, the images formed by the different wavelengths of light are of different sizes. This shows as color fringing of edges out in the lens field and is called *lateral chromatic aberration.*

Some of the light going through a lens goes past the edges of the diaphragm, and is diffracted—*diffraction* is another aberration. Theoretically a perfect lens would image a point object as a perfect point image. However, diffraction prevents this from happening. With any real lens that has almost perfect correction for aberrations, the image of a point object is a tiny round patch of concentrated light surrounded by faint rings of light. The size of the patch of light varies inversely with the *f*-number, so that a larger aperture lens has the potential of producing a smaller point image. The perfect lens that was just described is one that has no measurable aberrations, and it is said to be diffraction limited.

All these aberrations cause the image of each point object to be a *non-point*—actually a small circle (along the axis) or an odd shape (in the field). Some are improved by stopping down, while others are not. The lens designer tries to make each lens produce as small image non-points as possible, because the smaller they are the better the image definition is.

The manufacturer may not get all the lens elements exactly centered or exactly perpendicular

to the axis. This causes the focal plane to tilt and the point images to be "decentered." Such aberrations are manufacturing, not design, aberrations, but they can also lower image definition.

In the discussion of pinhole image formation, and image formation by a lens, it was assumed that the image would form as an exact replica of the subject—that the magnification would be equal all over the field. In practice, with real lenses, this evenness of magnification is difficult to achieve. When the lens creates an image with different magnification in the axial region than in the field, image *distortion* results. When straight lines near the field edge are imaged as curves convex toward the axis, the aberration is pincushion distortion. When they are imaged concave toward the axis, it is known as barrel distortion.

Illumination of Images. The exposure of images on film is directly dependent on the brightness (luminance) of the optical image. The brightness of the images of all lenses is essentially the same at the same *f*-number. Because of the way exposure meters, tables, and dials are calibrated, the photographer does not usually have to know the exact luminance values of the optical image in order to calculate the exposure. For scientific purposes they are calculated by this equation:

$$E = \frac{t \, \pi \, B}{4N^2}$$

where: E is the image illuminance, t is a constant factor for each lens (it is the transmittance of the lens, usually near 1.0 with modern, coated lenses), B is the luminance of the subject, and N is the f-number. The above equation is for distant objects. For close objects, the equation becomes:

$$E = \frac{t \, \pi \, B}{4N^2 \, (1 + m)^2}$$

where: m is the magnification (image size divided by object size). These equations are for axial-image illumination. Unfortunately, the illumination in the focal plane decreases away from the axis. Because the film is flat, the edges of the film are farther from the lens than its center. Light follows the inverse-square law. By geometry, this factor becomes a $\cos^2$ (cosine square) factor.

If the point image of light is a small circle on the axis, it is spread out into an ellipse in off-axis positions, so that it covers a larger area of film and loses illuminance by a cosine factor. If you put your eye at the corner of the field and look at the back of an opened lens, you do not see it as a circle but as an ellipse. Light coming through the lens at an angle has a smaller opening to come through than axial light. This loses another cosine factor of light. All in all, light reaching a position in the field has lost illuminance by a $\cos^4$ (cosine fourth) factor—that is, the cosine of the angle to the axis.

$$E_a = E_o \cos^4 a$$

This means that the illuminance at an angle a is equal to the illuminance at zero degrees, (the axis) multiplied by the cosine of the angle a multiplied by itself four times. The illuminance of most lenses follows this law pretty closely, although most do not have quite as much actual illuminance as the law indicates. However, due to their unusual light paths, reverse-telephoto wide-angle lenses actually have less loss of illumination in the field than the $\cos^4$ law indicates. Extreme wide-angle lenses of normal design may have less than half the illuminance in the corners of the format than in the center.

In many thick real lenses, the mounts shadow the extreme angular rays, lowering the amount of illumination in the corners of the format at wide apertures. This shadowing effect is called vignetting. Vignetting usually only affects the image at wide apertures and disappears when the lens is stopped down.

As a lens is focused on close objects, the relative aperture at a given f-number decreases, because the lens-to-film distance increases. Hence, for close subjects more exposure must be given. This can be calculated for a change in f-number by the following equations:

$$\text{Effective } f\text{-number} = \frac{v \times N}{F}$$

$$\text{Effective } f\text{-number} = N(m + 1)$$

where: N is the marked f-number, v is the object distance, F is the focal length, and m is the magnification.

Alternatively, a factor to multiply the exposure time can be found by the following equation, using the indicated f-number:

$$\text{Exposure Factor} = (m + 1)^2$$

These equations are valid for lenses that are symmetrical. However, for nonsymmetrical lenses, such as telephoto lenses and reverse-telephoto wide-angle lenses, the following equations should be used.

$$P = \text{Pupillary Magnification} = \frac{\text{Rear Pupil Diameter}}{\text{Front Pupil Diameter}}$$

$$\text{Effective } f\text{-number} = \frac{N(m + P)}{P}$$

$$\text{Exposure Factor} = \left(\frac{m}{P} + 1\right)^2$$

Sometimes a lens is reversed at very close distances to improve image quality. When the lens is reversed, the value of P changes because the front and rear pupil diameters are interchanged.

Illumination measurement is covered in the article LIGHT: UNITS OF MEASUREMENT.

Field Coverage. Lenses are designed to be used with certain format sizes of film. Film formats are rectangular, while the image of a lens is round. The circular field of the lens must be large enough to cover the corners of the film for two characteristics: illumination and definition. As indicated above, the illumination drops off as the field angle increases due to the $\cos^4$ factors and possibly vignetting. The designer usually tries to have the corner illumination no more than a half stop less than the axial illumination.

Usually, the aberrations cause the definition to become unusable at smaller field angles than the illumination. The designer tries to get the aberrations corrected for just the required field angle, because correcting for a wider field means that the degree of the corrections within the field usually have to be lowered or the lens has to be made unnecessarily expensive.

Lenses designed for view cameras must have a larger field coverage to allow for the use of swings and tilts.

Other Optics Subjects

The general subject of optics is usually considered to cover the study of light, its nature and behavior (especially refraction and reflection), illumination, lenses, prisms, mirrors, and various types of optical instruments, including cameras, telescopes, and microscopes. In this Encyclopedia, the subject is treated in various articles. As indicated in the first paragraphs of this article, the articles LIGHT, OPTICS, and LENSES are designed as a sequential series of articles.

There are special articles on REFLECTANCE, REFLECTORS, MIRRORS, and MIRROR LENSES that cover the reflection segment of optics. The article LIGHT: UNITS OF MEASUREMENT covers the measurement of the intensity of light and illumination measurement. Microscopes are covered in the article PHOTOMICROGRAPHY, while photography with telescopes is treated in ASTROPHOTOGRAPHY. As indicated earlier, seeing with light is covered in the article VISION.

• *See also:* ANASTIGMAT; APERTURE; ASTROPHOTOGRAPHY; BACK FOCUS; BRIGHTNESS; CLOSE-UP PHOTOGRAPHY; DEPTH OF FIELD; DEPTH OF FOCUS; DIFFRACTION; FIELD LENS; *f*-NUMBER; FRESNEL LENS; *f*-STOP; HYPERFOCAL DISTANCE; LENSES; LIGHT; LIGHT: UNITS OF MEASUREMENT; MICROPHOTOGRAPHY; PINHOLE CAMERA; PRISMS; RANGEFINDER; SHARPNESS; TELEPHOTOGRAPHY; T-STOP.

Further Reading: Cox, Arthur. *Photographic Optics.* Garden City, NY: Amphoto, 1974; Eastman Kodak Co. *Kodak Photoresist Seminar. Proceedings.* Rochester, NY: Eastman Kodak Co., 1970; Society of Photo-Optical Instrumentation Engineers, Seminar. *Image Assessment and Specifications. Proceedings,* Vol. 46. Palos Verdes Estates, CA: Society of Photo-Optical Instrumentation Engineers, 1974.

Orthochromatic

Strictly speaking, the word "orthochromatic" means "correct color" or "true color." Actually, the word was first coined when it was discovered that adding certain reddish dyes to a UV-plus-blue-sensitive emulsion caused it to become sensitive to green light in addition to the ultraviolet radiation and blue light. Orthochromatic films are not sensitive to red light, but the improvement in the tone reproduction of colors over the former blue-sensitive emulsions was quite substantial, especially for landscape photography.

Today, orthochromatic films have been almost entirely superseded by "panchromatic" (all-color) films, which are sensitive to blue, green, and red. No general-purpose, medium-contrast orthochromatic emulsions are currently made with the exception of Kodak Tri-X ortho film, which finds use in certain branches of commercial and portrait photography. Some special films for lithography and scientific work are made with orthochromatic sensitization. In the case of litho films, the main reason for the green sensitivity is to increase the speed of the film, rather than to improve its color rendition.

• *See also:* EMULSIONS; FISCHER, RUDOLPH.

Oscillograph Recording

The light-beam oscillograph is a "translator." It is one in a series of translators that enables the scientist or engineer to see, in the intelligible form of a graphic record, the magnitude and direction of the physical forces of an event with respect to time. The accompanying diagram represents this series of translators and describes the function of each.

The Light-Beam Oscillograph

The light-beam oscillograph uses a beam of light to record a trace on a piece of photosensitive material. Since there are no mechanical linkages involved, it has the advantage of being able to overlap these traces. Some present-day light-beam oscillographs can simultaneously record up to 60 channels

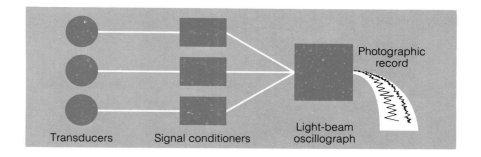

Transducers   Signal conditioners   Light-beam oscillograph   Photographic record

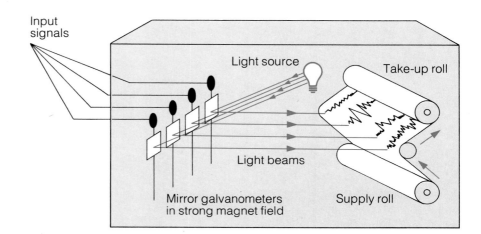

(Above right) Transducers sense the physical stimuli and convert them into usable electrical signals. These signals are amplified and smoothed by signal conditioners before being passed to the oscillograph where they are converted into light-beam movements that are permanently recorded on the photosensitive material. (Right) The light source illuminates all the galvanometers simultaneously. These, in turn, produce individual light beams that are moved across the photosensitive material in direct response to the input signal.

Input signals

Light source   Take-up roll

Light beams

Mirror galvanometers in strong magnet field   Supply roll

of data on a 12-inch-wide sheet of photographic paper or film.

The theory of operation of the light-beam oscillograph is quite simple. The accompanying diagram shows that the light from the lamp is reflected from a tiny mirror in the galvanometer onto a moving roll of sensitized recording film or paper. The diagram is typical of the basic light-beam path and does not attempt to include all the optical surfaces, which vary considerably among different manufacturers. All of these galvanometers are illuminated by a common light source, and each produces one trace on the sensitized material. Since the trace is "written" on the material by a light beam, the traces can be overlapped where necessary, as shown.

Types of Light-Beam Oscillographs. Light-beam oscillographs are classified in two categories: *develop-out* and *print-out.* These terms refer primarily to the manner in which the image is made visible after exposure.

The term develop-out indicates that the image is made visible by a chemical processing operation. Develop-out photorecording materials must be used and handled under either darkroom or safelight conditions.

The term print-out, or *direct-print,* indicates that image development is accomplished by the action of light, not by chemicals. A second exposure, made after the image exposure, causes the image to become visible. Print-out materials can generally be handled in subdued room light.

Light Sources. Although the terms develop-out and print-out refer primarily to the difference in the development technique used to produce the visible image on the recording material, there is also a difference in the light sources used.

Develop-out oscillographs generally employ an incandescent lamp as a light source. In this system, the paper is protected from room light during the exposing and processing operations. For this reason, emulsions of relatively high speed can be used; the light intensity of the incandescent source is then adequate to record high-frequency signals.

Print-out materials require a light source of higher intensity than a tungsten lamp, because print-out emulsions are relatively slow. Mercury-vapor and pulsed-xenon lamps, which are high-intensity light sources, are used for exposing print-out papers. The development of print-out materials having panchromatic sensitivity has made the use of high-intensity tungsten sources possible. This is important in many applications, since mercury and xenon lamps generally have larger power requirements and shorter lamp life, and are more expensive than tungsten lamps.

The Fiber-Optic Cathode-Ray-Tube Oscillograph

The cathode-ray-tube (CRT) oscillograph is a device that combines the high-frequency recording capability of a cathode-ray tube with the simple recording properties of direct-print paper. A fiber-optic faceplate is bonded to the face of the CRT to form a highly efficient lens. This fiber-optic lens is necessary to transfer sufficient energy from the light spot produced on the CRT's phosphor to the direct-print paper in order to produce a visible trace (see the accompanying diagram).

Photosensitive Recording Materials

Develop-Out Materials. The develop-out technique, as shown in the accompanying diagram, relies on the exposure of the photographic material while it is protected from room light in a lighttight enclosure on the oscillograph or under the proper safelights. This method of exposing is called *closed-magazine* exposure. After the trace exposure has been made, the record, still protected from room light, is processed in a conventional photographic development process or in a shorter stabilization process. The resulting records are high-quality black traces on a background that is white (paper) or clear (film).

Print-Out Materials. Print-out materials are almost as old as photography itself. It is the action of light, not chemicals, that "develops" the image on these materials. In many applications, the need for a quicker look at the data than that provided by the develop-out system led to further development of print-out materials. Most of the time consumed in the develop-out system occurs during the chemical-processing stage. The print-out system is a dry-process system, where the data are visible for evaluation almost immediately after the image exposure.

Two exposures are necessary. The primary exposure occurs at the recording plane in the oscillograph where the light reflected from the galvanome-

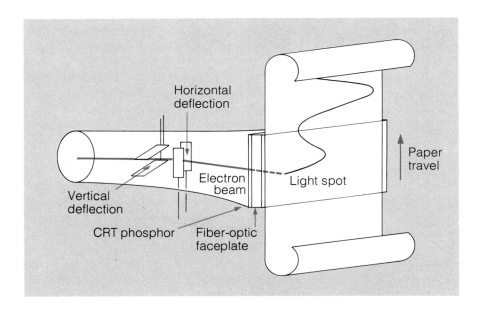

The spot of light created by the electron beam striking the phosphor is transmitted to the emulsion of the direct-print paper by a fiber-optic faceplate that acts as a lens.

Horizontal deflection

Vertical deflection

CRT phosphor

Electron beam

Fiber-optic faceplate

Light spot

Paper travel

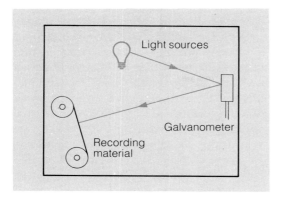

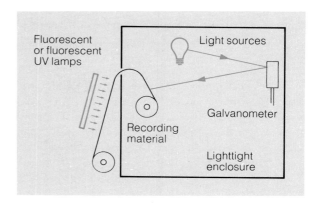

A diagram of a develop-out recorder is shown here. The entire exposing process takes place in a lighttight enclosure protected from ambient room light. The photosensitive material must also be protected from room light during processing.

This is a diagram of a print-out recorder. Two exposures are required: A primary exposure in the lighttight enclosure records the data trace; a secondary exposure usually by fluorescent lamps, "photodevelops" the trace to make it visible.

ter mirrors strikes the paper. The accompanying diagram shows that a secondary exposure (of lower intensity) of the entire record is then made, which causes the appearance of the record data as a dark trace. This is called "photodevelopment."

Writing Speed. Since the recording is being made with a moving spot of light, it is very important that the oscillographer select a paper with the capability of producing a visible density at the highest rate of spot movement. To do this, the maximum velocity of the spot to be recorded must first be determined and then a paper or film with a writing-speed (exposure) capability greater than this must be chosen.

Spectral Sensitivity. The spectral sensitivity of a photographic emulsion refers to its response to light of various wavelengths. This sensitivity is defined as the reciprocal of the exposure (expressed in ergs/cm²) that is required to produce a specific density (generally above minimum density) with specified processing.

In order for the oscillograph light source to do an efficient job of exposing the photographic emulsion, the emulsion must be sensitive to the spectral output of the source. This applies to the light beam reflected from the galvanometer mirror in a light-beam oscillograph, as well as to the light from the phosphor in a CRT oscillograph.

Reciprocity Effect. Since much oscillographic work is done with high-intensity sources, the reciprocity effect may become significant and is therefore an important factor in the choice of materials. The usual method of studying the reciprocity effect is to measure the amounts of exposure (Intensity [I] × Time [T]) required to produce a constant density at different levels of illuminance.

Developing Oscillograms

Photodevelopment. Two exposures are required to photodevelop a print-out record. The first, or primary, exposure occurs at the recording plane in the oscillograph, where a latent image of the trace is made by high-intensity light from a galvanometer or CRT. The silver-halide grains that are struck by the exposing beam form many small specks of metallic silver. These specks are too small by themselves to cause a visible image.

A secondary exposure of lower intensity is then given to the entire record. With this exposure, the previously formed latent image acts as a catalyst that reduces the remainder of the silver-halide grain to metallic silver. This process, called photodevelopment or latensification (i.e., latent-image intensification), amplifies the trace, which subsequently becomes visible.

The exposure received by the background of the recording material during this secondary exposure causes some density to become apparent. It is fortunate that print-out materials become progressively less sensitive to prolonged low-intensity exposure. This is due to failure of the reciprocity law.

Practical Applications. When the oscillograph runs at a low speed and the recording light-beam excursion is small, the trace will appear on the paper as the paper exits from the oscillograph into room light. In this case, the room lights should be cool-white fluorescent lamps providing 50 to 100 footcandles of illumination. These conditions will provide photodevelopment (latensification) in about 30 seconds. In general, slow, low-level (50 footcandles) photodevelopment produces the best image-to-background contrast. With reduced exposure (greater light-beam excursion and/or faster paper-travel speeds) or reduced photodevelopment times (faster paper-travel speeds), more intense latensification is needed to obtain sufficient image density, but generally at the expense of increased background density. This intense latensification can be obtained by the *blast method.*

The Blast Method. As the paper comes from the oscillograph after the primary exposure, it is passed under a lighting fixture called a latensifier, which has two or three fluorescent lamps. Some latensifiers combine both cool-white and black-light fluorescent lamps to increase the amount of ultraviolet radiant energy. With this method, image "pop-up" occurs very rapidly. However, since the ultraviolet radiant energy from the fluorescent lamps exposes both the trace and the background areas, the density of the background tends to increase, thereby decreasing the image-to-background contrast. The direct rays of these lamps should not be allowed to fall on the paper immediately as it leaves the recorder. Shielding the paper for a few inches will aid in preventing too much build-up of background density. Print-out records made on standard base papers have a better visual appearance than those made on extra-thin-base paper. These records can be stored for long periods without noticeable degradation of record quality, if kept away from ultraviolet radiant energy. The use of gold fluorescent or tungsten lamps while viewing print-out records will appreciably retard the latensification process.

Chemical Processing. Chemical processing of oscillograms generally falls into one of two categories: conventional processing or stabilization processing. Conventional processing requires four steps: developing, rinsing, fixing, and washing.

Stabilization processing substantially reduces the total processing time by substituting a stabilization bath for the fixing and washing steps of the conventional process. Converted silver, along with any excess stabilizer, is left in the emulsion and support after drying. Records processed in this manner are relatively stable under normal room conditions. However, since the chemicals are left in the emulsion, the record does have a shorter life.

Treatment for Improved Stability. Stabilized records must be treated in a fixing bath for 10 minutes before washing to improve stability. The amount of washing after fixing will determine the final print stability, as in conventional photographic processing. (*See:* STABILIZATION PROCESS.)

Do not wash stabilized oscillograms without first fixing them. Washing without fixing will remove some of the stabilizing compounds and may make the prints sensitive to light.

Processing Print-Out Papers. Print-out papers are designed to produce visible data without "wet" processing. These records can be viewed in room light for a considerable length of time. Eventually, however, image discrimination will be reduced because of the build-up of background density. Chemical processing can preserve the usefulness of some types of print-out papers. Consult the instruction sheet packaged with any print-out paper to determine if it can be wet processed, as this type of processing is not recommended for all print-out papers. Conventional processing and stabilization processing can also be used for wet processing oscillograph print-out papers.

Machine Processing. The long length of most oscillograms requires that some sort of processing machine be used to transport the photographic material through the processing solutions at a uniform rate. Rewind equipment utilizing a set of hand- or motor-driven spindles winds the roll from one spindle to the other, and back again, while the spindles and photographic material are immersed in the chemical solutions. Separate tanks are usually used for the various solutions; the reel is transferred from one tank to another.

The most popular long-roll processing method for papers is the use of a machine with four solution tanks for stabilization chemicals. The advantage of this type of processor is its drying drum. The paper can be passed over the drum after processing and then wound up dry.

• *See also:* CATHODE-RAY TUBE RECORDING; DEVELOPMENT; STABILIZATION PROCESS.

Further Reading: Hallmark, Clayton. *Understanding and Using the Oscilloscope.* Summit, PA: TAB Books, 1973; Herrick, Clyde N. *Oscilloscope Handbook.* Englewood Cliffs, NJ: Reston Pub. Co., Inc. 1974; Smith, Paul C. *Know Your Oscilloscope,* 3rd ed. Indianapolis, IN: Howard W. Sams & Co., Inc., 1974; Zwick, George. *Oscilloscope,* 3d ed. Summit, PA: TAB Books, 1969.

Ostwald, Wilhelm

(1853–1932)
German chemist, photoscientist, and professor at Leipzig University

Ostwald's major work was in the theory of the latent image and chemical development, in which he studied the growth of silver grains during the ripening of the gelatin emulsion.

He introduced a system of color classification that was based on the use of pure hues, to which were added amounts of black and white to match a given color. He published a *Color Atlas,* embodying these principles and establishing a system of tabulation for various colors.

Around 1903, Ostwald and Gros published an outline of a process for making color prints called "catatype," which utilized the catalytic properties of platinum to form the colored image.

Ostwald received the Nobel Prize for Chemistry in 1909.

Overexposure

Overexposure can be defined only in relation to correct exposure. Correct exposure is that exposure of film or paper that gives the desired results. Overexposure, then, is any exposure that is greater than the correct exposure.

Overexposure with Black-and-White Negative Films

Black-and-white negative films have a wide exposure latitude. Correct exposure is usually given in terms of shadow densities on the negative. A correct exposure is one that, in connection with the development given, produces a negative density in the subject shadow area of 0.10 to 0.20 density units greater than that of the film base. This is the area that is to be reproduced just lighter than black.

Overexposure on black-and-white negative film produces better shadow detail but will still give excellent tone reproduction in the highlight regions, even though they may be quite dense. However, this increased density results in increased graininess and decreased sharpness, which can detract from print quality. In this sense, the correct exposure is that which will just give adequate shadow detail to the print, and any more exposure than this is overexposure. It is for this reason that most advanced black-and-white workers use the shadow measurement method of calculating exposure.

Overexposure with Color Negative Films

Like black-and-white films, color negative films have a wide latitude. Thus, it might be thought that precisely the same definition for correct exposure would be given for both types of films—but there is a difference. All Kodak color negative films have two emulsions in each color layer—a fast emulsion and a slow emulsion. In a correct exposure that gives just adequate shadow detail, much of the exposure is in the faster emulsion, which has coarser grain than the slow emulsion. As the exposure is increased, up to a stop or so over the minimum correct exposure, a higher percentage of the exposure is on the finer grain emulsion. As a result, moderately overexposed color negatives have finer grain than correctly exposed negatives.

Under low-light conditions, where shutter speed and aperture require the use of the full film speed, correct exposure will be obtained by using the listed ASA speed. Under bright light conditions, as with flash or in daylight, an exposure index resulting in ⅔ stop more than that given by the ASA speed will result in finer grain and improved shadow detail. For example, if the speed is ASA 100, using an exposure index of 64 will give optimum results. In this special case, overexposure can be considered to be any exposure greater than the correct exposure, based on the lowered film speed rating.

Overexposure with Color Transparency Films

Unlike black-and-white and color negative films, transparency films have very limited latitude

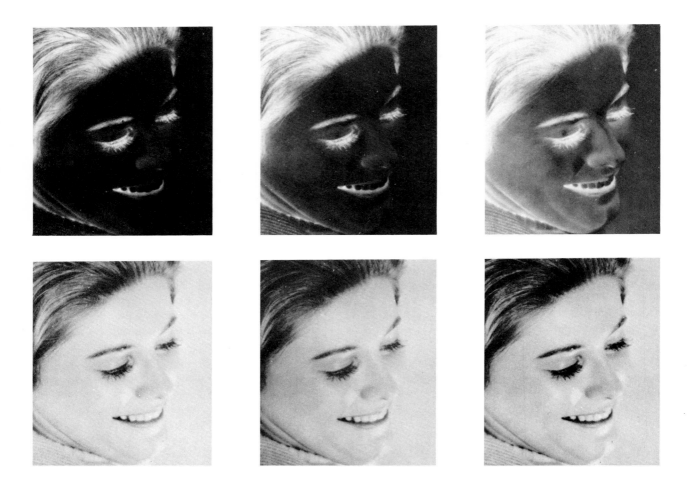

Some overexposure of black-and-white films can be compensated for in the developing process. Top row represents several exposure variations: (left) overexposure and overdevelopment; (center) overexposure and normal development; (right) overexposure and underdevelopment. Bottom row shows the resulting positive prints.

with most subjects. Negative films are processed to have relatively low contrast; typical negative density ranges are on the order of 1.00 density units. The papers on which negatives are printed have relatively high contrast, expanding the density range by a factor of about 1.5 to 3.0. For example, a black-and-white negative with a density range of 0.80 enlarged on a grade 2 glossy paper may produce a reflection density range of about 2.1, a factor of 2.5. The low negative contrast is responsible for the exposure latitude.

Transparency films must go from "white" to "black" as a result of each camera exposure, so they are made with a much higher contrast. The same subject that produces a typical density range of 1.0 in a negative film is likely to produce a density range of 3.0 in a transparency. When the subject luminance range is normal, there is only a fraction of a stop latitude in a transparency film. When the subject has an extended luminance range, there may not be enough range in the film to expose highlights and shadows correctly in the same exposure.

Highlight detail is nearly always more important in transparencies than shadow detail. Advanced workers use meter measurements of the highlights to calculate the exposure, and usually bracket this exposure to insure getting good results. In a correct exposure, specular highlights are recorded as clear processed film base, while diffuse highlights should have a density of about 0.10 above that of the film base. If the density is less than this, the highlights look washed out, and overexposure has occurred.

Hence, proper exposure of transparency materials is determined primarily from the scene highlights. In normal situations, the other tones will have good reproduction when the highlights are reproduced correctly. However, in some scenes with a very high luminance range, the midtones may appear underexposed when the lightest tones are reproduced as described above. To reduce the luminance range, reflectors or flash should be used. In the case of low-luminance-range subjects, the best procedure is to base the exposure on the midtones. In general, transparencies for projection should receive slightly more exposure than transparencies intended for halftone reproduction.

Overexposure of Photographic Papers

In the tray processing of black-and-white papers, there is some development latitude; that is, the developing time may be increased or decreased somewhat to compensate for exposure error. However, if the developing time is changed an appreciable amount from the recommended time, the print quality usually suffers. The correct exposure of photographic paper is that exposure which produces the correct print densities when the paper is developed for the recommended time. A longer exposure time that requires a shorter-than-recommended developing time is overexposure. Overexposure and underdevelopment result in prints with degraded highlights and weak blacks.

In all color and many black-and-white print developing procedures, there is no developing time flexibility, and all prints receive the same amount of development. In these cases, there is little exposure latitude, and overexposure results in prints that are either too dark in negative processes or too light in reversal processes.

 Overhead Projection

With an overhead projection system, large transparencies can be projected onto a screen in a fully lighted classroom or lecture room. The projector is placed in front of the teacher or lecturer, and the image is projected, by a mirror-and-lens system, over the shoulder to a screen placed above and behind the speaker.

The projector used for this purpose has a lamphouse on the bottom with a fresnel condenser that projects the light upward. Above the condenser is a glass stage on which the material to be projected is placed. Above this stage on a gooseneck arm is a housing for the lens with its associated mirror or prism. The mirror reflects the light beam at the desired angle and the lens forms an image on a vertical or slightly angled screen. The glass stage is usually quite large; in some projectors it is as big as 12″ × 12″, but smaller material can be projected if desired.

The projected transparency is large; hence magnification, even on a good-sized screen, is relatively low. This helps produce a very bright screen image, so it is unnecessary to darken the room. Due to this and because the operator faces the audience, there is little interference with communication.

The overhead projector is often used as an "optical blackboard." In this application, the glass platen is simply covered with a sheet of clear acetate plastic on which the lecturer can write or draw with colored felt-tip markers. In this case it is not necessary to prepare material in advance. The material can be drawn while the lecture is being conducted, just as it would be with colored chalk on a blackboard. The advantage, of course, lies in the magnification of the image in projection, which makes drawing or writing clearly visible to every observer.

More formal presentations, drawings, photographs, and other artwork can be prepared by a number of photographic and non-photographic methods. The resulting transparencies are usually mounted in cardboard frames for easy handling and to mask off unwanted light around the edges.

Preparing Materials
for Overhead Projection

Non-Photographic Methods. The following are examples of non-photographic methods that can be used in combination with photographic methods. Felt-tipped pens, variously colored, can be used to draw original art work and lettering or to color black-and-white transparencies produced by photography. Transparent tapes can be used in a similar manner. Grease pencils can provide opaque lines or, in some cases, transparent colored lines.

Photographic Methods. There are several simple photographic procedures for preparing transparencies for use in overhead projectors. Original subject matter can be in the form of line work, such as charts and graphs, or halftones, with either translucent or opaque background stock. Line copy is reproduced either as a positive, with black lines on a clear background, or as a negative, with clear lines on a black background, depending on personal preference. Color, used to improve the presentation, is added by hand or by the application of colored plastic sheeting. Overlay systems, consisting of several transparencies in register, allow an involved subject to be developed step by step.

The simplest photographic method for preparing an overhead transparency is the use of diazo materials developed with ammonia. To prepare a diazo transparency, a master is prepared with opaque lines on a transparent or translucent base such as clear acetate sheets or tracing paper. The master is placed in contact with a sheet of diazo film, which is commercially available in a number of dye colors. (Before development, the dye is not visible.) An ultraviolet source provides exposure. The exposed diazo film is developed with ammonia vapor in a closed container. Commercial exposing and developing devices are available, but the process is so simple that a light box and a wide-mouth gallon jar with a small cup of ammonia in the bottom are all that is required.

A clear-base, high-contrast graphic-arts film such as Kodalith ortho film or Kodak Autopositive film AC4 can be used to make high-quality overhead transparencies. Autopositive film can be handled in room light. It produces a positive image that is a duplicate of the original. A negative-working film such as Kodalith film can be used in the negative form or recopied to make a positive image.

In making transparencies with Autopositive film, the material is contact-printed through a transparent original with a high-intensity light source such as pulsed xenon, mercury vapor, or carbon arc. Yellow sheeting must be used between the film and the light source. Upon development in a conventional graphic-arts developer (see instructions packaged with the film), a positive image appears. The fixing, washing, and drying processes are similar to those used with conventional silver-halide films. If desired, portions of the image produced on Autopositive film can be re-reversed before processing by exposing the required parts of the film to an intense white-light exposure after the initial overall yellow-light exposure.

High-contrast negative or positive transparencies can be made on a graphic arts lith film, such as Kodalith ortho film, by contact exposure to the original. When it is necessary to reproduce subjects that are larger than the overhead projector can accommodate, a copy camera may be needed to make reduced-size transparencies. Negative transparencies made by camera reduction can be contact-printed to make positives. Of course, a composite transparency can be made by combining several negatives before making the positive print.

A continuous-tone black-and-white transparency can be made by printing a conventional black-and-white negative on a slow-speed, blue-sensitive film in an enlarger. Such a film can be exposed and developed in the same manner as photographic papers. While the density of lines or lettering will be lower than that achieved with lith-type films, the blue-sensitive film can also be used for titles or in combination with line and continuous-tone images. Check the results of exposure and development with this film by projecting the transparency; it is difficult to predict the correct density for projection when viewing the transparency on an illuminator.

Transparencies with Color Films

Where colored originals are available, it is, of course, possible to produce overhead transparencies with color films. If a large camera is available, the simplest method is to use a color transparency film such as Kodak Ektachrome sheet film, in sizes as large as 8″ × 10″. The processed film has only to be mounted in a cardboard frame to be ready for use in the projector.

When a large camera is unavailable, it is equally possible to use cameras as small as 35 mm to produce large transparencies. If the material has already been photographed, and 2″ × 2″ slides are on hand, enlarged transparencies can be made from these on duplicating film.

If color negatives are available, enlarged transparencies can be made on print film. Print film can also be used when a transparency is available by making an internegative from the transparency. The internegative can be made by contact and the final transparency by enlargement; or conversely, the internegative may be made by enlargement and the final transparency by contact. Of the two procedures, the second will probably produce a sharper result.

However, it may not be possible to use either method, for lack of contact-printing facilities. If, however, a medium-sized enlarger that takes negatives up to 4″ × 5″ is available, then it is well to enlarge the transparency to a 4″ × 5″ internegative, and then make the 8″ × 10″ transparency from the internegative on the enlarger.

Oxalic Acid

Oxalic acid is also known as ethanedioic acid. It is used as a preservative in pyro developers and as a sensitizer in platinotype paper. Oxalic acid is also used in toning and mordanting formulas, and in the preparation of the obsolete ferrous oxalate developer.

Formula: $(CO_2H)_2.2H_2O$
Molecular Weight: 126.07

It is made up of transparent, colorless, odorless crystals, freely soluble in water and alcohol.

POISON: Oxalic acid can cause skin burns if applied externally; it is poisonous if ingested.

Oxidation

In elementary chemistry, oxidation is considered to be the combination of elements with oxygen to form oxides. In more general terms, however, oxidation refers to the addition of either oxygen or some other electro-negative element to a compound. Oxygen in the air can cause the developing agents in black-and-white developers to oxidize. Sodium sulfite is added as a preservative to minimize the oxidation. It does this by combining with the oxygen (oxidizing) to form sodium sulfate. The equation is:

$$2Na_2SO_3 + O_2 \rightarrow 2Na_2SO_4$$

Sodium sulfite + Oxygen → Sodium sulfate

Oxidation is always accompanied by reduction in a chemical reaction, reduction being the removal of oxygen or other electronegative element. Thus, in the development of an emulsion, the silver bromide (AgBr) is reduced to metallic silver, the bromine being the electronegative element removed. At the same time, the developing agents are being oxidized, so that the final system remains balanced as far as both the total amount of reduction and oxidation to the electronegative and electropositive elements are concerned.

The following equation shows the black-and-white part of color development.

$$AgBr + H_2N - \!\!\bigcirc\!\!- NR_2 \rightarrow$$
$$Ag^0 + H_2N^+ -\!\!\bigcirc\!\!- NR_2 + Br^-$$

Exposed silver bromide + Color developing agent →

Metallic silver + Oxidized color developing agent + Bromide ion

The oxidized developing agent then reacts with the couplers, combining with them to form a dye.

The silver bromide is reduced to form silver atoms and bromide ions, while the developer is reduced. Chemists call a reaction involving both reduction and oxidation a *redox* reaction.

Other oxidation reactions in photography include the regeneration of bleaches. In some cases, air containing oxygen is bubbled through the bleach, oxidizing the used bleach back to its original form. In other cases, a chemical is used that causes a redox reaction and returns the bleach to its original state by oxidizing the used bleach. A simple example would be the bleach step in a color process where the metallic silver (Ag^0) image is oxidized by the bleaching agent to a silver ion (Ag^+) and removed from the film for reclamation, leaving only the dye image in the film.

• *See also:* CHEMISTRY OF PHOTOGRAPHY; DEVELOPMENT.

Painting with Light

Painting with light is a technique by which a large area can be photographed using only a single light unit—photoflood, flash, or electronic flash. The method consists of dividing up the area into a number of sections, each small enough to be covered by one light, and then making as many exposures on the one film as are needed to cover all of these areas.

As an example, photographing a long corridor in an office building is very difficult to do by conventional methods. A single powerful flash at the camera cannot be used; because of the inverse-square law, the light falls off very rapidly and the far end of the hall will be underexposed. Using a more powerful lamp will not help; it will merely overexpose the foreground.

Painting with Flash

One way to make this picture is to have all the lights in the corridor extinguished. The photographer should mount the camera on a tripod at one end of the corridor, open the camera shutter, and walk down the hall almost to the other end. Then one flash must be fired at the end wall, with the photographer facing away from the camera and shielding the flash unit from the camera lens with his or her body. Then, the photographer should move back about 5 feet, face the wall again, and fire the flash again. This action should be continued until the photographer reaches camera position and closes the shutter.

In many cases, this will provide an evenly lighted picture showing the full length of the corridor. However, there are some minor problems with this method. In theory, the photographer carrying the light should not appear in these pictures at all, because there is no light on the camera side of his or her body, but this is not always the case. There is a good deal of reflected light from walls and floor; in fact, it is essential to secure a natural result and to blend the successive exposures into a single, overall lighting effect that looks correct. But because of this, an eerie effect sometimes results—a row of disembodied feet appear on the floor of the corridor, or a series of ghost images of the photographer.

A better way to make such a shot is to keep the photographer out of the image area altogether. If the picture can be made after hours when there is no one in the building, arrangements can be made to have all the office doors open on both sides of the hallway. Then, the job consists of nothing more than firing a flash out of each doorway, aimed diagonally across the hall. The effect on the film will be the same as if the hall were lighted by illumination coming from the office lights. To make this even more natural, the camera shutter should be closed momentarily after all of these exposures are made; then all overhead lights in the corridor should be turned on and one more brief exposure made to register them in the picture.

Exposure Measurement

Because each area of the picture is separately lighted, the separate exposures are made on different areas of the film, and do not overlap each other significantly. Thus, the exposure for a picture

Flash #1

Flash #2

Flash #3

Flash #4

The photograph below is the result of a multiple exposure using the four different flash positions illustrated in the photos above. Flash #1 was off the camera, high and to the right to minimize direct reflections. Flash #3 was held low behind the cars to avoid directing light into the camera lens.

such as the one just described will be roughly the same as that for any one of the flashes. However, it is necessary for uniformity to make sure that all flash exposures are made at roughly equal distances from any walls or lighted areas, so that the final picture will not have too great a variation in bright and dim areas.

A fairly powerful flash unit is needed because pictures like this must usually be made at small apertures to obtain the necessary depth of field. For this reason, ordinary flash lamps are often more useful than small pocket-sized electronic flash units, since the latter seldom permit using small enough lens stops except with high-speed films.

As an example, referring again to the situation just mentioned, assume the corridor is 15 feet wide, and the photographer is shooting at $f/32$; simple arithmetic shows that the photographer will need a film/shutter-speed combination producing a guide number of 480. (*See*: GUIDE NUMBERS.) However since the flash is not synchronized with the shutter, it is necessary to use a lamp having this guide number for "open flash" with the film in use—such as a No. 5 flash lamp with film of ASA 400 speed.

With electronic flash, exposure is the same regardless of shutter speed; the problem is merely finding a unit that permits a 480 guide number with the film in use.

Large-Area Photography

The long-corridor type of picture is only one area in which painting with light is appropriate. Another and slightly different situation is the large, and particularly the wide, room that must be shown with uniform illumination. Restaurant and cocktail lounge interiors, manufacturing plants, and offices are typical examples.

It is difficult to light such pictures even when ample lighting equipment is available; the problem is to cover the area with light entirely from outside the photographed area. It is seldom possible to conceal light units within the picture area, and existing light is often inadequate.

Adding to the difficulty is the fact that such pictures must usually be made with extreme wide-angle lenses, implying small apertures and ruling out available light even if it were useful otherwise.

The "painting" technique here not only solves the problem of concealing the light sources, but also makes it possible to compensate, roughly, for the inevitable falloff in illumination toward the edges of the wide-angle field.

The method is to divide up the picture area into sections wide enough to be covered by the flash unit that is being used. It is well to have an assistant at the camera to uncover the lens for each exposure; this will avoid ghost images due to stray light in the scene.

To avoid blur due to camera shake, the shutter is not used. Instead, the lens is covered with a piece of black cardboard, close to, but not touching it. The shutter is opened on "T" or locked open on "B" with a locking cable release, and the exposures are made by drawing the card aside and then returning it. At the end of the sequence, the card is again placed in front of the lens, and then the shutter can be closed. View camera users generally use the dark slide from the sheet-film holder as the black-card shutter.

It is quite possible to make such a shot with the person carrying the light unit within the picture area at all times, but hidden behind objects in the scene. With the guide number having been decided as above, the photographer makes a mental note of the positions where he or she will stand for each exposure. The signal is given to the camera assistant to uncover the lens when the photographer is ready to fire each flash.

After all the wall areas have been covered, an additional exposure is given with the room lighting fixtures to determine positions of natural shadows. An additional exposure may be given with one or more flashes aimed at the floor. This will produce highlights on the floor, which give it the appearance of being highly polished.

An additional exposure may also be given if the ceiling appears in the picture; in this case one or more flashes are aimed from camera position at the ceiling. This is less necessary if light fixtures appear in the scene; but if in doubt, it is well to add the ceiling exposure for naturalness, especially in wide-angle pictures.

Intermittency

In theory, a group of exposures do not add up to the same overall effect on the emulsion as a single exposure of the same total duration. Consequently, it is often recommended to give additional exposure above the calculated amount when a number of exposures are superimposed upon a single film.

This effect seldom occurs in painting with light, simply because various parts of the scene are being exposed in succession. There is some overlapping, but not usually enough to have any effect. In any case, the intermittency effect is nearly negligible.

Painting with Incandescent Light

Painting with light can also be done with continuous light sources. This method is often used by news and police photographers outdoors at night.

A very useful accessory is a hand-held spotlight, which is plugged into the cigarette-lighter socket on the dashboard of the car. Such lamps put out a narrow beam of very intense light, and can carry for a considerable distance.

Method. The method of using such lamps is to stand at camera position, open the shutter of the camera on "T." Then simply aim the lamp at the subject and swing it back and forth in overlapping strokes, just like painting a wall. If this is carefully done, it will produce a quite even overall exposure, of a much larger area than any single source could possibly cover.

Exposure Determination. Exposure determination for this method is likely to be a bit difficult. There are several ways to handle the problem. One is to have an assistant hold the lamp, aiming it at a convenient part of the subject, while the photographer goes out and measures the light on that area with a conventional exposure meter. If a spot meter is used, the reading can be taken from camera position without assistance. With an incident-light meter at the subject position, aim the light directly at it and get a reading that way.

Another good way is to determine a guide number for the spotlight in use by making a few trial exposures at different distances. In any case, the result will only be an approximation; it can go completely out of line if the lamp is moved over the same area more than once during a given exposure. The technique is most valuable when any sort of picture is better than no picture at all, and the best advice that can be given is: If in doubt, *overexpose*

when using negative materials. The negative may be hard to print, but this is preferable to an underexposure or no picture whatever.

Long-Burning Flash Lamps

Two types of long-burning flash lamps, the FF-33 and the FF-33B, are made by Sylvania. While these are primarily intended as light sources for high-speed motion-picture cameras, they can also be used for painting with light, by using a simple and easily learned technique. The method consists of firing the lamp and swinging it in a sort of S-shaped arc across the scene. It is roughly the same size as an ordinary 150-watt lamp, and needs only a battery to fire it. Its light output lasts about 1.75 seconds down to half peak, but there is useful light output for a somewhat longer time; total burning time is about 2½ seconds.

The FF-33B is a blue-coated lamp intended for use with daylight-type color films. In the accompanying table, sample guide numbers are given for open flash and a total duration of 2½ seconds:

GUIDE NUMBERS FOR LONG-BURNING FLASH LAMPS*		
Color Film Speed (ASA)	FF-33 (Tungsten film with 81EF filter)	FF-33B (Daylight film— no filter)
50	332	245
100	470	346
400	938	693

*These guide numbers are based on the use of a 7-inch polished reflector.

It would seem that 2½ seconds is a very short time to paint a scene, but it is longer than one would think. If you wish to estimate the time, it can be done by mental counting. The average person, asked to count from 1 to 10, will count in almost exact half seconds, if not hurrying. Thus, the flash will last while you count from 1 to 5 at a modest tempo.

Painting can be done in a wavy pattern, or by describing an *X* in the air, or a letter *S* lying on its side. A little practice will make for proficiency in this technique.

• *See also:* ELECTRONIC FLASH; FLASH PHOTOGRAPHY; GUIDE NUMBERS.

Palladiotype

Salts of palladium can be substituted for those of platinum to sensitize papers for printing. The results are similar to platinum prints; the main advantage of palladium over platinum is that it is less expensive. The prints are considered to be as permanent as platinum images.

• *See also:* PLATINUM PRINT PROCESS.

p-Aminophenol Hydrochloride

Paraminophenol hydrochloride, paramidophenol hydrochloride, p-hydroxyaniline hydrochloride

A developing agent, formerly used to a large extent as a substitute for Metol by persons subject to allergic skin reactions; also used as a developing agent in tropical developers. A sodium salt of paraminophenol, probably sodium paraminophenolate, is the developing agent in many proprietary developers. In the form of sodium paraminophenolate, it has extremely high activity, and the stock solution is used at dilutions of up to 1:100. The Kodak name for this chemical is Kodak balancing developing agent, BD-86.

Formula: $C_6H_4OHNH_2.HCl$
Molecular Weight: 145.59

White crystalline substance, readily soluble in water, and to some extent in alcohol. Reduction potential 6.0. Paraminophenol developers produce pure black images free from stain.

Panchromatic

Panchromatic plates and films are sensitive to red, green, and blue wavelengths, as well as to shorter (ultraviolet) wavelengths. In films designed for photographing people and landscapes, red sensitivity is extended only to about 650 nm in order to avoid overexposure of red objects (such as lips). However, some products intended for technical applications have panchromatic sensitivity that has been extended to cover all red wavelengths—out to 720 nm in some cases.

Spectral Sensitivity

The spectral sensitivity of an emulsion describes its response to radiations of varying wavelength in the visible and invisible parts of the spectrum. Plain silver bromide, the fundamental light-sensitive element in negative emulsions, is sensitive to or absorbs only the blue and ultraviolet radiations. However, an emulsion can be sensitized optically by the addition of suitably chosen dyes that absorb radiations of longer wavelength. By this means, it is possible to extend the sensitivity through the green (orthochromatic sensitization), through the green and red (panchromatic sensitization), and into the invisible infrared region.

Choosing a Film

Spectral sensitivity, or color sensitivity, is an important consideration in choosing a film for a particular use. It determines the way in which colored objects photograph in tones of gray, the kind of filters that can be used with the material, and the way film must be handled in processing.

A film that is not sensitive to green or red renders these colors too dark in a black-and-white photograph. A panchromatic film that has a response to the visible spectrum similar to that of the human eye, records colors in tones of gray with the same relative brightness as they appear to the observer.

The relative brightness at which colors are rendered in black-and-white can be changed or corrected with suitable filters. Which filters can be used with a particular film depends, of course, on the color sensitivity of the emulsion. For example, a red filter can be used only with a red-sensitive, or panchromatic film.

The earliest photographic emulsions composed of silver halides—usually silver bromide and small amounts of silver iodide—were sensitive only to visible blue light and invisible ultraviolet radiation. Such films produced rather distorted tonal renditions of most naturally colored objects.

The black-and-white conversion from a color photograph, made on panchromatic film, illustrates the sensitivity of this film to red, green, and blue wavelengths. A panchromatic film that has a response to the visible spectrum similar to that of the human eye, records colors in tones of gray with the same relative brightness as they appear to the observer.

Panchromatic

Orthochromatic Films. Later, it was discovered that adding certain reddish dye compounds, such as eosin, erythrosin, and so on, to a silver-halide emulsion would also make it sensitive to the green section of the spectrum. Such films were called, with some exaggeration, "orthochromatic" (true, or correct-colored). They did, however, improve rendition of landscapes and portraits to a very marked extent.

Panchromatic Films. Early in the twentieth century, dye compounds were discovered that would also sensitize a silver-halide emulsion to red light; by combining one of these dyes with a green-sensitizing dye, it was possible to make an emulsion sensitive to red, green, and blue, as well as ultra-violet wavelengths. Such emulsions were named "panchromatic" (all-colored). Today, practically all general-purpose black-and-white films and plates are coated with panchromatic emulsions.

Obviously, by varying the proportions of the dyes, it is possible to produce panchromatic films with different sensitivity balances. For some time, panchromatic films were divided into three sensitizing classes, all with equal blue sensitivity:

Class A panchromatic, having relatively low red sensitivity.

Class B panchromatic, having approximately equal sensitivity to red and green.

Class C panchromatic, having greater red than green sensitivity.

All panchromatic films and plates still have a greater sensitivity to blue, violet, and ultraviolet than to red and green. For most purposes, however, the color rendition of a Class B panchromatic approaches the visual brightnesses of a scene quite closely. For this reason, almost all of today's films are Class B panchromatic. One or two Class C films are made for special purposes, while Class A panchromatic sensitization is practically obsolete.

Printing Papers

In recent years, a need has arisen for printing papers with panchromatic sensitivity. These are used for making black-and-white prints from color negatives (Kodak Panalure paper, Panalure portrait paper, and similar papers of other manufacturers). Another type of panchromatic paper is used, with filters, to produce direct color-separation positives from color negatives for photomechanical reproduction (Kodak Resisto Rapid pan paper, and similar papers of other makers). Such papers are used exactly like any other enlarging paper of medium speed, but require a special safelight if development is to be carried out by inspection. Generally, a standard safelight fixture with a Kodak Wratten safelight filter no. 10 (green) is recommended for these papers.

• *See also:* BLACK-AND-WHITE FILMS; BLACK-AND-WHITE PRINTS FROM COLOR FILMS; EMULSION.

Panoramic Photography

Panoramic photography consists of making a picture of more or less normal height, but of great width, often covering an angle of view as wide as 130 degrees; with some cameras it is possible to photograph the entire horizon (360 degrees) on a single negative. While special cameras have been made for panoramic photography, it is possible to make panoramic pictures with an ordinary camera by making several overlapping exposures and then mounting the prints side by side, matching detail carefully at the edges.

Panoramic Cameras

There are several types of panoramic cameras; the simplest is merely one that has a wider-than-normal format and a wide-angle lens. Cameras of this sort were often called "banquet" cameras, and were view cameras that made pictures either 7″ × 17″ or 12″ × 20″ in size, on flat sheet film or plates. In recent years, a few cameras have been made for roll film, which also produce a wide image, generally about 100 degrees in the included angle. These cameras use ordinary 120 roll film, they cover from one to two standard frames at each exposure. Examples are the Brooks Veriwide, which has a 100-degree angle of view and makes eight 2¼″ × 3¼″ pictures on a roll of 120 film, and the Linhof Technorama, which makes four 2¼″ × 6¾″ pictures on a roll of 120 film.

True panoramic cameras were made in the early 1900's; the Panoram Kodak was made in

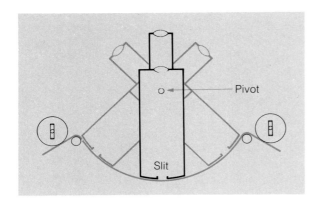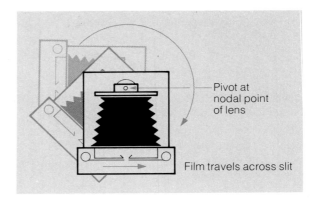

(Left) True panoramic cameras, such as the Panoram Kodak and the Widelux, use stationary film. The lens swings in an arc, exposing the film through a narrow slit. (Right) The entire Cirkut camera pivots around the nodal point of the lens, while the film is driven across the slit in the back.

two models, one using 120 film, but making 2¼″ × 6½″ pictures. The other used the now obsolete 123 roll film, and made 4″ × 10″ pictures. These cameras covered a wide field of view by having the film curved in an arc and the lens swinging on a pivot, exposing the film area through a narrow slit.

A similar, more recent camera is the Widelux, which also uses a swinging lens, but makes 24 × 59 mm pictures on 35 mm film; the included angle is about 140 degrees.

A different principle was used in the Cirkut camera, which was very popular for panoramic pictures and photographs of large groups of people. (It is no longer manufactured.) In this case, the camera itself was similar to an ordinary view camera fitted with a special back and tripod head. In taking a picture with the Cirkut camera, the entire camera was caused to rotate on the panoramic tripod head by means of a spring motor; at the same time, the film was wound from one spool to the other across a narrow slit in the camera back. The tripod head had gear teeth around its rim, and different sets of gears were supplied for the camera to produce the correct rate of rotation and film feed for lenses of differing focal lengths.

The Cirkut cameras used films either 8 inches wide by 5 feet long, or 10 inches wide by 6 feet long. Since the camera could be stopped at any point, only as much film was used as was needed for a given picture, and the number of exposures that could be made on a roll depended upon how wide a picture was desired. Obviously, it was quite possible to permit the camera to make a complete revolution, producing a picture of the entire horizon, or 360 degrees, in a single shot.

Because of the rotation of the panoramic camera, the perspective in the picture is necessarily somewhat distorted; it is similar to a photograph made on a cylindrical film. This type of perspective is therefore called cylindrical perspective. When printed on a flat surface, it makes a view of a city street appear to be convex. The objects directly in front of the camera appear to be closest to the camera (as they are), and the buildings at the ends of the street curve away and get smaller.

This effect is commonly seen when a large group of people are posed in front of a building. Usually, the photographer will arrange the subjects in a semicircle, so that all will be the same size on the film, and all will be equally in focus. The building in the background, however, will appear to be convex in shape, and may possibly be out of focus at the ends.

The rotational speed of these cameras is quite slow, and the exposure of an entire group may take from 15 seconds to a minute or more. It was a common trick, in the days when such group

Two photographs made with the Cirkut camera. Fitted with a special back and a tripod head, the entire camera was rotated on the panoramic tripod head, while the film was wound from one spool to the other across a narrow slit in the camera back. In the group photograph, the man in the vest appears at each end of the picture; this popular trick was made possible by the slow rotational speed of the camera, which gave him the time to be photographed at the left, then to run around behind the group to reappear at the right. Photo courtesy International Museum of Photography, Rochester, N.Y.

pictures were popular, for a person at the end of the group to run around and pose at the opposite end of the group as soon as the camera had passed him, thus appearing twice in a single picture.

Panoramas with Regular Cameras

It is quite possible to make simulated panoramic pictures, scenes, and interiors with an ordinary camera simply by exposing a series of negatives from one point, and then mounting the prints in one straight line. However, some precautions are necessary for optimum results; and, in any case, the perspective will be different from that of a true panorama. The reason is that instead of a smooth circular motion, the camera is moved in steps, and the exposure at each step is made on a flat plane, not on a section of a cylinder. Thus, if a wide building appears in the scene, it will be rendered, not as a cylinder convex to the camera, but rather as a convex polygon. It will have a series of rectilinear perspectives, rather than a continuous cylindrical perspective.

Yet, in many cases, the results can be quite satisfactory, especially where only a few exposures are made and the joining points (joins) are carefully chosen; if the subject is a street scene, for instance, joins are best made between buildings. Landscapes give little trouble.

For the very best results, a special tripod head should be devised, so that the camera can rotate about the optical center of the lens; while this point is not usually marked, it may be taken to be at the plane of the lens diaphragm, which is easy enough to locate.

An ordinary tripod head may be used without much error, especially with small cameras. It is essential that the head be provided with means for separately locking the tilt and pan movements; otherwise, when loosening the head to turn for the next exposure, there is a danger of tilting the camera as well, which will cause a mismatch between successive images.

For some years, a special pan head was provided by E. Leitz for the Leica camera. It had scales marked around the rim, and different scales were provided for lenses of different focal lengths so that accurate joins could be made between images. If no such head can be found, a panorama can be made with the use of the reflex finder.

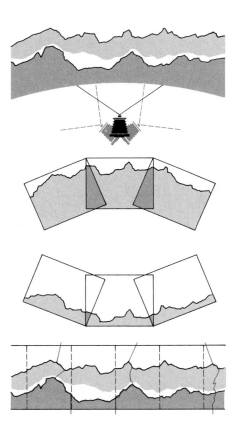

After making the first exposure, simply choose an object at one edge of the picture, turn the camera until that same object is at the opposite edge, and make the next exposure. As long as the same object appears in two successive pictures, there will be ample overlap for joining the pictures into a panorama. Actually, too much overlap is better than too little; in aerial surveying, for instance, as much as 60 percent overlap from one picture to the next is allowed, so that in pasting the pictures together, only a part of the middle of each image is used. This reduces image distortion and makes selection of the exact joining point easier.

The perspective achieved by this method is a combination of rectilinear and cylindrical. It is a series of rectilinear pictures arranged to create an overall cylindrical perspective. It will, therefore, have abrupt changes in the angles of straight lines that have a horizontal component. Decreasing the angular difference between each exposure decreases the angular change at the joins. Such changes are especially evident on the lines that are high or low in the pictures; central horizontal lines are not affected.

This means that the use of wide-angle lenses to create fewer joins is to be avoided because the angular change is greatest when this is done. Making many exposures with a telephoto lens minimizes the effect.

One other thing must be noted. If there are any moving objects in the scene, it is possible that they will appear in two successive pictures, in different places. This is of no importance, as long as the moving object does not run through the joining area of the pictures while the exposure is being made, otherwise there may be half an automobile in the final picture. On the other hand, having the same automobile appear twice may not be too serious, and no one is likely to notice the duplication unless it is pointed out.

(Top) The camera should be firmly mounted, and rotated through a fixed angle after each exposure in photographing a panorama. Views must overlap to allow matching up in the finished photo. (Center) If the camera is not absolutely level, the horizon line will appear to curve down or up. (Bottom) By following the outlines of prominent features in the photos, the joins can be unobtrusive in the final print.

Panoramic Photography

This panorama is composed of a series of photographs taken with a regular camera. After the first exposure was made, the camera was turned to the right until an object at the right edge of the first exposure appeared at the left of the next frame. The process was repeated throughout. This technique allows ample overlap for joining the pictures into a panorama.

One such problem is almost insurmountable, however. A panorama made on a windy day with rapidly moving clouds will be nearly impossible to join up. Probably the only solution is to join the landscape as well as possible, and then to retouch or airbrush the clouds into some semblance of proper form.

Making a Panoramic Picture with a Regular Camera. With all the above points in mind, making a panoramic photograph is simple enough, if the following steps are taken:

1. Set up the tripod at the desired viewpoint, without the camera on top.
2. Place a spirit level on the tripod head, and level it by carefully adjusting the tilt head and the leg length, until it can be turned through the complete circle without going off level at any point. Carefully lock the tilt head and the leg locks so they cannot slip.
3. Mount the camera on the tripod head, and check for inclusion of the desired view. If the top and bottom of the picture do not include the desired view, *do not* tilt the camera up or down. A small adjustment can be made by raising or lowering the entire tripod (with the center column, if one is available, to avoid tilting). Otherwise, use a wide-angle lens, and crop out the unwanted area in enlarging.
4. Focus and set the lens aperture and shutter speed.
5. If a panoramic head is used, make sure you have the correct scale for the lens you are using. Turn the camera to the extreme left of the image area, making sure it is at one of the click stops of the pan head.
6. If a regular panoramic head is not used, simply turn the camera to the starting position at the left.
7. Make the first exposure.
8. With the pan head, turn the camera to the right, to the next click. If an ordinary tripod is used, find an object well within the right-hand edge of the field. Turn the camera to the right until this same object is near the left-hand edge, but about as far inside this edge as it was inside the right-hand edge.
9. Make the next exposure, and repeat the above steps until the desired image width has been covered, plus a little more, for safety's sake.
10. Develop the negatives.
11. Since all these negatives were made at the same exposure, they should all be of the same density. Print all of them at the same exposure, making

sure to include the entire image of each negative, so that the overlaps appear on the prints. If any dodging or other exposure correction is needed, be sure it is done in an area that will not be in the overlap, otherwise it will be nearly impossible to match the density in successive images at the joins. Be sure the enlarger does not move between prints.

Assembling the Panorama. Lay out the finished prints side by side, and determine the width of the final assembly. Secure a sheet of mounting board big enough to take the entire panorama.

Locate the joining points of the pictures and mark them lightly with a china-marker pencil, which can easily be rubbed off after the prints are mounted.

Do not attempt to make a butt joint between pictures. Instead, after choosing the joining point of adjacent pictures, trim the prints about half an inch beyond this point to the left and right, so that they will overlap by about an inch, altogether. With a piece of very fine sandpaper, "feather" the edge of the first print so that it comes down to a thin edge at the joining point. Glue or cement this print to the board.

Before mounting the next print, determine its joining line to the third print, and again trim about half an inch beyond this point for the proper overlap. Now feather both overlap edges with the sandpaper and mount this print, registering the details at the left-hand edge with the previous print as closely as possible. Use a T-square to be sure the prints are being mounted in a straight line.

It may be necessary to modify the joining point to avoid a seam across an important detail. The overlap permits some modification, but it is better to watch for this problem when first choosing the overlap. It is not necessary that the joining edge be a straight line; it can be zigzagged around important details, so the lap is made in an almost featureless area. Slight mismatches, when unavoidable, can be retouched after the panorama is finished.

Continue the same process until the entire set of pictures is mounted, with all joins made as carefully as possible and all pictures in a perfectly straight line. Permit the glue to dry thoroughly, clean off any crayon marks still remaining on the prints, and touch up any defects in the joins.

If only a single copy is needed, it may be trimmed along the outer edges, or covered with a mat. If a larger number of prints is required, the assembly should be copied, using a large format, as big as 8″ × 10″ if available. Make as many prints as necessary from the large negative without further need for mounting or joining. Further retouching can be done on the copy negative if necessary.

Another approach is to print all of the negatives on a single sheet of paper, blending the joins. Make a layout sheet to place on the easel, indicating the edges of each image and marking important lines to aid in locating the paper for each exposure. This is done by projecting each negative on the layout sheet and marking it while the image is projected.

The edges are blended together by dodging. Use the edges of cards for the dodging, and keep the card moving into and out of the area for each image. A half-inch blended overlap may be about right for smaller prints, while large prints can stand somewhat more. It is helpful to have another person to dodge one edge while you are dodging the other.

Start several sheets of paper with the first exposure. It is easy to make a mistake when a number of exposures are made on one sheet of paper; if several sheets are used, you do not have to start over. It is also wise to mark the paper so you can tell which edge of the paper goes at the top of the pictures.

Panoramic Slides. This multiple picture technique can be used with slides and multiscreen projection. Panoramas projected on three side-by-side screens can provide very effective visual experiences. With slides, there should be just a little overlap between the pictures.

• *See also:* CAMERAS; COMBINATION PRINTING; MURALS; TRIPODS; WIDE-ANGLE PHOTOGRAPHY.

Further Reading: Darrah, William C. and Richard Russak. *An Album of Stereographs.* Garden City, NY: Doubleday, Inc., 1977; Okoshi, T. *Three-Dimensional Imaginary Techniques.* New York, NY: Academic Press, Inc., 1976.

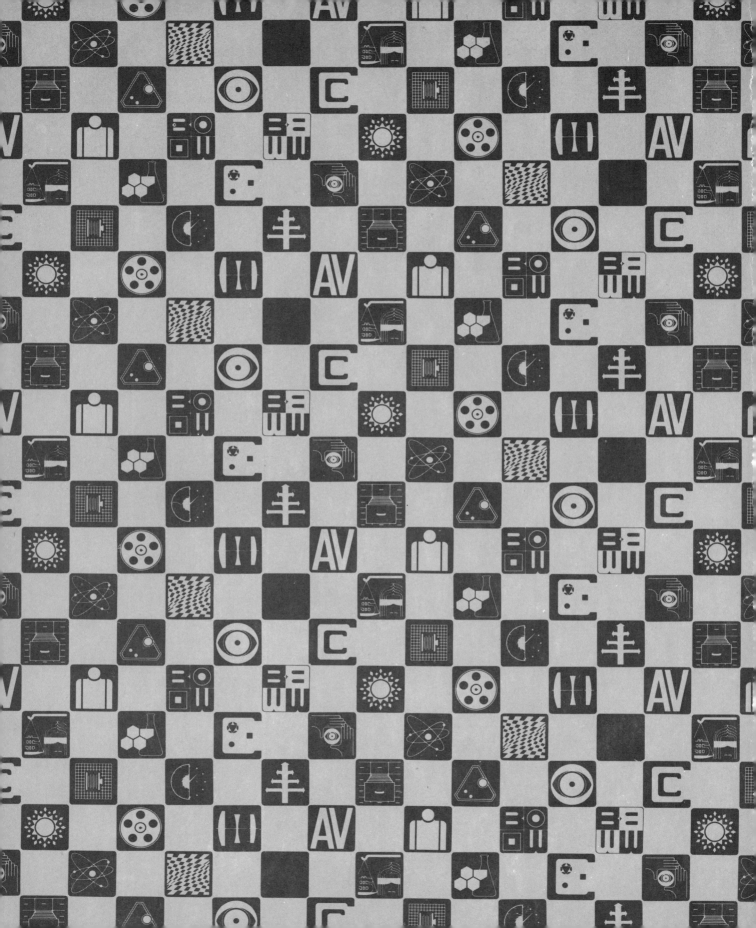